The First-Year
Urban High School Teacher

The First-Year Urban High School Teacher

Holding the Torch, Lighting the Fire

Paul J. Weinberg and Carl Weinberg

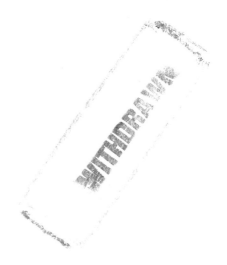

ROWMAN & LITTLEFIELD PUBLISHERS, INC.
Lanham • Boulder • New York • Toronto • Plymouth, UK

ROWMAN & LITTLEFIELD PUBLISHERS, INC.

Published in the United States of America
by Rowman & Littlefield Publishers, Inc.
A wholly owned subsidiary of The Rowman & Littlefield Publishing Group, Inc.
4501 Forbes Boulevard, Suite 200, Lanham, Maryland 20706
www.rowmanlittlefield.com

Estover Road
Plymouth PL6 7PY
United Kingdom

British Library Cataloguing in Publication Information Available

Library of Congress Cataloging-in-Publication Data

Weinberg, Paul J.
   The first-year urban high school teacher : holding the torch, lighting the fire /
Paul J. Weinberg and Carl Weinberg.
      p. cm.
   Includes bibliographical references and index.
   ISBN-13: 978-0-7425-6103-8 (cloth : alk. paper)
   ISBN-10: 0-7425-6103-8 (pbk. : alk. paper)
   ISBN-13: 978-0-7425-6104-5 (cloth)
   ISBN-10: 0-7425-6104-6 (pbk. : alk. paper)
   1. High school teachers—United States. 2. First year teachers—United States.
3. Urban high schools—United States. I. Weinberg, Paul J., 1979- II. Title.
LB1777.2.W44 2008
373.111—dc22   2007037781

Printed in the United States of America

∞™ The paper used in this publication meets the minimum requirements of
American National Standard for Information Sciences—Permanence of Paper
for Printed Library Materials, ANSI/NISO Z39.48-1992.

I dedicate this work to the students I daily endeavored to provide with an education that was worthy of their dedication, intellect, as well as their humanity.

—Paul J. Weinberg

Contents

~

Preface

Solutions to the critical problems of public education abound. What is not in dispute is the importance of high-quality teachers. Paul Weinberg, one of the authors of this book, is the kind of teacher everyone believes we need. He was a high-achieving math major at a prestigious university, trained to teach at one of the best teacher-education programs in the country, and deeply committed to teaching and to his students. The story of his first year of teaching math in an urban high school brings clarity to the complexity of the challenges of reforming education. It reveals a system of deeply entrenched and interconnected problems. Success in one domain—such as bringing in highly qualified teachers—is undone by failure in another. This book makes it clear that only comprehensive reform—a fundamental change in the way we *do* school—will bring meaningful improvements in student learning.

Paul starts his teaching career with great confidence and enthusiasm. Like so many new teachers, especially the most academically successful, his career was short. Fortunately, he teamed up with his father, an education professor at UCLA, to document the circumstances that explain the failure of most urban high schools and the departures of teachers like him. Paul had five classes of forty plus students a day. Many did not speak English. Some were supposed to be in a special classroom, but there was no space for them. The books arrived the third week of school. It would be easy to play the blame game—the legislature for not providing sufficient funds, the district office for disorganization, the principal for poor planning. All may be true, but this story has no villain. It has instead many victims of a system that is designed to fail.

The story is also not new. Paul's father, Carl, started his career as a teacher in an urban high school nearly a half century ago. The book documents the distressing similarities in their experiences. The details of the daily life of the school, the organization, fiscal priorities, use of sanctions in the classroom, standardization of content, and endless testing that is not diagnostic seem to be permanent fixtures in the history of these urban high schools. The Weinbergs are also not the first to tell the story of the failures of urban education. This book is unusual, however, because it is seen through the eyes of a novice teacher, and unique in the father-son collaboration that bridges decades of our failure to provide a decent education to youth who live in poor urban communities.

It is a remarkable book that vividly, poignantly, and with humor documents the experience of Paul's first year of teaching. We see close up and personal his day-to-day interactions with students, administrators, and occasionally parents. We see how the dysfunctional structure of a large urban high school plays out in people's lives. We experience their frustrations and despair and we celebrate their successes, small as most are. The authors cleverly pull us out of the drama regularly to force some reflection on the implications of what we are seeing and hearing. They do not pretend to have simple answers to the problems of urban education. To the contrary, a clear message of this book is that there are no simple answers. But the authors point us in some promising directions. The message is not one of total despair, but a warning that there is much to do and that little will be accomplished until society decides that it cares about educating all its children.

Deborah Stipek
Palo Alto, California

~

Acknowledgments

The following people played invaluable roles in the crafting of this work. Lois
A. Weinberg, Hayley Schore, Marca Weinberg, and Sarah Hasenmueller provided me both unconditional intellectual as well as emotional support
throughout this process. Rich Lehrer and Leona Schauble helped me gain new
and revitalized perspective on children's mathematical and scientific reasoning in the context of urban schooling. Min-joung Kim, Nina M. Knapp, Marta
A. Kobiela, Charles Munter, Wenyan Zhou as well as other doctoral colleagues have similarly supported my reconceptualization of approaches to the
teaching of science and mathematics. Maxine Axelrod, Alex Cardenas, Frank
Divinagracia, Charlotte Haynes, Cathy Klein, Hali Rosen, and Marco Salazar
were the teaching colleagues without whom I would not have been able to
survive to write this manuscript.

Paul J. Weinberg

Lois Weinberg and Deborah Stipek suggested the project and were supportive throughout the undertaking. Ed Young helped us formulate the organization of the book in the early stages. Rod Skager and Buzz Wilms, colleagues
in the School of Education at UCLA, read portions and offered feedback.
Art Pomponio pushed for a conceptual focus on the consciousness of the
teacher as he negotiated the daily practice of school life. Lois Weinberg ref-
ereed all disputes when the coauthors disagreed.

Carl Weinberg

~

Introduction

Carl is the father, Paul is the son; we both consider ourselves urban educators. Carl is ending his career. Paul is beginning his. The urban school encompasses both our careers. A half-century after Carl's experience some things have changed. Not nearly enough.

What we mean by an urban school is a school in a city where the students are poor minorities and the community is low income. We might add, to highlight a point we will often refer to, an urban high school is one where there is considerable standardization of almost everything, from the curriculum to the tests to the rules for discipline, to the allocation of resources, and to the placement of students.

Social problems abound in the neighborhood where urban schools are located. That hasn't changed much either in the time spanning our two careers. Unfortunately, at least in our view, the one good change, the movement to integrate schools racially, is undergoing a serious regression. Segregated schooling appears to be on the rise due to the inability, or unwillingness, of school districts to finance integration programs (Kozol 2005).

Actually, the evolution of the concept of the "urban school" is in itself a sociocultural phenomenon that contains the history of the relationship between education and economic disadvantage. Our book takes that history, in all its predictable consequences, for granted.

This work has two foci: (1) a new teacher's process of seeking ways to belong and contribute and (2) the way in which most urban students are denied the rights and the benefits of social justice. The two are frequently related. We

1

show how often the most important dynamic of learning for the new teacher in the urban school is seeing how so many of the practices in which he engages are those which deny students an equal opportunity, in relation to middle-class or private-school students, to succeed educationally.

No educated person needs to be apprised of the fact that schools are places where rewards for achievement and predictors of educational success are often associated with a student's race and socioeconomic status, which in turn is associated with where he or she goes to school.

Through January, February, and March 2005, the periodical *Education Week* reported a series of varied pieces on the call to revamp the American high school (*Education Week* January 26, February 9, and March 9, 2005). The issue of the failure of the comprehensive high school has penetrated with a vengeance into the political arena (state governors conferences, state and federal legislators, Department of Education) where it joins foundations (e.g., the Bill and Melinda Gates Foundation, the Marion Kauffman Foundation), university researchers, school district administrators, teachers groups, etc., to decry the shortcomings of our public high schools (*Education Week* March 9, 2005).

There seems to be general consensus, currently, that the "small school" movement, with a variety of models floating around, located principally in minority communities, is the way to go in initiating serious reform. But even small schools must deal with many of the same problems that large ones do. Small schools have been shown to improve student outcomes in general but not always and not in all areas (Darling-Hammond, Chung, Frelow 2002). Some studies have indicated that small schools do not always produce better achievement rates (Wasley, Fine, Gladden, Holland, King, Mosak, et al. 2000). Teachers in small schools that do not "cream" their students (take only those students who are likely to succeed) often complain of many of the same problems in dealing with students with low skills. Those are the kinds of issues we deal with here.

So, why another book about disadvantage, about problems that teachers in urban schools face in the classroom? What new needs to be dealt with?

The answer to that is in the *how*, not the "what" or even the "where" or "why." We know what the problems are, the kinds of schools where they become manifest, why they result in differential rates of student failure, and even why they don't seem to be fixable. But we don't know nearly as much as we should about how the dynamics are played out at the micro level. That is, the level of teachers' daily interactions with students, parents, staff, and administrators, how students are ultimately allocated to poor paying jobs and many to prisons.

The effects of Hurricane Katrina on the lives of the poor and specifically the poor black residents of New Orleans and Biloxi, Mississippi, as seen daily on TV in the weeks that followed the hurricane are an example of the "how" we are talking about. We already knew their economic status in the society, where they were, and what their condition was before the hurricane, and why poor minorities have difficulty rising in the social order, but it took television to show us how the combination of the elements of their condition played out under the circumstances. Where were their cars when they needed them? How was it they were left stranded on the roof while more affluent citizens drove north? How did it happen that relief was so delayed?

All the structures of obstruction we find in the comprehensive urban high school are revealed here day after day through the experience of a new teacher who is discovering them. Many of these structures that produce failure, regardless of the size of the school or the quality of the pedagogical model, involve conditions that will persist as long as society is made up of people of different races, different parental configurations, different socioeconomic levels, different neighborhoods, different degrees of support, different untreated mental health conditions, among myriad other circumstances. We may be a nation that has pride in our differences but we have found ways to discriminate based on those differences. Some of these ways are subtle, while others are blatant.

Why don't we have more literature from the teachers themselves in the schools where the particulars of socioeconomic and racial discrimination operate? They are the ones who are constantly negotiating the dynamics that comprise the school day. Perhaps because teachers are too busy with too much to do or perhaps they don't see themselves as qualified academic writers. Many individual teachers, we believe, have stopped worrying about the many failures they have to witness and concentrate their limited energy exclusively on the small number of successes they are able to achieve. How they arrive at this decision is part of our story.

The goal of the present work is to explore in the human drama of the everyday urban classroom, found in the interaction of the teacher with students and their parents, colleagues, and administrators, how minority students from low-income families are too often disserviced in their quest for equal opportunity and equal attainment—that is, social justice.

Our first theme, the socialization of a new teacher of a different race and class to both the cultural world of the urban adolescent as well as the role of the teacher in the bureaucratized institution of schooling, is an issue that needs constant inspection. All experiences of this nature, how one learns the world of the urban classroom, how one struggles to gain trust and acceptance, are unique to the teacher/learner and must be explored within the context of the character and personality of the individual teacher and the characteristics of the individual students with whom he interacts. We are operating on the assumption that a teacher's development as a quality urban high school teacher is directly related to his[1] insights about how social injustice occurs in the classroom and what might be done to turn things around.

For the beginning teacher the classroom is where, in the midst of a barrage of mixed messages, contradictory expectations, bursting illusions, competing egos, and the needs of legions of complicated adolescents, one discovers one's self as a teacher. One also finds how hard it is to gain the respect of urban students, particularly if one is white. What we have here is a story of struggle, resolve, and openness to reinventing oneself, and about the desire to survive and ultimately prevail in a problematic enterprise. And if one is led to the call of teaching out of a desire to aid the cause of social justice, the urban classroom is the place where the beginning teacher learns the obstacles to attaining that goal.

Paul, the teacher in this work, as well as the coauthor, is the heir to a long line of people committed to poorly paid careers associated with the social and educational welfare of the under classes. It's not an uncommon biography. His great-great-grandfather was a rabbi with a congregation of newly arrived, mostly destitute immigrants. His great-grandfather was a union organizer during the Depression. After that it was a family of teachers, men and women who taught primarily in the urban ghettos of North Philadelphia. His father started out the same way: same place, same struggles. His mother spent seventeen years fighting school districts for educational services for children with disabilities from poor families. So Paul's choice to go into teaching in an urban school was probably set in his social genes long before his father, a lifetime educator, started to try to talk him out of it.

The book follows Paul's career as a first-year high school teacher from a teacher-education program in a highly esteemed education department through a year of regular classroom teaching in an urban high school. It's an excursion into the process of learning what it means to teach in this kind of a setting and, as such, exposes some of the institutional arrangements that make teaching in the urban school such a difficult enterprise. Difficult, that is, for those who are focused on making the kind of difference that a social-justice consciousness requires.

We will frequently be juxtaposing the problems of the daily work of teaching in an urban school with what was or was not dealt with in Paul's training program. The purpose in doing that is to implicitly suggest what should be dealt with in any teacher-education program, if possible. But the book is in no way to be read as a critique of the particular training program that Paul went through or even teacher education programs in general. The failure of low-income minority students to achieve in the urban high school is a product of many collaborative forces such as the teacher-training program, the school, the community, the society, and the teacher. Each of these forces, as well as many more, will be seen to play a role in the events we will be describing.

As far as our concern with social justice goes, in a local newspaper recently there was an article about a group of upper-class private school students in Los Angeles who were touring the Ivy League universities of the East Coast so these wealthy students could differentiate one elite institution from another, to find their "fit." The article was more or less a blatant exposé of the differential effects of privilege, demonstrating how students with distinct economic and, therefore, educational advantages can parlay that advantage all the way up the educational ladder, and almost certainly beyond. When one of the students of this privileged tour was asked how she felt about having a leg up in the race for academic opportunity, witnessed by the tour, she answered, "Yes, we do have an advantage, but we pay for it" (Ritsch 2002).

No pretense of meritocracy here. It's all in the open—clear and present opportunism, advantage, and social reproduction. Nothing hidden. For these students the system works. Schooling works. Those who can "pay" for a superior education usually get one.

What kind of system or society can we envision where this isn't the case? Imagine a city with a freeway system. Every major city has one. Los Angeles has a large one. Now, whether you can afford a Jaguar or a Kia, the problems of congested traffic are every driver's problem. And if pressure is put on the powers that be to improve congestion it will be improved because it is everyone's problem.

What we have now, rather than a freeway system, is an escape system for those who wish to distance themselves from the poor. The escape mechanism is the private school or the flight to suburbia or exurbia. As public school quality decreases, private school attendance increases. And as we might expect, white students are considerably more likely to opt for private schools than students of color (Saporito, Yancy, and Louis 2001; Lott 2002).

How can we influence change when the problems of schooling are not seen as everyone's problem? Perhaps it's because most people don't understand how most urban schools fail most urban students. When people see how injustice is caused, when they see injustice at work, seeing children in the process of failing, having their futures downgraded, we would hope they would want to do something about it. We hope to be able to provide some suggestions as to how the cause of public education can be supported.

What role did his father's cynical attitude about the possibility of reforming mass education play in shaping Paul's career decision? It was something along the line of "If things are that difficult, that obstructive of quality education in urban schools, then it is a challenge worthy of me."

Perhaps because he is a mathematician, Paul thinks of problems as something to be solved rather than complained about. In general, we would submit that problems could be challenges, not always hardships. Teachers who are not subject to high levels of stress in the classroom seem to have this attitude (Weinberg 1989). We suspect success stories in all occupational areas would tell the same story.

The history of a first-year teacher's success and failure in the classroom is more often than not a question of the particular fit between the biographical experiences and character of the teacher and the character of the school and the student body. So we begin in chapter 1 with a brief autobiographical note about the teacher, which we think could explain much about Paul's struggles in adapting to the world of urban schooling. Included in chapter 1 will be a discussion of the character of the school and Paul's initial experience in the orientation held for new teachers. The remaining chapters will follow the pattern we have sketched below.

Organization of the Book

The book consists primarily of vignettes of school and classroom life that are organized around our two major themes: (1) the making of an urban high school teacher and (2) the structures of social injustice in the school and classroom. Each chapter (after chapter 1) will contain an introduction by Carl in which he will attempt to connect the experiences of his son to his own almost a half century earlier. This will set the stage for looking at some of the reasons why schooling remains, in general, an inflexible institution rendering change more than difficult.

An analysis will, at the end of the chapter, comment on the important social implications of the vignettes. The analysis is our joint effort to put into more general terms the significance we find in the particular encounters between Paul and members of his school community as well as to reference others whose research can illuminate parts of the problems encountered in the vignettes and suggest solutions. We intend to make recommendations in two areas that we hope will have positive consequences in the classroom and the school at large. The first area will be recommendations directly related to problematic classroom situations. The second area focuses on recommendations regarding current educational reforms.

Other organizing components included in the analyses will involve not only general interpretations of particular school and classroom dynamics, but also commentary on what went wrong and what could have gone right, as well as moments of regret and moments of gratification. It is our intention to make suggestions about how some problems for the new teacher can be overcome and how teacher education can be improved to help the new teacher deal with these particular problems.

The journal of Paul's encounters at Olympia High School (not its real name) covers the period from his orientation to the close of school for the summer in the years 2002 and 2003. During free moments at school Paul was able to jot down the details of what he felt were significant events in his school day, and on the long (timewise not distance) bumper-to-bumper sojourn from school to home he would call his father and they would talk through the occurrences and what they felt they signified. On weekends we discussed what we felt to be the implications of the experiences for generating policies for improvement in each problem area covered by the vignette.

Note

1. We will be using the male gender reference rather than both genders in all pronouns since the book is about the experience of a male teacher. When referring to students he or she will often be used.

CHAPTER ONE

~

Autobiographical Note from Paul

I'm twenty-three-years-old, though my students believe I'm in my thirties. I think that gives me more "adult" credibility, not to mention authority and at least the illusion of maturity. I identify myself as upper middle class, Jewish, and liberal. Within the context of my school, I identify myself as white. I'm conspicuously white with the exception of most of the teachers. I'm not ready to make anything of that.

In my life, I never spent much time with the same population of kids I teach (urban African Americans and Latinos). My schooling, although always in public schools, took place in a social environment where, despite some diversity, peers of similar ethnicity and socioeconomic status surrounded me. Through tracking students into ability groupings my schools implemented policies of de facto segregation. These policies began in my elementary school and continued through high school.

I was schooled in the Los Angeles Unified Public School District, the second-largest school district in the country. My schools were ethnically diverse, exclusively due to busing. Despite this fact, I never saw much of the school's minority population in my advanced placement or honors classes because I had long since been tracked to the college preparatory track where bused-in students were in short supply.

I entered the teacher-education program at UCLA in my senior year at the university with an undergraduate major in mathematics. In the math department, it was pretty clear that both the professors and most of my fellow math majors looked down upon careers in teaching, regarding careers in business, technical sectors, as well as academia, as superior choices. These so-called superior choices didn't feel right to me. I knew I'd always enjoyed working with kids and I knew there was a population of poor kids who were put at a disadvantage by being in the schools they were in, and I was hoping my qualifications and my desire to help them gain access to opportunities they would otherwise not have could work together to help with this population.

Where does the compassion that motivates me to try to provide equitable education to students in an urban school come from? My parents have a history of concern for the struggling underclass in American society that I can trace back several generations. However, I believe I developed my own inclinations in this direction. When I was in high school I was very aware that the kids that were bused in were being tracked into "regular" classes while all my friends from the neighborhood were in honors or AP classes. And as far as I could see, it didn't seem to have anything to do with ability or intelligence. Actually, some of the kids in our honors classes didn't seem to be nearly as bright as those I knew in "regular" classes. But their papers were neat and clean and turned in on time. And for the most part, they did their homework and turned it in.

The teacher-education program gave me an opportunity to observe a wide range of schools of the type that interested me. We were given courses that attempted to show us how we might teach math to second-language learners and that was attractive to me. I was quite aware that the Latino population in the schools was increasing rapidly. Also, we were given courses and readings that appealed to our social justice commitments, ideas that dealt with student empowerment, community-school collaboration, overcoming racism, multicultural education, democratic education, critical pedagogy, ideas which, when put into practice, could transform schools from institutions of selective allocation based upon race and socioeconomics to places of genuine equal opportunity for all students regardless of family demographics.

I understood these abstractions to mean through the use of the subject matter we were teaching, in my case mathematics, we would be able to help students gain insight into ways to elude a future predictably determined by their socioeconomic limitations. We were encouraged to believe we could help these kids to see they could break the cycle. How? By achieving, by learning to like math, by getting the math problems right, by understanding particular formulas, by getting good grades, by learning about the markers of achievement (what teachers reward), by hearing teachers tell them they are worthy, by giving students success experiences. If I think of my classroom as a social world, a world with social issues that impact my students' lives I can push the social justice agenda. At the time, since I wasn't teaching yet, I didn't have to relate the ideas to what I could actually do in the classroom.

What remains by way of introducing myself is to mention that my major concern, my major question going into the work of teaching in an urban school, is to discover how all the social justice ideas I absorbed in my teacher-education program play out in the real world of urban schooling. At this point I'm not even close to having an answer.

Paul Finds Social Justice in Westwood

We begin the biography of a teacher's process of becoming an urban school-teacher with the touch of irony that training for teaching in the inner city begins in one of the most affluent suburbs in the world.

The University of California at Los Angeles is located in an upscale, actually very rich, very green, community in the western end of Los Angeles called Westwood. The faculty can't afford to live there. It's surrounded by Beverly Hills on the east, Bel-Air on the north, Brentwood and Pacific Palisades to the west along a meandering street of riches called Sunset Boulevard, and on the south by the actual "downtown" of Westwood, an upscale professional community of high rises peopled by business executives and corporate lawyers. Westwood at one time was very much a student-oriented town with bookstores, pizza and hoagie shops, cheap restaurants, and a Jewish deli. Now it's a town that almost ignores the campus, replete as it is with legal firms and mid- to large-scale business enterprises—and coffee shops where a latte or a Chai tea will set you back four bucks.

UCLA itself is a self-contained city of almost 40,000 members; it is a remarkably clean, well-kept, sun-drenched, luxury of a campus with a recreation center that rivals well-appointed country clubs, parklike grounds where you can lounge in the shadows of trees with esoteric names, and a student store that approximates an upscale market. There are a half dozen gourmet coffee shops spread around the campus and a sculpture garden of statues that are never touched by graffiti.

This is a curious context for Paul's socialization to inner-city teaching yet no one in his teacher-education program seems to find it at all contradictory. Ironically, the subject never came up.

The Program

The training program Paul experienced was, in both of our opinions, woefully unrealistic in giving him either the insight or the experience that would prepare him for the kinds of difficulties he would encounter. And while the academic faculty was able to infuse the students with a wide range of social justice principles and arguments, the actual praxis of the social justice curriculum was never clearly communicated, nor did it prove to be helpful to either Paul or a number of his peers who had also come through the same program.

The main principles and assumptions underlying the philosophical theory of the "social justice" training program were:

1. To understand the relationship between socioeconomic factors and student outcomes
2. To see that the battle for meritocracy, by which middle-class students achieve more than low-income minority students, does not occur on a level playing field
3. To see how tracking, the procedure by which high-achieving students are separated from low-achieving students and maintained in homogeneous tracks, disserves poor, minority students
4. To view the role of the social justice–oriented high school teacher as someone who seeks ways to provide low-income minority students with resources to help improve his or her possibility of obtaining opportunity and access to future success
5. To work toward creating a diverse caring, socially responsible learning community in the school
6. To view and to develop learning as social inquiry and dialogue within communities of practice
7. To blend theoretical models of social justice with classroom practice
8. To attend to the moral, cultural, and political dimensions of teaching

While the goals of the program were infused into the consciousness of the about to be urban high school teachers, the connection between theory and practice was, in Paul's view, never clearly made. Not only was the appropriate pedagogy left to the devices of the new teacher, but also the training program did not attempt to examine the nature of the high school student him- or herself. There was no adolescent psychology that would explain why some kids have tinderbox fuses and, at the moment of anger, are unable to process their desire to fight or hit out against the sanctions they know will be imposed should they lose control. It would be too often the case that Paul would be faced with the question, "Why in the world would he do that when he knows how much it will cost him?"

The School: Location, Location

Down the heart of Los Angeles County from UCLA runs the 405 Freeway which serves, at least for much of the way, as a socioeconomic divider, approximating the notion of "tracks" as in the right and wrong side of. To the west is the Pacific Ocean with its attendant up-market real estate that happens, not coincidentally, to translate to "better" schools than their cross freeway counterparts. To the east of the freeway are communities that have reputations as minority ghettos where the schools reflect the low level of expectations for the school success of all but a small portion of the student population. This is indicated by the paucity of advanced placement courses, overcrowding of classrooms, large numbers of second-language learners and the difficulties teachers report in the area of classroom management.

Olympia High School is located in a predominantly Latino community. On the main streets are the predictable fast food establishments, tire shops, auto body shops, mom and pop groceries, 7-11s, barber shops and beauty shops called Luisa's or Angelina's, nothing with fancy names like Epic, Estetica, or Papillion.

School Characteristics

Physically, Olympia High School is a typical Southern California school configuration of one-story buildings with one main building that is occupied by the administration. At the beginning of the year, there were 3,006 students in attendance, too many to be accommodated within the district plan and California regulations with the number of available classes. Plans were on the table to hire more teachers but until that occurred, the classes would be large, many containing over forty students.

The ethnic distribution within the student body is 58 percent Latino, 27 percent African American, 8 percent Asian, 3 percent Caucasian, 2 percent Filipino, 1 percent Native American, and 1 percent Pacific Islander. This is not far from the typical distribution of minority students in large urban schools nationwide (National Center for Educational Statistics 2003). Diversity, for "good" or "bad," is available. The good lies in the possibilities for an enriched curriculum in which ethnic difference can be shared, not only for understanding others, but also for understanding oneself and how one's own cultural experience can enrich the lives of one's classmates. The "bad" or unfortunate lies in the real possibilities that ethnic difference can be the source of conflict and violence in the school environment.

Early in the semester Paul and all the teachers received a memorandum from the principal citing six incidents of fighting taking place between African American and Latino students, all in the last few days. As a result of the fighting, twelve students were placed on five-day suspensions, three students were arrested, four students were transferred to other schools, and four others were being considered for expulsion. The teachers were asked to read aloud to their students a list of consequences that would follow for students involved in fights.

The fact that students attend school in an environment clearly tinged with the possibility of erupting violence is not only made apparent by news of or even the witnessing of acts of interracial violence but also the daily presence of seven uniformed security officers wherever students walk—reminders of the circumstances surrounding their education. Analogically, it is not all that different from the awareness that students at elite private schools have of the number of college counselors around keeping them focused on the importance of good grades and extracurricular activities. The question about the effect of a large number of security officers is whether the students feel more secure knowing that the officers are within quick call, or do they think this is primarily a feature of security for teachers? Or are they offended by the thought they have to be patrolled in order to be educated?

Salad Days: My Orientation

My first feelings about being at Olympia High School are very positive. I'm anxious but enthusiastic. I've come here knowing the school has problems that are typical of low-income, large, comprehensive urban schools dominated by diverse, nonwhite minority groups: fighting, disrespect for teachers, students who don't do homework, high failure rates, and high rates of absenteeism and transience. These I take to be abstract facts. They don't scare me. I suspect my biggest problem will be working with a lot of kids who don't have a good grasp of the English language and those who have low skills in mathematics. Those are the problems; the solutions for them are not as obvious. I'm new.

At our orientation the new teachers are treated very well; I'd even say made to feel special. The administrators and the staff make us feel very welcome. They're going to pay us our full hourly pay for attending the orientation since it's before school is to start, and they consistently provide us with a first-class breakfast and lunch. They even have lox to go with our bagels and cream cheese. My first impression is that the district doesn't lack for money. I don't know, of course, anything about allocation of finances or even how affluent the district is. How schools are financed is something we never touched upon in our teacher-education program. I wonder why teachers are never familiarized with any of the finance issues involved in running a school, particularly since so much of what we do or want to do is affected by financial considerations. I'm wondering if this apparent affluence will carry over to teacher resources. My father has warned me to be on the lookout for inconsistencies but I'm not as cynical as he. I hope I never have to be.

Details about the demographics of the school and the student population are certainly helpful. I think, on the other hand, the problems we're likely to face are not being dealt with in a way that might reduce our initial anxiety. It doesn't feel like we're being deceived but there isn't a whole lot of time spent on any logistics about discipline problems and how they might be routinely expected and managed, especially in the kinds of classes to which most of the first-year teachers will be assigned.

What I am to find out a little later is that our school is being watched by the California Department of Education as one of the schools in danger of being taken over by the state because of our low achievement. Our students have not been performing very well on the three standardized tests that chart our position in relation to other schools in the state. We are actually, along with a number of other urban schools, on the bottom rung of the achievement ladder. The consequence of not improving (all schools on the bottom rungs are given an improvement goal) is that, after a number of warnings, the state will take over and monitor the school. Administrators will be fired and many teachers will quit rather than be supervised and given extra work by the state. This would involve having to turn in detailed lesson plans aligned with state mathematics standards months before a lesson is to be taught.

When the orientation at the school ends we're put on a bus and driven around the neighborhood. It looks to me a lot like the neighborhood I live in now, a working-class, ethnically diverse community. The houses are modest, small one-story stucco structures, sometimes with single garages, sometimes carports. When there are garages it's surprising to me to see people living in them, sometimes a bunch of people. Some of the lawns are well kept with hedges and flowers. Sometimes the lawn in front of the house is a plot of dead brown grass. These houses have flaking paint and sometimes broken windows. I expect to see that some of them are unlived in but that's never the case.

I don't see many Mercedes or BMWs parked on the street or in driveways but it is not unusual to see a new car in the driveway of a run-down stucco building. Most of the cars and trucks are older models and could use a body shop. The main streets that cross the neighborhood are wide with a lot of traffic and a great many stores pinched together. There's a lot of noise in the neighborhood. That's about the same ecology as I have in the neighborhood I live in, except where I live the food places, aside from the normal fast foods, are Italian and Jewish. Here it's mostly fast food and Mexican with a couple of Asian establishments.

My Classroom

After the orientation I'm told where to go to find my classroom. I'm informed that the room to which I'm assigned was inherited from a math teacher who had retired the year before. When I walk into the room, I can't help thinking about the man who had been doing for thirty-four years what I was just hired to do. One of the reasons his presence is so present, so to speak, is that it looks like he'd left a part of all those years behind him when he went. It's like he took off running at the final bell on the last day of school and never looked back. He didn't bother taking much of those thirty-four years with him. There are files and files of past years' student papers, books, and magazines, well out of date, and protractors and compasses and a box of 1,500 pieces of white chalk. There are no chalkboards in the room anymore. In one of the locked bookcases, which I force open, there are about thirty expensive-looking calculators that don't look like they'd gotten much student use. On the bulletin board are pictures turning yellow from age and there is next to nothing on the walls. It doesn't look like there ever was much on the walls. I notice this because I'm coming prepared with a bunch of posters that I thought my students could relate to.

The walls are clean enough and I'd arranged with an artist friend of mine to paint a mural, which we later did, without the approval of the administration. I'd assumed that if we had asked for permission to paint a mural the request would have been immediately denied. I also assumed that once my principal saw the mural, he wouldn't ask us to repaint the walls. I hope no members of the administration come in to my classroom before we complete the mural (they did).

About a week after the mural is painted, as I'm walking in the hall, the principal begins to walk along with me. He tells me how much it means to him that I'd spent so much time on such a beautiful mural; it shows him that I really care what my students' learning environment looks like. As I was about to thank him, he concludes with, "But, if you ever do anything of that magnitude without administrative approval, you will find yourself in my office before you even have a chance to leave for the day." I tell him he'd made himself crystal clear. We then part and I feel reprimanded, but I have my mural.

Before I put my posters up (here again I didn't think to gain approval which I should have, since some of them were controversial) I decide to remove the musky smelling, dirty curtains that give the room a heavy, dark look with a thin film of dust floating from the windows. When I remove them, caught in one of the folds is a long deserted bird's nest. I can't help but smile wondering how many math classes the bird or birds sat through before they decided they were bored and took off.

Then I put up my posters: Che Guevara in a revolutionary pose; Malcolm X with his fierce strong gaze; culture heroes César Chávez, Martin Luther King Jr.; and singers Bob Dylan and Ani DiFranco, two of my political musical heroes. I was later to find out that more of my students than I thought would be were familiar with Bob Dylan, even though he's well past the age of any of their own cultural heroes. I was also surprised that more than a few had heard about Che Guevara, and one of my students early in the semester stole a copy of a book on Che by one of my university professors from my desk. I've been meaning to write to him and tell him that his book was stolen. He'd be proud his book was the one chosen for theft.

My goal in putting up these posters is not to make revolutionaries out of my students. I couldn't do this under any prevailing circumstances. I know they want to succeed within the norms and values of the larger society. They want security; they want money and cars and houses and opportunities. I want them to want these things too and I want them to succeed in ways that will allow them to attain what they want in life. That means to succeed in school. But I also want them to become political, to realize that certain changes in the fabric of society have to take place before students who have to go to a school like ours can take advantage of the opportunities that exist in the world.

My class assignments start out better than they will end up. I'd been given three Introduction to Algebra classes and two Algebra II classes, one honors. I'm pretty happy about that since I'd expected worse. Some senior teachers, the friendlier ones, had told me that new teachers are usually given the classes that nobody else wants, or, looked at a slightly different way, the more experienced teachers select the more advanced classes. I feel no resentment. I'm thinking the more experienced teachers have a right to carve out their special teaching niches in the classes they feel they can teach best. And in addition I think my ideals about social justice will be better served with the lower-achieving students. The truth is there just aren't that many advanced classes to be divided up. Where I went to high school there were a large number of advanced placement and honors classes. Here, I can see, there aren't enough to go around.

Before I teach my first lesson, I lose my one honors Algebra II class to a more experienced teacher and one of my regular Intro to Algebra classes is replaced by something called a "sheltered class," which is also an Intro to Algebra class for non-English speakers.

The Introduction to Algebra class is the lowest level math class offered in the school and it's a long trip from being in this class to accumulating enough higher-level math credits to attend a state college or university. The work in the Intro class is intended to provide the mathematical skills students need to handle Algebra I. This consists of a variety of integer, fraction, and decimal operations: addition, subtraction, multiplication, and division with both positive and negative numbers. It also presents students with a minimal introduction to geometry. In the second part of the Intro class, labeled Intro B, students graph and solve simple linear equations with two variables.

The "sheltered" classes are for new English-language learners. The students, presumably, are being sheltered from having to compete with fluent English speakers. I think maybe this will be a test of my ability to teach math to students who can't speak enough English to be in a regular Intro class, as easy as these classes are supposed to be.

So, the stage is set. I know a lot of the logistics about how things are organized. I know what kinds of problems to expect. As far as the subject matter is concerned, I know I know my stuff. So am I ready? I'll have to wait until after the weekend to find out.

CHAPTER TWO

∼

Incoming

Introduction

The important issues of the first school days of September involve the problems of Paul getting his feet on the real classroom ground of teaching in the inner city and away from the Halls of Ivy. My own experience in moving from the teacher-education program into the inner-city high school was not quite as dramatic as Paul's. My university *was* in the inner city. For miles around in every direction the university community was an African American ghetto, very run-down, very poor. My first teaching experience in Philadelphia was in an inner-city high school. When I moved to California I resumed teaching, this time in an inner-city junior high. My students were still primarily African American with a small percentage of Latinos and Asians. Between my days in the classroom (late 1950s, early 1960s) and Paul's, the state of California has experienced a dramatic demographic shift in schools, from a majority to a minority dominated public school system. Other major cities have witnessed the same demographic shifts. There are considerably more high schools like Paul's today than there would have been not so many years ago (Kozol 2005).

To compound the problematic nature of Paul's task it should be kept in mind that with the passage of Proposition 227 in California, it is unlikely that the children of the dominant Latino minority who are not English proficient will be taught in their own language. For a new teacher planting one's pedagogical feet on the classroom ground is doubly challenging. Everything is new and often unfamiliar, as there are many ambiguous expectations and hopes to be clarified and tested.

The main point to be emphasized in contrasting the population demographics of my teaching experience with Paul's is that we both taught poor ethnic minorities and I felt, as we went through Paul's experiences day after day, the problems were almost always the same, only the skin color and the language had changed, not the socioeconomic conditions nor the way society regards the education of its poor and working class minorities.

We both experienced the initial anxiety of standing before a *large group* (overpopulation of inner-city classrooms is not a new phenomenon) of students we had almost no contact with until that point. And we were both aware of being teachers in segregated schools. While in my day, the explanation was entirely geographical (no such thing as busing); in Paul's situation it was also geography even though now busing is recognized as a legitimate integrator.

This much was the same: Will the students like me? Will my colleagues accept me? Will my students respect me? Am I adequately prepared for the challenge? How will I react to having to teach five classes a day five days a week? So far the most we had taught in our student-teaching assignments was two. And for the new teacher with a head full of ideals about social justice (yes, I had this too), what are we going to be able to do about that?

September is, in the mind of the beginning teacher, a time when most experiences are new and most affecting. It is our goal, within the context of the daily class and school experiences, to establish a base from which Paul's development can be traced. The first month for both of us was and is a time when we can't help but make the most comparisons between our teaching situation and the context in which we received our own high school education. I don't believe it can be helped that when we first walk into the arena of the classroom, our knee-jerk reactions to problems will be reflected in the recollections of our own high school experience. It will take a little time for a teacher to recognize that the problems most teachers have in the inner-city high school are not the same as their own and therefore require different strategies than the ones we knew. Put another way, it appears that what school is for the individual student is what students experience, and we don't have to convince anyone that what students experience is significantly different from community to community. For Paul, September is a time when he discovers he's not in Kansas anymore. Nor is he in the same California his father taught in. But he is in a school, and that's where many important differences, despite the passage of many years, are hard to find. The issues Paul will be dealing with in this chapter have a great deal of commonality with my own teaching experience: oversize classes, lack of resources, students with low expectations, dealing with noise levels, dictatorial administrators, and dealing with my own stereotypes and prejudices.

In all the years I taught in teacher-education programs at two universities, the one concern that was always uppermost in the minds of the students preparing to be teachers, even before they hit the schools, was how do I deal with a problem student. That never changed, probably because nobody ever came up with an answer that worked for all teachers. Students were and remain anxious about confronting the world they don't know much about. How to best structure the subject matter content was a secondary concern of most teacher candidates, even though teacher-education professors typically try to have students understand that good management is supposed to begin with good lessons. Teacher prospects were always encouraged to keep that in mind, but when push came to shove in their actual teaching experience, they were frequently forced to accept the fact that their lessons weren't quite good enough to validate the point.

So we begin Paul's journey on an eye-opening experience.

First Day, September 4: Tower of Babel

Well, here I am, a real teacher, albeit a non-Spanish-speaking white teacher, looking around at the faces of a lot of brown and yellow skinned non-English speakers. They're all looking up at me, all forty-seven of them, wide eyed, nicely dressed, fresh young faces, probably wondering what was going to come out of my mouth. What were they going to understand? Not all of the students are Spanish speakers, although most are. Some speak Korean, some speak Tagalog (a language from the Philippines), and a few speak Vietnamese. One thing is certain: the superficial Spanish I remember from high school and college isn't going to help me much.

Another problem I have, besides my inability to speak Spanish, is I don't have enough desks or chairs in my classroom for all the students. We're eleven short. It seems to me that that's a lot but I'm new to this enterprise. The solution I come up with is for students to share desks and I borrow some chairs. I allow one student to use my desk. Ultimately he is responsible for stealing a considerable amount of the school's as well as my personal property from that location. My naïveté is profound.

The first thing I ask is, "How many of you speak some English?" Two hands go up unenthusiastically and I realize I'm going to have a very difficult road ahead of me. I'll have to use those who speak some English to help me communicate my instructions to those who don't. These "translators" would command much power in my classroom once they realized how indispensable they were. On one occasion later in the semester, Omar, one of the two "bilingual" students, refused to translate for me until I agreed to meet certain of his demands for special treatment. This I can't allow, of course, so I fire Omar; then Wendy, a new student, who doesn't make demands, becomes my primary translator.

As an afterthought, I have to credit Omar for showing entrepreneurial savvy. If you have something that's in demand and special you want to find a way to capitalize on it. It's too bad I can't reinforce his entrepreneurial gambit. I admire it, but I don't want to be the victim of it.

I spend most of the first day trying to get their names right. I haven't yet discussed anything about the course. One small attractive (am I allowed to notice?) Latino American girl's name I mispronounce and she corrects me. I apologize and she accepts my apology in quite good English, with a smile. I notice she isn't one of the two students who had raised their hands. Why is she suppressing her English fluency? I ask her to see me after class and she nods. I think this isn't the first time she'd been caught speaking more English than she was willing to admit. At the moment I don't know which is the bigger problem, having students who *don't* speak English or having some who do and say they don't.

After the class the girl informs me of what I'm already beginning to suspect, that the more English you admit to, the more will be expected of you. I ask her if she wants to be transferred out of this "sheltered" math class to a regular Introduction to Algebra class. She says no, her English isn't good enough.

Meanwhile, back in what seems to be a never-ending first period, time is passing and I know I'm not able to teach this class anything I have in mind to teach them today. I don't even know yet what they are ready to learn. I have a little quiz in mind to see how much math background they have but I don't want to give a quiz before I figure out how to talk to them. It might have been easier if I had enough books to go around—probably not. A related problem of the size of the class and the nonavailability of enough chairs or books is that students are close to each other, some sharing books whose directions they can't read. Later I will discover that a number of them couldn't read the book if it were in their native language. This means to me that much of my instruction will have to be oral and of course that means it will have to be translated.

I'm feeling like the kids really got the short end of the stick when their counselor assigned them to me. I have no idea how to teach a class of forty-seven with approximately forty-five non-English speakers. I'm under the impression that there's a legal mandate for ELL (English Language Learner) aides to be assigned to all sheltered classes. Where is this elusive aide? I need help.

The purely procedural tasks seem to be taking forever, but they're killing time until the aide shows and then maybe we can embark on some serious mathematics. I have the available books passed out, so I decide I might as well begin instruction, writing concepts on the board that I want them to know. We begin with the addition of positive and negative integers. This should be manageable. I ask them to take notes in their notebooks. I have no idea whether they're familiar with these concepts I am addressing. Some students are copying them down, but not all. This feels like rote memorization. There is no interaction between the class and me. At this moment I'm feeling teaching is not what I'm doing but I don't know what else I'm here for.

As far as the anticipated aide is concerned I'm treading water. Even with translation help from my two crutches, Omar and Wendy, I'm feeling very little of what I'm doing on the board or any place else makes any sense to the students. Most of them understand the word for "homework" though and I do remember the Spanish translation for some of the expressions they use in response to that. I don't know if my students understand anything more than they are being given homework. What the homework is I don't think matters much to most of them. It's unlikely they intend to do it but, based on what I'm seeing, I don't know this for sure yet. So why are they groaning? Probably a conditioned response to the word "homework." Most likely, if they don't understand the lesson, the homework assignment will be equally meaningless.

During class there's considerable talking, mostly in Spanish. I guess if they can't communicate with me, at least they can communicate with each other. So here's my first challenge: understanding how much talking I can accept, or tolerate, which may be the same thing. There are a lot of words being muttered that I hadn't learned in high school Spanish. Some of those words cause the majority of the class to burst out laughing. This is distracting and especially annoying since I have the distinct impression I'm being left out of the action in my own classroom. I'm a stranger in a strange land, and I'm supposed to be in charge.

After class finally concludes at the end of what felt like an interminable period, I call the head of the English Language Learner program from my classroom phone and report that an aide never showed. She wants to know if I had requested one. I tell her I didn't know I had to request one, being that I spoke no Spanish. I thought it was automatic in such cases. She informs me, as if it were my error, that it is policy to request resources and they would be provided, if possible.

If possible? I can't imagine what my semester will be like if it isn't possible. I ask if, in this case, it's possible to get an aide and she says it is and that one would be assigned to my class. I meekly add ASAP please, thank her, and hang up. One day in class and I'm already being exposed to what seems to me to be logistical absurdity.

The aide shows up a few days later midway through my class. I'm struggling with some assistance from the couple of students who can translate the limited directions I give them. I'm explaining how to subtract positive and negative integers using the good old number line. I'm having students attempt problems at the board. The aide helps make my goal here clear to them. She is a friendly, articulate young Latina who is getting a teaching credential at a local state college. She also has a math background that is good enough for those tasks for which I need her.

She gives me a list of all the days she won't be able to assist my class, which are considerable. I figure half an aide is better than none. I'm a week in and I'm learning the meaning of compromise. I'm a little uncomfortable about going back to the ELL program head to see if a full-time aide is available. I'm learning Spanish as fast as I can, but I know my own good intentions will have no bearing on the logistics of resource allocation.

What turns out to be the most trouble in this class, besides the communication problem and the fact the aide is only there half the time, is the sheer numbers. The class started with forty-seven, was eventually trimmed to forty-one in accordance with state law, but it doesn't look like the prospect is good to have it reduced much beyond that. I assume if I complain they'll put the original six back. This is my first experience with the paranoia that comes from thinking the system is there purposely to frustrate teachers. I do register a mild complaint with the administration later on and am told that my classes can be made smaller if I would volunteer to teach another class during my preparation period. I can't imagine surviving without a preparation period. I know I can't teach six classes a day my first teaching year. Other teachers had made that deal in the past, I'd been told, and were given classes with only slightly fewer students. I accept that I'll have to do the best I can with this class.

One thing turns out to work in my favor. The sheltered, or class with non-English-speaking students, is held during fourth period, the first lunch period. Even though there are forty-one students in the class and I have only thirty-six chairs, it turns out I almost never have more than thirty-six students attending class at the same time. Apparently many students don't think one lunch period is enough for them. Thank god for small favors.

Also, I'm told by the brother of one of my students that his brother and their mother have moved to Chicago. This news is quickly followed by another report that another student has moved back to Mexico. I decide not to report the departure of these two students because I've heard that the attendance office rarely catches such cases. If I report it I'll have two more students the next day to take their seats, provided seats are available. It turns out that teachers have developed their own methods for managing class size. I'm beginning to sense an us-against-them kind of maneuvering. I suppose I'm part of us but I'm not happy that we're not more of a team.

September 5: A Surprise Visitor

The principal of Olympia High School is Dr. Jason Williams. Everybody calls him "Doctor" as far as I can tell. No one I've talked to, even teachers who have been in the school for many years, refers to him as Jason. I'm sure he believes the Dr. title confers greater authority upon him, which I have no doubt he thinks is needed, but I suspect he could do it without the title, be authoritative that is. He is about six feet two or more, stands very straight and tall in his tailored suits, and has a voice like a tuba. When he's angry with someone his voice carries throughout the school. Students stiffen and close their mouths when he addresses them. I guess he's in his fifties but he moves like a much younger man. I've heard he chases students across the yard on occasion but I haven't seen him in action yet.

Anyhow, I'm in my Algebra II class where I am most nervous. I know the students are intelligent and while I know I'm intelligent, I'm not certain I can communicate it this early in my first semester. It's only the second day of school. I got through yesterday with getting all the names straight and passing out books and a few other clerical chores, but today I'm expected to teach something.

So, I start with a review of what basic knowledge I think they'll need for the algebra class I intend to teach. I'm reviewing whole numbers, integers, rational, and irrational numbers. I'm also reviewing basic properties of functions. The students are looking smug and saying, "Yeah, yeah, we know all this stuff, let's move on!"

I'm growing more nervous and a little annoyed as well. I decide to rise to their challenge and up the ante on them. I tell them I'm going to teach them about something called transcendental numbers, numbers that cannot occur as a solution to an algebraic equation. This isn't really fair but I need to let them know that I know more math than they do.

I put examples of algebraic equations on the board and show them how one would solve them using their algebra I knowledge. I then try to explain how certain numbers can't be solutions to these equations. I can tell nobody has any idea why all real numbers couldn't be solutions to any algebraic equation. But they're not complaining either. Actually they're the quietest I've heard them. I'm looking around the room for a face that doesn't look confused. That's when I see Dr. Williams standing in the doorway. No wonder no one was calling out or complaining. I thought I was dazzling them with my mathematical knowledge.

It seems strange to me that he could have slipped in and stayed invisible for a while and then once I noticed him, he's about ten feet tall. I tell myself not to panic but I can't help feeling tense. No matter where in the room I'm looking I see him out of the corner of my eye. Any teacher who has ever been visited by the principal in his first semester probably knows this sensation. So, instead of panicking, I decide to quickly capitalize on his presence, as well as decrease my anxiety. I say to the class, "Well that's what we call a transcendental number. We'll get to it before long." I doubt we'll ever get to it.

I know my comment to the class sounds intelligent but I have no idea what Dr. Williams is thinking when he hears me say it. Does he think I'm posturing for his benefit? I am of course. Does he realize that transcendental numbers don't appear in the California mathematics standards? Then I quickly shift back to the review material and they don't complain at all.

When Dr. Williams leaves, the noise starts up again about this being old stuff so I make a deal with them. I'll give them a review quiz of the material they say they know and if they do well we'll move on. They agree. So I give them a test on algebra fundamentals and nobody passes. I'm in good shape. I don't need to revise my lesson plans.

September 5: Paul Befriends a Student

It's the third day of school. Nothing catastrophic has happened yet. It's the beginning of fifth period. I've almost successfully completed my third day of real life teaching and I'm feeling pretty proud of myself—a little lighthearted and cavalier actually.

I notice a muscular, African American student, Dejaun, whispering something that looks salacious into his neighbor's ear. I figure it'll be fun to have a laugh at Dejaun's expense. He walks and talks tough, but he looks like he'd be a fine sport to joke with. I say to him, "Dejaun, would you mind removing your tongue from Alberto's ear so we can begin the lesson?"

Dejaun immediately stands up, takes two steps toward me, and yells at the top of his lungs: "Who the fuck you think you are? You think you can say shit like that to me?"

I don't think he intends for me to answer those questions. I take a deep breath. My heart is pounding. How am I going to handle this? I respond to his tirade with, "I'm sorry Dejaun. What I said was totally inappropriate." The whole class sits silent, waiting for Dejaun's response. He apparently has a reputation for mouthing off to teachers. I'm thinking it's my first week of school and I'm about to be punched out by a student.

Fortunately, Dejaun thought about it for a stressfully long few seconds and then said, "It's cool." There was a long silence. He then concluded with, "I'm sorry too," and sat down. I'm incredibly relieved. I'm also of the opinion that Dejaun had not heard many apologies from teachers in his school life.

I then begin the lesson on adding positive and negative rational numbers and decimals. This is the first time I've exposed my Intro to Algebra class to fractions and decimals. But neither the class nor I were finished with the Dejaun incident. About five minutes later, I'm feeling compelled to apologize again for my comment and I tell him I appreciated his apology. Stupefied by my behavior, he again apologizes himself. I'm feeling that I'd successfully weathered the storm that Dejaun apparently brings with him to all his classes. I went back to the lesson with a relatively clear mind.

There was, of course, in that confrontation with Dejaun, more to be learned than I could think about during the emotional intensity. Afterward, in reflection, I realize I'll have to seriously rethink the way I relate to students. That is, how familiar can I be and not endanger my authority.

September 11: Jason Looms Large

On this particular day I hand out a lunch-detention slip to a student, Jason, a husky, tall, Latino boy who had pushed me farther than I was willing to go. It wasn't anything in particular; it was everything in general. He was showing nothing but disrespect for the class and for me: talking loudly, yelling out everything but answers, standing up, strolling around the class, and annoying students at their seats. Apparently my approach to teaching addition and subtraction of fractions isn't able to grab his interest.

Unfortunately, in my haste and unfamiliarity with the various disciplinary paperwork, I fill out the wrong referral slip and hand it to him. I meant to fill out a slip requiring Jason to spend his lunch during the next day in the guidance room. I had, apparently, given Jason a form requiring him to go to the guidance room during this one class. This form is traditionally used for students who need to be removed immediately from class on specific occasions for disruptive behavior. After three days, I discover Jason hasn't served his "lunch detention." When I confront him with this, Jason argues that he was never given a lunch detention, but rather a referral that he had served. I was sure I had given Jason a lunch detention and had checked with Mr. Winkler (the teacher in charge of the guidance room) to ascertain whether or not Jason had been in the guidance room that week. Mr. Winkler assured me that Jason had not. I believed this called for more severe disciplinary actions. I then give Jason a lunch detention that requires him to spend his next three lunches with Mr. Winkler. I also resigned myself to call Jason's father and request a conference. I had already talked to him on the phone (with the help of a translator), but that seemed to be fruitless.

Jason insists that he isn't going to serve the lunch detention. I tell him that is fine, but there will be consequences. Jason continues to argue that in the note that was now in the hands of the vice principal that I was "lyin' on him."

The next day, just as I'm about to go to lunch, the boy's father shows up on campus without a guest badge (badges that indicate visitors have been cleared by security and are legally permitted on campus). He's waving the lunch detention slip that I issued his son the previous day, which he found between the cushions of the couch at home. Jason was apparently not intending to bring the form that required him to serve the detention. Jason's father wants to know what it's all about and he is yelling at me in Spanish. Unfortunately, my Spanish is not adequate to understand him. We're at a standstill.

I run around campus for twenty minutes with the father at my side, pretending this is school protocol, looking for someone to translate. Normally two translators are in the main office since this is a common issue. Unfortunately, the two translators had been reassigned to other tasks because the school is understaffed. Finally, I run into someone in the hall who speaks Spanish who explains to the father what I tell her about the lunch detention slip. The father is also told of Jason's daily behavior problems that range from not sitting in his seat, to talking excessively, to total defiance. The father says the boy will serve the detention and he will talk to his son about the other issues. Meanwhile, my lunch period has passed. When the boy shows up later in the day he tells me that he won't serve a lunch detention because I originally gave him a referral slip, not a detention slip.

After another three days have passed and Jason has not served the lunch detention, I am ready to recommend Jason for suspension. I place a suspension request in the box of the assistant principal (AP) in charge of discipline. I also have a call made to Jason's father, letting him know what actions will be taken for Jason's gross misbehavior in class as well as his general defiance. Again, while I'm trying to eat my lunch, a secretary from the main office and Jason's father enter the teachers' cafeteria. The secretary, a middle-aged Latina translating for Jason's father, tells me that Jason's father wants to have an immediate conference. In fact, she tells me that he demands it. I don't believe he's in a position to demand such accommodations, but since he's about twenty years my senior and looks very angry, I think I should arrange it. The secretary tells me I should give him the conference because the school has kept him waiting for me for nearly two hours. It would have been nice to have been informed he was on campus waiting for me. It was also nice to later find out that the secretary was merely absolving herself of blame for the whole incident, since the father had been waiting for two hours in her office.

Jason, his father, a translator, and I go into the secretarial lounge because it is the only room currently available for conferences. Jason had been called out of PE to attend this conference. Leslie, a fellow member of my UCLA math team, is covering my class. Before the conference even begins, or perhaps at the beginning of the conference, Jason looks at me and angrily asks, "Why the hell did you pull me out of my class?"

His father immediately verbally admonishes him. What ensues is a fifteen-minute verbal argument, in Spanish, in which both father and son look like they're about to strike one another. They're both bigger than I am so I feel compelled to call for backup. Finally, the translator interjects. Actually we're not using an official translator because they're at lunch. The translator on this occasion is my new friend Lucia, who is in charge of the school's data processing department. Lucia is fluent in Spanish and sizes up the situation as something I need to wiggle out from. She tells them that we need to deal with why we're all here today. Lucia says that Jason insists that the AP in charge of discipline has a copy of the referral, which really no longer has anything to do with this whole mess. I tell the group to hold on and I will get the AP and we will finally get to the bottom of this.

I walk into the AP's office and ask him if he has a minute. He tells me he has exactly one so I'd better start talking. My minute-long speech culminates in my telling him that it is irrelevant whether I gave Jason a referral or a lunch detention because I intended to give him the latter. I tell him that Jason's behavior since this whole thing began has been deplorable. He deserves the subsequent three-day lunch detention whether or not I initially gave him a referral. I finally ask, in light of everything I've stated, that regardless of whether the initial form was a lunch detention or a referral, that Jason be held fully accountable for not serving a detention. I then further recommend him for a three-day suspension. The associate principal looks at me as if we're in an episode of *The Sopranos* and says, "I'll take care of it." He then tells me he'll be in to talk to everyone in about twenty minutes.

I go back into the room with Lucia, Jason, and his father. The two males are again at each other's throats. I tell them that the associate principal will be in to check the status of Jason's disciplinary record to determine whether he was given a referral or lunch detention. I had to leave to teach my next class. As I leave the conference I feel confident that, even though I was negligent regarding the referral, the school would to some degree, hold Jason accountable for his bad behavior.

Later that day, Jason and his father arrive at my classroom door while I'm teaching my final class. Jason bursts in on the lesson and waves a piece of paper in front of me. This document from the associate principal with whom I had spoken absolves him of all disciplinary action taken against Jason by me since I filled out the initial referral two weeks earlier.

The associate principal made me aware later that there are too many serious discipline matters to deal with simple complications. I also sadly and painfully learned our school administrator did not back me up when I specifically asked him to. What can I expect when I don't ask?

September 12: It's Not Like She's Naked

Today a male security officer walks into my classroom and asks that one of my students, whose name is Penelope, and I step outside. Things are going well in the class. The students are actually interested in graphing quadratic functions. Penelope is an exceptional student, working away on the assignment. She is a vivacious, young Asian woman. I have not yet found anything about Penelope to complain about. The girl stands there quietly outside the door as he puts the question to me, "Don't you think that this student is in violation of the school dress code?" It was rhetorical, of course. I'm surprised he asked me and not Penelope, who is breathing heavily and trying not to look too embarrassed. I take a moment to try to see what he is seeing and objecting to. She is wearing a short skirt but so do many girls in the school. She is wearing an abbreviated top that reveals a navel that has been pierced with a ring. I'm pretty sure that's the problem. It doesn't seem like a big deal to me but I don't make the rules. I have a sense if I throw the officer's question on to Penelope she would have a lot to say about who can and can't tell her how to dress. I can picture a debate ensuing about rules and personal freedom so I tell him I see his point and I'll deal with it. Then he leaves and we go back into the classroom and I look at Penelope and she nods and puts on her coat and that's the end of it—except for the feelings about it that I come away with. The truth is I didn't even notice it. I just left college. Girls there dress like Penelope all the time. And the algebra lesson was going so well. What's important around here?

The school dress code, for me, is a damned if you do, damned if you don't regulation. My thinking goes along this line—because I am a young single male I am not supposed to be noticing the exposed flesh of my young female students. On the other hand if I don't notice, which often I don't, I am not alert to my responsibility in enforcing the dress code. I would prefer it if female teachers dealt with female students and male teachers with male students.

Let me explain more about our school's dress code. As might be expected, a number of codes to regulate the behavior of students, intending to combat the possibility of gang- or race-related on-campus eruptions or the disruption of gender relations, are in effect. The dress code orients to the provocative. What is provocative is the sexual in girls and the violent in boys. For the girls anything that is too tight, too revealing of flesh, too short, too skimpy, is problematic. For the boys, clothes that suggest gang affiliations: caps, hats, bandanas, baggy pants, tank tops (referred to affectionately as "wife beaters") are outlawed.

Administrators sometimes prowl the halls and look into classrooms to make sure the code is being followed. The security officer in Penelope's case served notice that I was to be more on top of violations. I have a hardened position that teachers should not be enforcing the dress code. Our jobs are not to scrutinize the visible flesh of our students. While we are teaching, administrators, staff, and security should be issuing dress-code violations. Many teachers regard their enforcement of the school dress code as an annoyance.

September 13: The Lockdown?

I'm having my lunch in another teacher's room when one of the senior teachers, a union representative, pops his head in the door and tells us there's a "race riot" going on in the student cafeteria and we should all go to our classrooms and lock the doors. I tell him I thought there was a lockdown bell that's supposed to ring under such circumstances, but he says we haven't yet had the teachers' meeting where we are to be instructed in the lockdown procedure. Until that time, the lockdown bell is not to be used.

I run back to my room as instructed, pull down the shades, lock the door, and wait for some all clear sign. I have visions of bullets spraying through my window glass. I dial my mother to tell her how terrified I am but she isn't home. I call another teacher to find out how he's handling the situation. He responds, "What situation?" He has not heard about any lockdown or any race riot either. Then the lunch bell rings. When students in my next period class start knocking on the door I assume all has returned to normal. Apparently not all teachers had gotten the lockdown message.

Later that week we have a teachers' meeting and are given instructions about a lockdown bell. This is a very important meeting where all teachers are taught how to differentiate between all of the school's bells. Numerous teachers had difficulty differentiating between the fire and the flood-watch bell.

September 17: I'm Raked Over the Coals

I learned something today that was very painful to learn, but I think it was a worthwhile experience. A male student named Chris, an African American boy with a lot more energy than he can contain, has upped the ante on me. I've let a little talking and restlessness and moving out of his seat slide for him but today he's totally out of control. He refers to me as his "homey," and is in a nonstop chatty mood. He can't stay in his seat for more than two minutes. I won't make the same mistake I made with Dejaun and cultivate a closer social distance by accepting that I'm his homey. I decide to call his mother.

I call after school and introduce myself as his teacher and lay out the problem as I see it. She listens quietly for a couple minutes and the conversation goes downhill from there. Without dealing with my concerns about Chris's behavior she wants to know how he's doing academically. I tell her it's very early in the semester and I only have a few assignments from the students. "Well, how did he do on those assignments?" I tell her I think he did all right but that's not what I'm calling about. She asks about a class project that he turned in. She wants to know how he did on that. I tell her I haven't graded it yet. I've given the same assignment to 140 students and haven't finished grading all of them. She then tells me that she, too, is a teacher and she would never think of calling a parent unless she had all the information about the student's work right in front of her. She adds that I shouldn't expect all problems to be resolved in the home. She implies that I'm irresponsible for making the call under such circumstances and tells me not to call her unless I have all the information at my fingertips. She hangs up with a bang.

I hang up the phone slowly and shake my head. I have to admit she had a point. Ok, I'm calling her back tomorrow with all of Chris's work and grades in front of me. It turns out he turned in the project two days late so she should not have expected it to be the first to be graded. I have to remember to tell her that even though it wasn't the reason I called in the first place. It's the first time I've experienced trouble from a parent. It hadn't occurred to me that relations with hostile parents could be one more challenge in my quest to become an urban schoolteacher.

September 19:
"Special" Needs and "Cultural Disability"

Today, I was made aware of the difference between a student with special education needs and a student with general education needs. The idea was not new to me and had been talked about in my training program, but now the idea became manifest in the person of Angel. In my Sheltered Intro class, at least in the initial stages of the class, I find it difficult to differentiate between kids who can't learn math because they speak no English and students who can't or won't learn math no matter how much English they speak. I am aware numbers on a page don't need to be translated and I know if they can add or divide they can do it in any language. I have enough students in my four Intro classes that don't speak much English but can do the basic problems. They can but some just don't care to.

One of the boys in my sheltered class, Angel, a quiet, almost silent, thin faced, shorthaired Latino boy, however, seems to have a unique problem, which is not only that he can't learn math; he can't learn English. On Angel's Individualized Education Program (IEP) form, it is specified that he needs a lower-level math class taught in Spanish or a special education class. The fact that he has an IEP defines him as disabled in the first place. He was, in fact, recommended for placement in the most restrictive special education math class offered by the school, a special day class (SDC). The learning goal on his IEP for math is that he will learn to count to one hundred. So, I wonder, why is Angel in my Intro to Algebra class when he can't even count? The counselor has told me that for placement purposes he has to be in my class because it is the lowest-level math class which, for all intents and purposes, is "taught in Spanish." Though legally, sheltered classes are to be taught in English, the counselor was suggesting that in our school this is the best place for someone who cannot learn English. The rationale is that once the teacher realizes he can't learn anything in English, he'll find a way to teach him in Spanish. The fact that I don't speak Spanish is unfortunate for Angel. I'm strongly advised by other teachers that I shouldn't waste my time investigating special education placement issues. It doesn't yield anything useful. Unfortunately, I can't take such advice so I continue to look into what I consider egregious placement screwups.

I consult the associate principal in charge of student placement and learn there is a special day class where the teacher is fluent in Spanish even though the class is to be taught in English. Then Angel is transferred out of my class into the special day class. I, of course, wonder why this placement wasn't made without my intervention. Why, in a school with a 60 percent Latino student population there isn't a single special day class taught in Spanish? The answer is Proposition 227.

Angel's case, I suppose, is unique, and so, I also assume, is Jesus'. Jesus had been placed in my sheltered class a few days after the class started. I had never met anyone like Jesus. He had just arrived from Mexico and I've been informed that he is from a very rural area and has never had any formal schooling. On the day Jesus entered my class, his guardian took my hand and said, "Take care of him, he is a simple boy." I have no idea how to "take care of him" except to let him be. Jesus never attempts to do any work in class but as long as he isn't disruptive, I'm content to have him there. Since the class is forty-one, now forty-two, strong and difficult to manage, there is little chance of Jesus getting anything out of it if he won't or can't do anything, and I can't give him special attention because of class size and because he never does anything to be helped with. I have given him some individual exercises but he just doodles on the paper. The parameters of what counts as "teaching" in the real world of the urban classroom have just expanded. I'm at sea here and it's about to get worse.

A few days later Jesus grabs a girl's butt, the girl screams, and I know I have a new kind of problem. I send him to the office and Jesus is suspended for five days for sexual harassment. It is my observation that sexual harassment is frequently exercised at the school but seldom punished. Usually the girl just hits back or curses the harasser out or gets her homeys to jump him.

Friends of the harassed girl are closely watching Jesus. When he first returns to school he is brutally beaten by the sexually harassed, her boyfriend, and his friends. I didn't see this nor did I hear of it being reported, but I heard later that Jesus would not be back in class for a while. I feel a little like I let the old man down who asked me to look after him. I don't think there's any way I could have looked after him. I'm just a teacher and see students only fifty minutes a day, if they show up.

I consult an associate principal who, after getting full information about the boy's progress from his teachers, calls the boy's guardian and recommends that Jesus be sent back to Mexico, not as an expulsion or deportation per se but as well-intentioned advice about where he will fit in best. Jesus' learning difficulties, according to the associate principal and the ELL department, are substantial. They say the boy has little hope of doing well in the culture of an American high school. I don't have a sense that the AP is engaging in a discriminatory or racist act, but that he does believe it would be best for Jesus to return to a familiar environment where he can be successful and at the same time place him out of harm's way. It turns out, from further discussion I have with the AP, that he has frequently recommended that boys be sent back to their country of origin, particularly when it looks like their involvement in gang activity puts them in danger of arrest, serious injury, or worse.

Analysis

In the analysis following each chapter we want to cohere the individual instances of problems that Paul faces in the classroom with the more general issues of which they are instantiations. Throughout the teaching year different events of classroom activity will refer to some of the general issues we discuss in this chapter. The point is that such issues as lack of resources, racial conflict and sensitivity, how you teach algebra to students with third-grade arithmetic knowledge, culture conflict, and problems of classroom management will have different faces. We want them to be seen as indicators of the same social and organization problems facing educators in most urban high schools.

The first point to reiterate is that Paul is new, naive, and he has questions. Why, he wonders, have the powers that be allowed forty-seven non-English-speaking students to be taught by an English-speaking-only new teacher? Well, what are the priorities? There's a reason for everything. Paul just doesn't know the reasons. Nor is he ever likely to. Teachers are not typically in the loop.

A second question he has is how much can he trust these kids? His awakening to the problem of theft is quickly achieved as the student using his desk relieves it of a number of his possessions, as well as the school's. His basic instinct is, in his admitted innocence, to trust students. This question will be revisited frequently as the year proceeds.

Paul has discovered that some students don't want to admit to being able to speak English. In his own mind he knows that being a member of an advanced class will advance the students' opportunities to go on to higher education so he is, at first, befuddled as to why they would deny themselves that option. The more he understands the urban student's mind, in this case a Latina, the better he will understand student priorities and how these may not correspond with his sense of what all students should want.

The problem of classroom noise is central to the issue of classroom management. Again, it begins as a typical new-teacher question. How much uninvited talking should Paul allow, which is not the same question as how much can he tolerate, although that's not irrelevant.

Most new teachers are generally not young people who were students themselves in troubling classrooms. In their own high school classrooms they probably had few models for how serious discipline problems were to be handled. And it appears that for most new teachers their student-teaching experience occurred in the more advanced classes with stronger master teachers and more motivated students. But the image of the urban classroom is pervasive in the culture. Movies and TV series showing unruly, often violent students and struggling teachers have helped to create for them a worrisome specter. Unfortunately, most teacher-trainees hold the mistaken belief they are going to learn how to handle these problems in their training program.

We are suggesting here that the control of classroom talking or noise while posing a challenge to teachers also turns out to be one of the circumstances associated with social justice. We will return to this theme in several other contexts. Suffice it to say for now as a provocative notion, it is our view that the less children are encouraged to talk to each other, the less opportunity they have for learning. There is no end of educational text that argues the value of group learning (Medcalf 2004), though educators must ensure the activity structure is compatible with the nature of the student tasks. However, the more urban a school, it seems the stricter teachers are encouraged to be in what they can allow by way of student freedom. The suspicion (perhaps the paranoia) of the association of group work with noise and conflict probably accounts for the restraints some administrators place on their teachers.

One thing Paul will learn about his Introduction to Algebra classes as the days pass is many of the students will opt for an extra lunch period rather than attend class, giving him a more manageable group. At this early point in his awakening to the problems of urban schooling he suspects he shouldn't be happy students are ditching his class. But he is pleased for the benefit of those who do come as well as his own peace of mind, that ditching is not treated as a big deal in the school. It would be interesting to know which and how many urban schools are, shall we say, "relaxed" about students ditching class.

Early in the process Paul came face to face with the issue of the school bureaucracy and its top down administration. The first visit of the principal, now seen from Paul's perspective as an evaluation rather than a mentorship and therefore a threat to Paul's career goals, is the first real test of his nerves. The several things that he learns from this visit is (1) he needs to keep his cool and act like his confidence in his skills is greater than his anxiety about being judged, (2) the kids behave much better when the principal is in the room, and (3) the evaluation of his teaching is a formal procedure conducted by someone who represents himself as an evaluator rather than a resource. As the year progressed, the principal's visits were never made in the spirit of wanting to help. I suspect he didn't know how to help in a way that would actually be helpful. The only advice he would offer later on was, "Toughen up. Get strict." We don't believe any teacher evolves in skill and confidence in this way. It is the first of many interactions that reveal the structure of large, comprehensive high-school schooling as a formal affair.

On another subject, more fundamental than Paul's relationship with an authority figure, is his realization that the students in the advanced class know considerably less math than he assumed they would. The problem of math failure in urban schools is well known. We are not sure that the word "failure" is at all appropriate or communicates anything more than the students are not nearly ready to learn what Paul is expected to teach them. It would be like saying that a person who understands nothing about computers failed to solve a computer problem. He has already accepted that the students in the Intro classes have mathematical deficits but he did expect more from his advanced algebra class. On the one hand this is useful information as Paul sizes up the work in front of him, but it is highly disorienting to see just how little they do know. If the advanced class knows so little, what can he expect from the pre-algebra group?

We know from the research on math skills, even in small schools, that urban students do very poorly on standardized math achievement tests. The evidence is there. Forty percent of twelfth grade students of color scored "below basic" on standardized state mathematics tests. The statistics are certainly even higher for those below the twelfth grade who were not part of the study since they had already dropped out (National Research Council 2004). The consequence of poor math proficiency is that very few students will have the ability or the credits to jump to the next educational level. One interpretation of this fact—and of math deficiency in general—is that students are mathphobic. Is it that students are mathphobic or that for the most part they don't find math interesting? It's not surprising that lack of interest is frequently taken by some observers as a phobia. We agree that the math curriculum in most schools is too fundamental to ever bring students to the interesting part.

There is much argument in the mathematics education community that suggests there is no specific "interesting part." We believe much of the conceptualization of mathematics education present in schooling is wrong. Though mathematics learning is traditionally conceived of as a linear accumulation of skills toward a particular end, it is rather an integrated web of mathematical artifacts that should not be memorized, but instead reasoned around. For example, the algebraic formula $d=s(s-3)/2$ can determine the number of diagonals for any n-sided polygon. This algebraic formula is not interesting in and of itself (nor is any formula), but we can motivate mathematical reasoning by studying the relationship between the sides and diagonals of polygons (Lehrer, Kobiela, Weinberg 2007). This investigation may begin with any polygonal form the student chooses. The learning does not occur in the manipulation of formulae, but in student processes that lead to an understanding of these formulae.

We are not suggesting teaching is placing a student in front of an artifact (e.g., a polygon) to investigate and then waiting for knowledge to accumulate. What we are suggesting is students can begin to reason about many concepts by just being presented with an artifact as seemingly simple as a triangle. Lehrer, Kobiela, and Weinberg demonstrated this in a research study in an urban middle-school classroom. Students can come to, individually as well as collectively, ask questions about this artifact (any questions), raise conjectures about it, and argue their intuitions in table groups as well as among the entire class (classroom norms must be in place that support these practices). Students in this study posed the following questions within this process:

1. What is a side?
2. What is an angle?
3. Why do the exterior angles sum to 360 degrees?
4. Do the exterior angles of all polygons sum to 360 degrees?
5. Why do corresponding interior and exterior angles sum to 180 degrees?
6. Why do the interior angles of a triangle sum to 180 degrees?
7. Can we create a generalized way of expressing the interior angle sum for all polygons?

These questions can be treated in a manner that will render them mathematically rich or alternatively, uninteresting and trivial, depending on the nature of instructional intervention.

Mathematical practice operates through repeated cycles of questions, conjectures, and argument about mathematical artifacts. There is no reason this should not be the practice within high school mathematics curricula. This model of instruction places all mathematical content as a locus for mathematical reasoning (Lesh and Lehrer 2003).

It seems to us most middle-class students are able to overcome the problem of boredom owing to a psychology of delayed gratification. We are quite sure middle-class students will accept the tedium of instruction as the price one pays to do well and go to a good college. The abysmally low scores in math achievement from urban schools suggest to us that these students do not buy into the delayed gratification psychology since the gratification that they would be delaying is neither of particular interest nor in many cases achievable. There is much need for teacher-training programs focusing on math teaching to invest time in developing, in their prospective teachers, a theory of teaching mathematics that takes into consideration how students learn. The National Research Council publication *How People Learn: Brain, Mind, Experience, and School* (2000) provides such a framework. Some such theories treating the questions of how students specifically learn mathematics, posited by Lehrer and Lesh (2003), are characterized in the previous paragraph.

The rather dramatic confrontation with DeJaun is a rather gross example of the way in which the nature of a student-teacher interaction shapes the classroom management dimension of teaching, specifically the way the door to conflict gets opened. Throughout the book we will see a wide range of ways in which this conflict dimension is organized. Research in this area is not extensive but needs to be looked at by urban schoolteachers where it does appear.

Teachers make fun of students all the time and students seem to generally appreciate the attention and the act of familiarity. But this is something teachers have to earn the right to do. And what it takes is a balance between maintaining one's authority at the same time as loosening the strings of control. Of all the things that take time this is one of the most difficult to achieve. Actually, the time would come much later when the same remark could have been made to Dejaun without arousing conflict.

The general issue of the potentiality of physical violence in the urban school is another important focus of Paul's conscious and subconscious awareness. It shapes attitudes and adaptations of all concerned: students, parents, teachers, and administrators. The incident of being confronted with the possibility of real physical conflict from a huge adolescent, Jason, is important to our theme of social justice.

Three things that Paul learned from the events with Jason and his father are: (1) bad things happen when you fill out the wrong form, (2) parents can't be a lot of help if you don't speak their language and vice versa and there aren't available translators, and (3) probably of greatest significance is, you don't want to give up your own lunch period to deal with discipline problems. During the first year of struggle you need all the energy you can muster—not to mention the respite from students—that your lunch period provides.

Another theme, which will have a variety of faces throughout the book, focuses on the idea of culture conflict. Simply put, the way students think things should be is often in conflict with what the rules of the school require. The dress code confrontation, and it was a confrontation all the way around, is for us very troubling. Paul was in the middle of teaching a lesson when the security guard interrupted his class. The classroom is, or at least should be, the teacher's sacred domain. Yet, that having been said, it is one way in which, in the urban school, the tail can be seen to be wagging the dog.

The major rationale for dress codes in urban schools seems to be to diffuse the impact of gang membership in the school. And for this reason there is an extension of the dress issue into the domain of the adornment of the body with tattoos and piecing. Hats in particular are anathema, not only because the color identifies gang membership but also how the hat is worn: backwards, sideways, or over the eyes (Garot and Katz 2003).

Paul has learned in this encounter with the dress code that he himself cannot be the arbiter of what is or is not appropriate in his classroom. Nor is it the consensus policy of the teachers. He has learned that the various structures established by the administration for avoiding problems, like the dress code, detention rooms, policing by uniformed officers, prohibition of talking, gum chewing, smoking, leaving your seat without permission, etc., are strategies that raise classroom control above the level of classroom learning as the higher priority. There are certainly structures of student control in the best schools but they do not take precedence over learning, achieving, and getting ahead. Once more Paul sees how students in urban schools are disadvantaged in the struggle for equal opportunity.

The issue of race and racial conflict is an omnipresent phenomenon of urban-school life. Some aspect of the issue is almost always present in Paul's mind. As to his first encounter with the rumblings of racial strife it was simply a matter of a shoe ready to drop. Potential racial conflict is a threat that consumes the consciousness of all members of the school community. All pedagogical issues take a back seat. Not only are the African American and Latino students wary of each other, there are a large number of both ethnicities that are members of gangs, and engaging in violence can be part and parcel of gang membership, not only across but also within racial groups. The consequences to these gang members of suspension or expulsion or being shipped to a continuation school don't seem to matter to them much. They know that such actions are not likely to put a dent in their future plans, if they have any.

There are a number of factors operating to account for racial conflict, or at least the likelihood of it occurring. The general idea is that social underdogs, living in proximity, are likely to bite each other, especially when both experience discrimination from those that stand above and apart from them (Rosenbloom and Way 2004). One study of this phenomenon in urban schools went so far as to claim that the prospect of potential violence was responsible for increasing the rate of dropouts for urban students (Clark 1998).

As to our feelings that some placement problems are resolved by sending kids back to Mexico, well, we have a lot of trouble with that notion. We suspect this kind of recommendation would not be a policy that would be considered in schools that aren't compromised by problems of size and resources and the constant need to integrate recent immigrants. We would like to believe that under better circumstances, all matters of integrating new students into the culture of the school and the community would be better accommodated.

CHAPTER THREE

~

Making Decisions

Most urban high school teachers find teaching tough, even those who love the challenge. When I was teaching in an urban school back in the days when busing and legal integration of the schools were just being considered, there was always a teacher who, already burnt out by the end of the first month, used to plop down in his seat in the lunchroom after a particularly rough class and exclaim, "Only a 150 more days until summer vacation!"

The feeling, which I remember well because I experienced it five years in a row, was: all my rethinking during the summer, all the resolutions I've made, all the energy I've stored up from a relaxed summer, all the knowledge I've processed from things that went wrong last year, damn, here it is only October and nothing's changed. And I need another summer vacation.

I don't want to delve into the reasons why little has changed here, nor do I want to try to account for why, after enough of those dismal fall realizations little *has* changed for them, teachers give up and leave the urban school. There is considerable study that has gone into that issue and we doubt if any educators, or knowledgeable noneducators, would find any of the explanations surprising (Hanushek, Kain, and Rivkin 2003; Ginsberg, Schwartz, Olsen, and Bennett 1987). Too many students, too many students with no hope of succeeding, too little administrative support, too few well-prepared students, little support from parents, the threat of violence, poor remuneration, and on and on. It's not an easy job.

New teachers are probably not wiped as early as October. They have the energy of beginners and fortunately they have other things on their minds, a very different agenda from experienced teachers. They have the advantage, or the disadvantage, of being probationary. In my day it took us teachers three years to escape the probationary condition. It still takes two to three years. Is that because there is sound reasoning grounding the decision to make probationary status two or three years? Or is it because the more things change the more they stay the same?

As the first month is drawing to a close and the second getting underway, Paul feels he has shifted somewhat from a discovery mode to a decision-making mode. You begin by experiencing the situation, and then you make decisions about how you are going to deal with it. It's a predictable sequence. Now that he has at least a working knowledge of how things work, what the problems are, and what is expected of him, he is beginning to look at what he needs to resolve in himself, or if resolve is too strong a word for this point in his career, what he has at least to encounter in himself.

Probably the most complicated variable in the early stages of decision making is the process of choosing classroom-management techniques the teacher hopes will work for the kind of teacher one thinks oneself to be. And that has to be the first step for the beginning teacher: deciding how he wants to be perceived by the students and in which mode he is the most comfortable. The subjective processing of the observations so far will bring this step on. But now the beginning teacher is processing a number of questions he had no reason to consider before beginning to teach. Is the classroom to be a democracy or a dictatorship or something else entirely? Am I a friend or a foe, or something else again? Does an authoritarian style suit me? Can I put up with a lot of noise? Can I handle what may seem like chaos? Can I accept criticism from administrators for allowing a class to have the appearance of chaos even if I know that students are learning? And most of all, can I handle it if I feel the students don't like me? Can I achieve respect without being liked? Ambivalence is fatal in the long run but normal in the beginning, which is why it's so damn tough in the early years.

My own experience in this area, and the challenges and questions I have mentioned remain the same for Paul, was to tolerate more in the way of disruptive behavior than did most of my peers and much more than the principal liked. Fortunately, I outlived him; unfortunately the next principal, the one who fired me, was less tolerant of my brand of individualism than the first.

Paul at this point is, like most new teachers, ambivalent about whether he is suited to the task, but he is constantly learning about himself and how to be in the classroom. At this stage in the process he would like to be lenient, give students the benefit of the doubt even if he himself has no doubt. What is his level of tolerance? One thing he can be sure of is the students want to know that level too and will be pushing to find where it lies.

The issues we had to deal with in common across the generations that are represented in this chapter are: dealing with threats from threatening students, overcoming our own stereotypes of our school and our students, filtering the conventional wisdom from our more experienced teachers, looking for keys to awaken the interest of disinterested students, and handling the disappointment of seeing some really good, cooperative students flip-flop and become serious problems.

When I began teaching in 1956 many of the senior teachers were men who had come out of the military after World War II, gone to college on the GI Bill, and came into the classroom with a military perspective regarding what we called "discipline." The term "classroom management" replaced it in modern times although the military approach, as far as I could tell from my observations of teachers in the urban classroom over the years, has not varied much. Start tough, stay tough, and punish deviance, hopefully fairly. Should a student meet the classroom goals and have comported him or herself respectfully, the military equivalent of a medal is called for, a good grade and a pat on the back.

As for dealing with threats from physically large students, I have to admit I had to more than once call upon one of the physical education teachers, who were African American like the student, to communicate to the student that there would be very serious consequences if he ever confronted me again. Here was a case of my being too racially conscious to handle for a number of years a prospective physical confrontation between a male African American student and myself. It's a complicated dynamic and something white middle-class teachers, like Paul and most others in the urban school, will need to make peace with. The last few years of my urban school-teaching experience was relatively free of these racial confrontations, which I suspect, or want to believe, was due to the fact I had completely dumped my dalliance with military discipline and most of my prejudices and was seen as the students' best friend—which in the long run led to my being squeezed out of the system. And I have to say, metaphorically speaking, saved my life. We begin this chapter's experience then on that topic, an urban teacher's worst fear, and the threat of physical violence.

September 20: Potential Violence and Fear

Jason, the young man who wouldn't take the lunch detention and set up my difficult encounter with my Spanish language inadequacy, made it clear to me today that he has something to prove to me. It isn't the quadratic formula.

If I could have found just one mathematical concept that captured his interest I don't think he would have caused me so much difficulty. But that's true with other students who have no interest in math, even hate the subject. Not all of them take it out on me.

Since Jason has few demonstrated math skills and spends most of his time disrupting the class, I would be a lot better off with him out of here. He is getting in the way of my teaching students who are showing interest in the material. After a number of disruptive actions on Jason's part, I tell him to leave the room, in probably a bit more confrontational way than I should have. I have a lot of anger toward Jason and I am struggling to constructively channel it. He, more than any other student, renders me a significantly less effective teacher than I would be otherwise. I can't easily let go of my anger toward him.

It took my experiences with Jason for me to rethink the benefits of removing an extremely disruptive student from the class. The problem this day began when I took from him a pair of drumsticks he was pounding on the desk, as if this were band practice instead of pre-algebra. He is clearly annoying other members of the class who were trying to do their work and making it impossible for me to continue with the lesson. I feel this type of disruption bordered on insubordination. So, I order him to give me the drumsticks, telling him I would return them at the end of the period. He gives me the drumsticks, but continues to fool around for much of the period, talking to other students and wandering out of his seat. I, at one point, order him to stand in the corner, telling him if he sits or leans against anything he'll be given a thirty-minute lunch detention (we both know how effective those are). Is this the social justice I promised myself I would bring to the urban classroom? When the period ends he walks out of the room, apparently forgetting about his drumsticks. I find this amusing.

Then a minute or so before the next period bell rings, he storms back into my room and tells me to give him back the drumsticks. I ask him to try asking again, except this time in a polite manner. He responds more angrily, "Give me my damn drumsticks!" I tell him I'll return them to him the next day. This is apparently the last straw for him. Jason, about six feet three and 270 pounds, looks at me with his face drawn in anger and proceeds to shout, "If I see you on the grounds after school I'm going to kick your fucking ass!" This is the first time I've been so angrily threatened for doing my job. I do not know what to do, how to reconcile this experience with the picture of urban education presented by my teacher-training program.

This scares me more than a little but I just nodded and smile to make it seem like I couldn't take his threat seriously. I ask him if he wants to leave or should I call security. I walk over to where my phone is and Jason stomps out without backing down. Apparently there is no cost too heavy to pay for maintaining his masculine dignity. I don't know if what I am dealing with is a particularly Latino macho attitude or might it have happened to any male student in the face of being criticized. The Latino teachers in the school are convinced that such confrontations are definitely the result of the machismo attitude they say pervades their culture. I'm not comfortable applying stereotypes, but it does sensitize me to being careful about seeming to emasculate any student.

At any rate I have to report to the administration an instance of being physically threatened by a student, be it a cultural phenomena or not. Jason is suspended for a week and then transferred to another math class. Later I ask the associate principal (AP) in charge of discipline why, given the nature of the transgression, he isn't being transferred to the local continuation school. I'm told that the list for transfers to the continuation school is already much too long, and he's deserving of another chance. I have no idea how many chances a student like Jason "deserves." I don't even know the basis on which he does deserve another chance but I'm not in charge of discipline. When I've been here a while I'll delve into that.

Jason has since been transferred to three new teachers, a kind of sharing of the burden. It becomes kind of a game after the second transfer. Math teachers are lining up to tame the untamable student.

This in no way resembled what I'd learned in UCLA's social justice program. Our mission is not to take "at risk" students and turn them against us. We were not trained to "tame the savage beast." I'm at a philosophical impasse.

September 24:
I Grab a Bite and Confront a Stereotype

On a regular basis, after school I grab a bite to eat at a sandwich shop on the more affluent side of the freeway. It isn't that I want to escape the neighborhood; I just like the food there. I also like the idea I won't run into any of my students while I'm eating.

On this particular day, I was ordering a sandwich when one of the two young women who work behind the counter—same age as most of my students—recognizing that I come in frequently, asks me what I do. I tell them I am a math teacher at Olympia High School. They both register horror. One of them asks, "How can you teach those kids?"

Instead of dealing with that question I ask them where they went to school and they tell me in Inglewood, a nearby neighborhood, which I would have thought had the same school problems and a similar reputation as my school. It seems, I conclude, that there are various levels of differentiation of communities with problematic schools.

I tell them most of my students were really nice young people who are in school to learn but I can see they're waiting for me to smile or indicate in some way I'm kidding.

I ask them why they think otherwise, what's wrong with the students at Olympia High? From what they tell me about encounters they have had with some Olympia students, I infer they don't agree with my assessment that they are nice kids or even teachable.

The way I read it in reflection on my drive home is both young women were reacting to rumors, stories, tales that circulate in the adolescent subculture in their part of the city in their reaction to my teaching, I sense there is a matter of asking me if I fear for my life.

I feel bad that my kids are being stereotyped that way, as threats, but I also know they aren't stereotypes and that such stereotyping is problematic and probably wrong. By now these stereotyped kids are my kids and they are real people. I think it strange that kids from one so-called ghetto community would label my kids as lower on the ghetto hierarchy. You know, more troublemakers, tougher school. This is not a topic we spent any time thinking about in the training program. We knew that some schools where we observed had reputations as being tougher than others, but we never talked about how the students might feel about their reputations, or how we as teachers might feel about the reputation of the school and how it reflected upon us.

September 26:
A Serious Test of My Management Skills

Some days in some classes the dynamics of student behavior play out in ways I couldn't possibly be ready for this early in my career.

It happens to be my second period Intro class but it could have been almost any class. The student ability level is superfluous to the issue. What is not superfluous is that it is a math class and in a unique sense relevant to my math teaching. Two young women students, one Latino, the other African American, sit at the same table and they share a "head." I've never seen this before in a class or anywhere else. It's a hard rubber head of a girl with a lot of hair. They use this head and hair to practice braiding. Braiding is important in our school; it is major in both the Latino and African American cultures. Many students of both genders wear braids. I was well aware of the fact and the result of braiding but knew nothing about how braids were done. The two young women pass this head around the room and some of the other girls stop doing their math to try their hand at braiding.

So, of course, since this regulation size head is hard to keep from my eyes, and because it has nothing to do with the class assignment, at least at that point in my thinking I couldn't imagine it having any math-learning possibilities.

I insist on it being put away. Amy, a small Latina and her friend Loquitia, an African American student, argue with me about how I'm interfering with their developing some skills they will need to make a living as beauticians. They have an argument (absurd as it may be) and I have to give it a moment's thought. Finally, I realize if I let them get away with this on those grounds I will have nowhere to draw the line. It could quickly get out of hand, so I shake my head and smile and eventually they laugh and put away the head. Two minutes later, Amy jumps out of her seat and runs to the corner of the room, grabs a broom I keep there and starts to sweep the room.

I ask her what she's doing and she says she has to sweep the room because it's dirty and besides, she has to do something before she has a nervous breakdown.

Meanwhile the class is in hysterics and I'm focused on a girl who tells me she has to do something to keep from having a "nervous breakdown." All I can think of is she needs to be braiding hair like it's some kind of nerve pacifier.

I ask her why she's anticipating a breakdown and she tells me she hasn't had a cigarette since before school and she's nervous. I notice now she's chomping on a mouthful of gum. Normally, I tell students there's a rule against chewing gum and to spit it out, but I'm contemplating how that will sit with Amy in her current mood.

Finally I decide, the way she's arrogantly chewing, I have to say something so I say, "Amy, spit out the gum."

She says, "I can't not chew and not smoke. Do you want me to start smoking? It's bad for my health."

She's playing me all the way. She's locked me in a power struggle. I'm not going to get into a discussion about her health.

"And if I tell you to go to the guidance room."

"Then I'll have to stop at the girls' room and have a smoke and I don't want to do that."

I ask her why she doesn't. She says she might get caught and she knows it's a serious violation.

It occurs to me this debate could go on for the entire period. What the hell am I doing? I've completely abandoned my lesson plan and am engaged in ridiculous argument that is doing nothing more than wasting everyone's time. The problem is I have no idea how to get back on track. Amy is not the kind of student who ever runs out of comebacks. I tell her, ok, enough, now take your seat and I know you are strong enough to get through the day without smoking or chewing gum.

"How about sweeping?"

I tell her we pay somebody to do that and he's a member of a union and we don't want to get in trouble with the union, so no sweeping either.

Amy sees she can't push me any further at that particular moment and returns to her seat. I feel that derailing the class has been made into a game. Amy's basically a good student. She doesn't want any serious trouble.

Later, I find how braiding can interface with math. Fortunately, and surprisingly, there has been research done on the subject and this will be discussed in the analysis segment at the end of the chapter.

October 3: A General Observation from Paul

I'm beginning to relax enough now to be able to notice little things that escaped my attention while I was consumed with the larger problems of overcrowding and classroom management. One thing I noticed today was that the students never take off their backpacks. Funny it would take me a month to notice something that obvious.

Students sit in class all period with their packs on their back and cart them with them wherever they go in the room. They take them with them when they go to the bathroom (presumably for legitimate reasons though intuition suggests otherwise) and to the board when they are asked to work a problem. The boys, instead of opening their backpacks at the end of class to put their work papers in them, stuff the papers in their back pockets. Late in the day the pockets look like they contain a bag of Ruffles potato chips. It seems to me the only things most students keep in their backpacks are loose pieces of blank paper, various disorganized class assignments, pictures of all their friends, and markers in a variety of colors. I will not make any assumptions as to their uses of these markers. I need to clue them in to the fact that backpacks can also be used to transport pens, pencils, and books. Students too often show up without any of these. I asked one boy why he doesn't take off his backpack. He looked at me like I was suffering from stupidity and responded, "What, and have somebody jack it!"

October 7: "Don't be too Good with the Bads"

A teacher who had been in the school for several years tells me that if he doesn't send enough students to the discipline offices he'll get a reputation as being too able to handle problem students and overcrowded classrooms. You don't want to be a resource for accommodating too many students that other teachers can't control. This is conventional wisdom, of course. I'm unclear about how true it is. I've already decided most of the older teachers are a very different breed than the ones I've entered with. Still, I like many of them and I'm sure their experience counts for a great deal. I'll just have to decipher for myself what "wisdom" I want to absorb and what to discard. I have an intuition that the senior teachers I like are the ones I should listen to—like Claire next door. She's a white woman probably in her late forties, has a New York accent, and a potty mouth. The kids really seem to respect her. She throws paper wads at them. She stores them up like a squirrel saving nuts for winter and when some kid talks out of turn she hurls one at him. I talk with her a lot, not just because she's next door, but because I think I want to relate to the students like she does. In teacher terms Claire is like chicken soup for the beginning teacher when they feel a cold coming on.

October 9: Turnaround Students

My students aren't always consistent with respect to attitude. There seems to be little that is consistent in my work. I'm starting to get the message you don't want to push a kid on his inappropriate behavior too hard in front of the class. There's a thin line between what needs to be said then and there and what needs to be said in private. I'm starting to get a feel for that line.

Today one of my better students, Lupe, clean cut, nice looking, usually a hard-working kid, seldom a problem, decides that his brain has been too overworked lately, so he's decided to take the day off and just mess around. I tell him to get to work but he ignores me; then I threaten to send him to the guidance room, and that is the point at which he decides to take a stand about his right not to do his work today. It's a complete surprise, the way his attitude has changed. He tells me he doesn't care where I send him. Then I tell him he's pushing me to call his parents and still there's no back down in him. "Yeah, call whoever the fuck you want, I don't give a shit."

I was very disturbed by Lupe's turnaround. Whom can I count on? Do I have the ability to handle any classroom-management problems? I do call his parents, commenting on both his refusal to work and using vulgarity in class, and the next day he comes in with a note of apology, written by him, but after this incident he stops being the model student he had been. His grades take a nosedive. It's obvious he's stopped caring, irrespective of what work he does.

What is so damn difficult is knowing exactly what kind of treatment each kid requires to keep him or her on track and when to give it to him. My most disappointing experiences are standing by and watching students turn around, from cooperative and hard working one week or two like Lupe was, to being uncooperative and disruptive the next week. Nowhere in my training was I helped to think about just how to deal with huge fluctuations in student classroom performance and behavior.

October 10: Another "Not in Kansas" Moment

When I was in my high school six years ago we bothered the hell out of teachers for recommendations for one thing or another, especially for getting into college. Today one of my students came up to me after class and asked me for a letter of recommendation. He is a better than average student so I told him I would be happy to write one for him. I felt impressed with myself that I seemed occupationally important enough to be asked for a letter of recommendation. I asked to whom should I address it? He told me the Juvenile Court, Special Gang Unit, and he'd be by to pick it up before his court date the following day. I've since learned there are more requests for letters to keep kids out of juvenile hall than for going to college.

October 11: The Key to Dejaun

Dejaun could never manage to make it to my class more than one or two days a week. When he did come he was not prepared to do anything but sleep. Most of my colleagues would consider that a blessing, but he is exceptionally intelligent and it was my responsibility to get him to learn, pass my class, and graduate.

Dejaun is an obsessive body builder so I try to connect with him by indicating my own interest in weight training, which truthfully has not been of serious interest for years.

Last week Dejaun decided he's going to take it upon himself to get me in shape. He set about planning a workout regimen for me that starts with my doing fifty pushups and sixty sit-ups twice a day. I told him if he comes to class every day with his homework done, completely and correctly, I would consent to following his program. I also have him figure out the percentage increase or decrease in the numbers of pushups I do per day. This class is still working on percentages so it's my sneaky way of getting him back into the flow. I'm thinking of shifting the assignment to the whole class but I'm worried they may all have tasks to challenge me.

He proceeds now to come to class every day to find out just how many pushups and sit-ups I'm up to. Some days I'll get down on the floor to show him I've been working on the program (which I have) after we go over his homework. Meanwhile, Dejaun has been doing his work in class and is demonstrating a great deal of intelligence. I am considering signing him up for an independent studies math class that would challenge him. I'm really glad to see that he's smart because this makes it easy for him to turn things around. It is certainly easier to succeed academically in any kind of school with ample intelligence, but in the urban school it is more important for students to understand the behavioral strategies that students in middle-class schools employ. I have the probably erroneous belief that school is less difficult if you're intelligent. I don't think this is necessarily true in this environment. You have to not only know how to behave but also care enough about succeeding in school to behave that way. When I consider I have a bachelor of science in pure mathematics and a master's degree in math education, it is a bit demoralizing to think that I am on the cold floor doing pushups just to get a student to do his work. But the truth is, all I really care about is that I've gotten a disruptive student interested in mathematics.

October 15: The Bird in the Classroom

I'm administering a chapter test; the class is quiet and uncharacteristically peaceful. About halfway through the test, a small bird has managed to flit through a small opening in the window and is zipping back and forth, helter-skelter, across my classroom. Students are screaming and laughing and ducking. One of the students, Antonio, is trying to whack it with his math book. It's the first use he's had for it this semester. Since my classroom is comprised of long windows on two of the four walls, the bird, I'm guessing, believes it had many convenient escapes. Unfortunately it doesn't realize most of the windows are closed. Like a kamikaze pilot the bird dive-bombs into one of the windows directly above a student's (Derek's) desk. The class assumes, from their oohs and aahs, that the bird has "committed suicide" as it plops down right in the middle of Derek's test paper. Derek screams and runs out of the room. I do not see him again until the next day.

Derek is a wisecracking, African American student who spends more time wandering the classroom than in his seat. It is ironic that this bird crash happened the one time he's sitting at his desk. I imagine he won't be sitting in his seat much in the future.

We all assume the force of its very impressive collision with the window has broken the bird's neck. Antonio volunteers to put the bird out of its misery and climbs up on Derek's desk ready to stomp on the bird with his shoe. I order him off the desk. Another student, Alberto, stands over the bird pretending to administer CPR. I order him back to his desk as well. Finally, I ask Celia, my teaching assistant, to take the bird outside and dispose of it in the bushes. I then tell my students that they only have twenty-five minutes remaining to complete the test. I don't think this will be effective because this is my most distractible class but they do go back to their tests. At the end of the period, Celia returns to announce that the bird regained consciousness and eventually flew away. Antonio states angrily, "It flew away? Now I can't stomp on it!"

Analysis

From the first incident with Jason, in the matter of the wrong referral form, Paul learned just how complex and sensitive the whole business of disciplining students is. In the second incident, he learned about his reaction to threat. With so many failing, angry students of ethnicities other than his own it was inevitable that a confrontation would someday occur. And it did, not long into the semester. Yes there was fear, but he learned he could deal with it.

Racial difference and violence emerging from it are always part of the puzzle of inner-city teaching. Based on conversation with several Latino teachers, Paul was led to entertain the possibility that Jason's inability to back down had something to do with Latino social norms. We suspect these social norms as well as Jason's reputation in the subculture of which he is a part. Unfortunately, Paul ended up convinced that Jason knew better than he that not much in the way of institutional sanctions would come from his threatening a teacher with physical harm. In this school, and he wonders how many other comprehensive urban high schools, the system doesn't always have the teacher's back.

So Paul now knows violence can be tied to racial difference as well as the student's standing on the ladder of academic achievement. There isn't really much that can be done to prepare a teacher for all eventualities in the classroom, but dealing with the possibility of actual confrontation of the sort that Jason's anger represented was conspicuously avoided in his training program. True they, the teacher-educators, don't want their future teachers heading for the inner city with disabling fear, but social justice goals must find a way to incorporate social reality. The truth is, and it would be an egregious error of judgment to deny to teaching candidates, that the potential of violence is a real fact of life in the urban high school and has been for many years (Wilson 1995; Noguera 2003).

There are many ways that the issue of classroom management emerges. Many of them seem unique and are unlikely to occur on a regular basis. Paul is beginning to get the idea there is no such thing as a predictable way. Anything can happen to disrupt the progress of the class, as we shall see over and over. The incident with Amy, the "head," and her gum-chewing and floor-sweeping behavior is a case in point. The most general facet of this incident seems to lie in the battle of wills and the contest for power. Moving from a teacher-education program that espouses giving students power to affect their own education has put Paul, initially, on the horns of a dilemma. Clearly, he knows he needs to be in control of the context of the learning in his classroom regardless of the way students engage him in a power contest.

Paul is willing to accept that students can call some of their own shots if he sees it contributes to their learning. The instance of the rubber "head" is a case in point. It turns out, curiously enough, there has been some work done on the subject and we can affirm that math teachers in minority schools can definitely find a place in their curriculum for the relation between braiding and learning mathematics (Gilmer and Porter 1998). However, teaching mathematics through hair braiding is only as powerful as the theory of mathematics learning that motivates it. Without an understanding of how to leverage the geometry inherent in hair braiding teachers can produce only very superficial tasks.

Probably the most difficult aspect of the problem of classroom management, in relation to Paul's processing of conventional wisdom, is the amount of time he devotes to difficult students. How should he manage his time, how much time does he want to devote to the problem student when this will take time away from the students who appear to want to learn? The conventional wisdom, a clear survival strategy, is not to bother with those who don't show they want to learn. There are enough who do. Our question is: are these to be throwaway students? Many teachers would argue these students have chosen to be throwaways, and they don't care.

As Lupe's incident illustrates, classroom management is not always a line-up affair, where the teacher can depend on the class breaking along the lines of the "troublemakers" and "good" students. Surely, teachers must begin to assume, even cooperative, hard-working students have problems of their own, at home and within the culture of the school. Middle-class and wealthy students unquestionably have their own problems but as we know from extensive sociological research (Weiss and Fine 1992; Coleman 1969; Kozol 1991), the problems of personal and social disorganization in low-income minority communities are considerably more pronounced and students do become victims of their social conditions. What these conditions are should be obvious: poverty, fractured homes, early pregnancy, crime, violence in and out of the home, and substance abuse. In a recent study of adolescent students in similar urban neighborhoods (Pastore, Fisher, and Friedman 1996), half of the students surveyed indicated they knew someone who was murdered, 61 percent indicated they had witnessed a robbery, 59 percent had witnessed a beating. Many students in the same study who had witnessed violent crimes reported having thoughts of suicide. The deleterious effect of observed violence on the school success of urban students based on the neighborhoods in which they live is a social reality that has no easy solutions but has provoked extensive sociological inquiry (Aber, Mitchell, Garfinkel, Allen, and Seidman 1992; Jencks and Myer 1990).

Although Lupe apologized and returned to class with obvious support from his parents, he never quite turned back around again. Paul considered it an opportunity lost but he doesn't know how he lost it. Before too much time passes he'll learn to accept the likelihood that he had nothing to do with it.

Paul has discovered that, for many of his students, there is a significant relationship between the educational system and the juvenile justice system. At this point he doesn't quite know how to integrate the two, but rather than see the two systems as distinct, they exist in both the education and rehabilitation enterprises. A number of papers reporting attempts to partner these two institutions have appeared in recent years. A number of U.S. counties have incorporated school-based probation officers into their educational programs whose responsibilities include (1) notifying the school of the student's conditions of probation or parole, (2) monitoring the attendance, school behavior, and performance of students on probation, and (3) counseling students in danger of being expelled for truancy or school discipline problems (Juvenile Justice Bulletin 2000). In many states, however, the courts operate heavily according to a punitive model and pay little attention to programs for integrating school and juvenile justice functions (Office of Justice Programs 2002). None of these approaches, however, are familiar to anyone at Olympia High, and Paul is on his own to contemplate his resources for dealing with students who are not only trouble in the classroom but also have their own troubles with the juvenile justice system.

Everyone who ever went to school knows there are events that are not expected and therefore disrupt classroom routine. They are, for teacher and student alike, abnormal occurrences. Not that what is normal is particularly better educationally, but at least it is predictable. It never takes much out of the predictable to turn a classroom full of nose-to-the-grindstone students into a circus, celebrating the fracturing of their boring routines. A hard rain against the window panes could do it; a shouting match between two arguing students about to turn violent could easily do it; a thunderclap from a plane flying at Mach 2, a car crash on the street below, something that sounds like, or is, a gunshot. And God forbid there's an earthquake in California, or a tornado in Texas.

The problem for Paul in the bird incident not only involved taking action to get the bird out of the classroom but also normalizing the situation before the students went totally ballistic, which they would be happy to do if only someone or some fluke of nature would give them the opportunity.

Similar events would disrupt classes in Paul's own high school as well but the situation was easily normalized there, since most students had an investment in learning within the normalized context (e.g., preparing for AP tests). Here, in this class, since most of the students don't feel much of an investment in classes proceeding normally, the normalizing process would take much longer. It is one more feature of the social forces at work in the urban classroom.

CHAPTER FOUR

~

Dealing with Failure

The teaching year is well under way but it is still the first year and Paul is still a new teacher, discovering almost daily new features of the way urban students are deprived of an equal chance to compete for the rewards of higher education. He is discovering this through the number of ways they fail to learn what he is trying to teach them, which is algebra. My own teaching subject was English, which can easily be related to teaching math in that the major topic in English classrooms required by school systems, on both coasts, at the time was grammar. Teaching the rules of grammar to low-achieving African American students who spoke their own cultural grammar in the community was as difficult I'm sure as teaching algebra concepts, through rote memorization, to low-achieving Latino students. Many have suggested that the actual teaching of these subjects should involve teaching content through contexts that are familiar to the students. We, however, are not so naïve as to believe a simple "correspondence" principle is the answer (i.e., because this mathematical concept corresponds with some aspect of student experience it will necessarily foster student learning). Though this is a sensible theory, without an understanding of how this theory corresponds with theories of how students learn mathematics it is useless. From what I see in viewing the texts and mathematics standards used in contemporary urban secondary schools, I don't believe there is any theory of how students learn mathematics at their foundations.

Not only will at least half the students at Olympia fail to receive a high school diploma, but many will not even enjoy any part of their long drawn out failure experience. This was also my experience and I don't think the dropout figures are any less in the urban school of my day than they are in the urban school of Paul's day.

Failure rates in urban high schools, indicated by dropout and failure to graduate statistics, are currently staggering. Balfanz and Legters's (2005) data-based study on 250 urban high schools show that less than half of the entering freshmen make it to the twelfth grade. Other data show that less than 50 percent of students in large urban areas graduate from high school (Campbell 2004). Compare that to 1960 to mid-1970s rates of dropout data for urban-school students which for blacks were in the 25 to 40 percent range, declining steadily until the early-to-mid-1990s when they began to rise again; data for Latino students was very similar (Hauser, Simmons, and Pager 2000). These figures are certainly comparable between Paul's time and mine, which means we each had problems dealing with students we couldn't reach and probably many who didn't want to be reached. Some research suggests black students currently drop out more often than Latino students (Campbell 2004), while other studies suggest the opposite (Hauser, Simmons, and Pager 2000), but for both groups the numbers hover somewhere in the 50 percent range. It should also be kept in mind that for most of those who graduate high school, it is the end of their formal education.

It is one thing to be bored and fail, it is another to be underserved and fail, although both can be viewed as structures of guaranteed failure—in most cases what we're calling social injustice. What we're trying to show here, given that we know the rates of student failure, is what students are up against, how the odds are stacked against them, how so many are lost before they start. There seems to be no end of ways of illustrating that.

In this chapter we will be presenting some of the most blatant circumstances that sort students into paths of failure. The areas where our experiences intersect are: our concern about being white (which also contains an element of class difference), overhearing teachers sit around the teachers' room blaming the "victims" for their failure, seeing students placed in programs they weren't at all suited to, and using the test as a classroom management technique.

I have to admit, apologetically, that one strategy I would use to calm down a class going bananas was to open the Bible and start reading from it. I'm of the opinion that technique wouldn't work very well in today's urban classroom, but I'm sure there isn't any data on it. The students still go to church but don't seem to be intimidated or influenced much by church doctrine. We also, as a collection of new teachers, had the same opinion of our principal as Paul has of his: an authoritarian martinet who wants no input from the troops. This led inevitably to a morale problem in my day and, as we will see, a similar phenomena in his. I should mention parenthetically that it is as true today as it was in my time that if we're talking about an urban high school we're talking about a school with lots of new teachers. The reasons behind that are certainly not mysterious.

We begin this chapter with an example of how very little emphasis is placed upon executing one of the few policies that are in place to salvage an individual student from falling by the wayside in the rush to efficiently locomote unmanageable masses through the public school system.

October 16: I Discover the Teacher's Role in an IEP

The Individualized Education Program (IEP) meeting—something that my mother, a special-education advocate, has frequently participated in—is lodged in my mind as a routine procedure that was facilitated in schools as a matter of course. It is a serious legal function and as such, I assume, will be treated in a professional manner. And while I know there are often competing points of view and often disputes between the parties, my sense of an IEP meeting is that it is intended in the best interest of the child. I know, should I ever become involved in one, I intend to do my part to make the child's educational experience an appropriate one. I am looking forward to having the opportunity.

I get my chance on October 16. The student's name is William. William is a feisty, skinny, African American, whose hair seems to be his claim to fame, or if not fame then at least notoriety. Some days it's an eight-inch Afro and other days it's braided in cornrows, and a combination of rainbow colors a la Dennis Rodman, depending on his particular mood that day. William is short. I find it humorous when he wears his hair in an Afro that is almost as big as he is. William is always dressed in what is current school fashion. He hasn't been to class more than two days in any week. He tells me I'm not helping him learn math. I tell him to come after school and I'll give him individual attention. He never shows up after school let alone to the actual class sessions. He tells me he doesn't need help after school; he needs it right now. This is a problem since the bell has rung and my next class is filtering in.

The counseling office has requested my presence at an IEP meeting for William, which is to take place today. It isn't a lot of notice but I tell them I'd be happy to participate. Experienced teachers tell me I don't have to accept. Most teachers don't. At this point I can't imagine why not. I want to learn what accommodations and modifications I can make to help William be more successful in my class. I'm about to discover why not.

The IEP meeting is to take place during one of my class periods and should I choose to attend I have to find my own substitute. I have a real problem with subs because most are assigned to classes where they know nothing about the subject matter. I've heard subs in the faculty lunchroom compare subbing to babysitting and how easy it is to be a substitute since they believe they don't have to do anything. I want my substitutes to teach my students something. I will soon learn this is too much to ask.

So I reject getting the substitute and find another teacher who teaches math to take the class and I hurry off to the IEP meeting room. The IEP, legally, is required to be attended by an administrator, a parent, a general education teacher (i.e., me), and the student's case carrier who is also a special education teacher at the school—and of course the student if considered appropriate, in this instance, William.

When I arrive at the assigned room, only the case carrier is there and she doesn't know where William is. She doesn't even know who William is. Case carriers were formerly referred to as caseworkers, but in my opinion the name has been changed because they only carry their caseloads around and never actually work on them. Sorry, this is too cynical. I'm sure they work hard but with their heavy caseloads they don't always have a chance to meet all of the students whose cases they manage.

I call the counseling office, which was responsible for arranging the IEP meeting. They don't know where William is either. They also tell me they don't know what he looks like because he failed to take his "mandatory" school ID photo so it isn't in the computer and they can't call it up. I know he's in school somewhere because he was in my first period class this morning.

The case carrier is going over the rules of the IEP meeting in Spanish since she expects to have to communicate them in Spanish to the parent or surrogate. I tell her not to bother; William is African American.

By now the period is ending and William hasn't shown. The bell rings so William's lunch period is next. I feel like playing the hero in this drama and saving the IEP meeting so I decide to try to find William because nobody else seems to have any idea what to do. Nobody seems to care that I am not teaching, something that is infuriating me. I check the lunch area since I know it's one period William won't skip. I ask a group of kids from my first period class who know him where he hangs out. I'm told he hangs out everywhere. William likes to keep moving.

I can't find him so I go back to the IEP meeting room. By now the counselor has shown up and another teacher, strong-armed by the secretary, takes my sheltered class so I can give my report. I've given my lesson plan for this class to my sheltered class aide, but unfortunately she doesn't show up. We are still waiting for William in the IEP room. I'm running back and forth. I'm curious to follow this exercise to its conclusion. Because my aide hasn't shown up with my lesson plan I have to call a substitute for that period and we negotiate between what I had planned and what he would like to do.

The IEP meeting is ultimately postponed until the last period of the day. I will need another substitute and I want to find someone from the regular faculty. After a number of calls, I find a teacher from the regular faculty who is willing to take my class while I attend the IEP meeting. I'm now free to teach my fifth-period class. I begin by telling my students that I'm in a bit of a bad mood and would appreciate their sensitivity. My UCLA supervisors have often said that students respond well to honesty. Then my phone rings. I answer it and it's the teacher who had agreed to substitute for my sixth period calling to tell me she is going home sick. Now I have nobody to cover my next class so I call the counseling office and tell them my situation. They tell me I'm responsible for finding a substitute because I've committed myself to attend the IEP meeting. I feel like telling her I no longer am willing to participate in an IEP handled this dysfunctionally, but instead I tell the secretary that I'm trying to teach a class at the moment so they have to find a substitute and call me when they have. I hoped I was in a position to make such demands. It sounded reasonable but by now I have the feeling they think they're doing me a favor by finding a sub so I can do what they've asked me to do in the first place.

I now reiterate to the class that I'm in a particularly foul mood. One student says under his breath, "What, did your mom break up with you." I don't even know what to make of this comment, but it infuriates me.

I strongly inform my students they'll be sent to the guidance office if they create any problems for me. "I repeat, the guidance office, not the guidance room."

As I'm about to go over the homework, one student, Anthony, yells out, "What's the difference between the guidance office and the guidance room?" This student had checked into my class that day and was already mouthing off. I tell him it's in his best interest to be quiet. I'm about to fly off the handle. He insists he needs to know the difference. By now I feel teaching describes hell more adequately than Dante's Inferno. I turn and yell at him, "I don't give a shit what you want to know!"

Within seconds I come to my senses and ask him to step outside with me. I apologize to Anthony for cursing at him. He tells me it's ok with him, everybody he knows curses at him all the time, especially his parents.

He returns to the room happy and not in the least bit interested in the difference between the guidance office and the guidance room. I then apologize to the class for my grossly inappropriate loss of self-control.

The counseling office manages to secure another teacher, not math, but someone with a teaching credential, to teach for the twelve minutes I am being allotted to give my report on William and I rush down to the IEP room ready to give my report. When I arrive only William and a secretary are there and she's yelling at him for not showing up when he was supposed to. After a few calls and a short wait the counselor and case carrier are collected. William did not have a parent or guardian present. When I asked why, I was told his grandmother, with whom he lives, found it to be "too much of a hassle" to bring herself to the school for these meetings. I give my report quickly, sign a form, and go back to class, thoroughly disenchanted with the IEP process. I imagine William's grandmother has also become disenchanted with this process.

October 18: An Amusing Racial Slur or Racism?

Camilla, a bright Chicana with a bit of an attitude in my Algebra II class, presented me today with yet another how do you deal with this kind of problem puzzle. It seems for every math problem I hand them they repay me by behaving in ways I don't know how to handle. I was making a point in class about the importance of homework in preparation for an upcoming quiz and when I came to the end of my point I heard Camilla's voice say, "Yeah, whatever white boy!"

I looked over at her and I didn't see any hostility. She seemed actually to be working on a problem we were doing before I talked about the homework. My first reaction was to be amused so I did what I usually do when I'm amused. I smiled. But before I went on with the lesson I found myself hesitating because I wasn't sure a smile was the best response. I looked over at Camilla and waited until she looked up at me, then I told her that comments about the color of somebody's skin are not appropriate in this class even if they are not meant to be put-downs. Camilla lowered her eyes and I heard, "Yeah, whatever." Maybe that was followed by "white boy" in her mind, but at least it didn't come out of her mouth. I've discovered that even the best students have little familiarity with what types of behavior are appropriate in the classroom. I, for some reason, assumed norms surrounding classroom behavior would not be something I would have to emphasize just to create an environment where I could teach.

October 24: "Sometimes They're Just Too Weird."

I call my dad from my cell phone on my drive home from school. The traffic is always bad when I leave school so we both take this opportunity to go over the day's events. Many of the vignettes reported here are recorded from my drive-home calls from the rush hour traffic on the San Diego Freeway. I call in particular today to talk about Robert. I just don't know what to do about him. Robert is Latino, has no special-education identification, although I suspect of all the students I've yet had Robert has the most special-education needs. His English isn't bad but his words don't constitute intelligible sentences. He laughs at things I say that are not meant to be funny and says equally unfunny things himself and laughs up a storm. He pays no attention to classroom tasks, fails all of his tests but doesn't seem to care; he daydreams and draws and when I ask him questions, his affect is impossible to assess. He gives bizarre answers to basic questions. It feels sometimes like he's talking to somebody who isn't really there.

I've secured a copy of Robert's transcript and see that the only classes he's ever passed in his two years at Olympia High are art and PE. Then I check with some of Robert's other teachers, teachers who have seen every type of deviant student behavior but with Robert the response is the same from all teachers. "The kid is weird." The advice is the same as well, "Since he's quiet, just let him sit in the back and draw until he's old enough to leave school."

I put in a request for a meeting of a student study team (SST) to assess Robert for special-education needs and am told by the counseling office secretary not to expect a response any time soon because the last thing the school needs is more special-education students. She told me that all special-education classes have reached their enrollment caps.

My dad asks me (we're still on the phone and I'm still on the freeway) why I'm having such a hard time taking the advice of my colleagues. I tell him, "Because his education needs are not being served. I believe I can show Robert what's interesting about mathematics. I could begin with the important relationship between math and art. I know I can do more for him now than anyone else is. I can't believe other teachers have just given up on him."

My dad then asked me, "What is the relationship between math and art?"

I told him I hadn't figured out yet how to find a relationship that will seem important to Robert. I ask him if he knows of any work that's been done in that area. He tells me that he does but it's not a fit topic for freeway driving. He also raises questions about why I didn't get to deal with it in my teacher-education program. I tell him it's a good question but we can finish the discussion later. My cell phone bill is rising out of sight.

October 25:
Coffee Time Wisdom—Blaming the Victims

I go to the teachers' cafeteria before school for coffee every morning. The coffee is not good, but I like the settling feeling of catching my breath between the stressful freeway and the start of classes. I sit with a few experienced teachers who are also settling down. I like to chat with this group although I'm somewhat bothered that the chatter often leads to complaints, mostly complaints about troublesome students. I sense the right to complain comes with tenure and experience. It seems to me to be very much a reflection of poor morale. I'm also very aware that the students who are complained about, actually blamed, are victims of the fact we've found nothing to motivate them to care. This is our job and we're failing miserably.

I raise some questions, based on my confusion about how Robert had ended up in my class, about the placement problems in the school. The teachers blame it on incompetent administrators and counselors, then go on to complain about how none of these issues ever get dealt with at faculty meetings because the principal listens to all the views and then does whatever he wants anyway. Again, it's a morale issue, a reflection of how little input teachers feel they have in the way things get done. What I'm most surprised by is that they seem to take placement screwups as a fact of life and not a problem that urgently needs fixing. I leave the cafeteria convinced they are wrong placing the blame on incompetent counselors and administrators. Sometimes they blame the parents for not caring what happens with their children, not overseeing their children's placements. At this stage I don't blame anybody. I'm pretty convinced the logistics are just unmanageable. We all need to try to work together as effectively as possible.

October 26: Another of My Soul-Searching Moments

I'm troubled because I think I'm becoming too mean to my kids in my attempt to get a handle on the classroom management problems. They make me angry by the way some refuse to respond to my efforts to develop personal relationships with them. I let them know it is their classroom, that they have the power, that I am concerned about their welfare, individually and as a group. I think this anger may be leading me to provoke them to confront me after I've singled them out for disrupting the class. They may interpret it as a kind of betrayal, a betrayal of the friendship hand I've held out to them. If I come across to them as a mean, punitive teacher, I'm going against my every intention. It's very troubling.

My teacher-education program impressed upon me the notion that if students are allowed to construct their own rules, there will be nothing motivating them to break them and everything motivating them to work within them. Even when students create classroom rules for behavior, I am the one who unilaterally has to enforce them. The problem is many students push the boundary no matter whose boundary it is. When they do I become the evil dictator that maintains order. I'm uncomfortable with this role but feel compelled to play it to maintain classroom control. I'm in limbo between UCLA's theory and my classroom practice.

October 29: Getting Antonio's Attention

Antonio, a Latino with short, spiky hair, in a class loaded with discipline problems (Antonio is the boy who was so concerned with putting the bird out of its misery with one emphatic stomp), is out of control again. I can't spend a lot of time trying to get the troublemakers to behave in this class or none of the students who are willing to learn will get any work done. I tell Antonio I'm going to call his parents. He tells me, "I don't give a fuck!" This is a predictable response. I smile and continue with the lesson and Antonio sits and thinks about it.

After class I make the call. Antonio's mother tells me they can't control him either so I can't expect any help from them. I then ask her what does she think I should do with him? After a pause, his mother tells me I might be able to get some support from his probation officer. She gives me the number.

The next day Antonio is misbehaving in class. I tell him that he probably wants to control his behavior. He looks over at me incredulously. "Why?" he asks, rudely chuckling.

"Because," I say, "I have a phone number you probably don't want me to call."

The whole class is now interested. Antonio, still thinking I'm full of shit, says, "Oh you're not going to call my mom again." He and a couple of his friends bust up laughing. I inform him that I'm not going to call his mom again. I tell Antonio that the person whose number I intend to call probably doesn't want to hear he's been misbehaving in school. Antonio still thinks I'm bluffing. "OK, what the fuck is the number?"

I read the number aloud and Antonio loses it. He starts yelling to the class that I'm harassing him and he's going to go to the principal. He stomps out of the room, slamming the door. I shouldn't have embarrassed him in front of the entire class. It's difficult in the moment to always make the best judgments. He would be hostile toward me because of this humiliation for some time to come.

After school I call Antonio's probation officer who tells me he'll deal with it and Antonio will be much improved the next day. Antonio's behavior *is* much improved the next day. I know it won't last but I appreciate the hiatus.

October 29: The Brer Rabbit Gambit

Today I discovered a wrinkle in the overall management of discipline cases. I saw it on the face of one of the students whom I had sent to the guidance room. The boy was smiling as he left the room. I asked the class why they thought he was smiling and one student told me that in the guidance room he won't have to do any math, all they do is hang out with their friends and write an essay. Frequently they write the same essay they've written several times before. Nobody keeps a record of the essays. Of course I don't like the idea of rewarding students for being kicked out of class and it troubles me how many students would rather write essays in the guidance room than do math. At the same time, I have to accept that the class runs smoother when the kids who hate math are in the guidance room rather than in mine.

October 31: When Is a Loss a Gain?

Today I've learned that two problem students in my Intro classes are being transferred to other schools. My first reaction is relief, my second ambivalence. I did have hopes of being able to get through to both of them. Once again I'm reminded by senior teachers to be grateful for small favors. "Concentrate," I'm told, "on the ones you don't have to fight to get through to." I'm not there yet. A third student, Pablo, one of my best students, someone I can always count on to ask good questions and motivate his peers, has transferred out to a school with a better reputation for sending students to good colleges. I know he will have better opportunities there and I'm happy for him, but I wish he had the same opportunities here.

October 31: Happy Halloween

Today I feel I've really gotten through to my students. They told me that I passed out better Halloween candy than any of their other teachers. It made my day.

Analysis

The IEP experience with William shook Paul's dependence on predictability and convinced him even the most of what he took to be official and serious functions can and often do go awry. This occurs in part because they are not taken seriously. In another part, as one author assesses it, the execution of the IEP does not necessarily guarantee its implementation (Byrnes 2004).

Paul is starting to learn that when more than one or two people are involved in an IEP, from call for, to set up, to execution, there is much more room for mis- or noncommunication. Also he feels many teachers don't want to participate. It's too much trouble for harried teachers to worry about failing students.

It is our sense that the inability of many urban high schools to salvage capable students is the main indication of the failure of the role schools play in the pursuit of social justice. The case of William suggests how it is more than that, that even students who will have no interest in or possibility of higher education can have a chance of a better future if they can graduate high school and be motivated to attain certain skills that will help them get work after high school. In William's case nobody seemed actively engaged in paying much attention to him at all, and Paul's experience with William's IEP meeting exposed him to this sorry circumstance.

Paul learned he doesn't know the best ways to deal with some issues that call attention to the fact he is involved in a multiracial, multiethnic, and multicultural enterprise. This is the kind of thing the training program needed to confront but didn't. The training program did emphasize in many ways the fact of these racial and ethnic and cultural differences but never helped the students develop ways of responding to troubling events that exposed these differences in conflictual ways. We are not talking here about proactive multicultural exercises that teacher-education programs include; we're talking about latent feelings about other races that sometimes become manifest, even when students aren't aware of what they're saying or when they're joking. Paul doesn't think Camilla was trying to be hostile. She's a savvy student and is focused normally on doing well and not causing trouble. Paul needs to be asking how other white teachers have dealt with similar issues. Presumably white teachers in minority schools (by far the majority) should be color-blind. At least, according to one survey (Schoenfeld 1986), they say they are. But is color-blindness enough? Perhaps understanding the way race operates to inform student relationships with teachers, and others of different races, is more important than color "blindness" in understanding how to be effective in a classroom. One study (Johnson 2002) concluded that one's personal experiences prior to becoming a teacher are more important than the assumption that one is "color-blind." Another suggestion based upon Johnson's study is that it helps to have men and women of color in your teacher-education program. Paul's teacher-education group had a significant number of Latino students which he found helpful in helping him orient to working in a Latino environment.

The conception that all students can be placed in the most appropriate slots (classes) for them in a school the size of Paul's, with its attendance fluctuations, overcrowding, and failure rates, is naïve. Placement in Paul's school is a work of manipulation that makes the resolution of a Rubik's Cube seem like child's play. Often, as Paul has related, counselors don't have all the data they need on students and it isn't always easy to get, and to make the counselor's work even more difficult, as discoveries about where kids really belong are uncovered, the classes suitable for them are often filled to legal capacity. Consequently, Paul has students in his Intro classes who have passed Algebra I, and there are students in Algebra I who have failed both Intro A and B. Paul has also discovered that there are a number of seniors in his Intro class who have passed all the way through geometry, but just need credits to graduate. Of course the consequence of this for Paul's classroom management is the latter group of students, bored with the elementary material, joins with students who have no interest in learning the elementary material to foment disorder. Unmanageable logistics explain a lot about why some classrooms are unmanageable. The question we are left with in an environment where teachers often blame the students for their failure is whose fault is it that the logistics of student placement are unmanageable. If we look carefully at a number of factors that could explain the placement dysfunction, we would have to conclude the interaction between legislative support for personnel and resources, coupled with the inability of the organizational structure to compensate for the shortfall, leads to placement errors. It appears to boil down to administrative priorities, where considerable resources need to be funneled into the student safety factor with reduced support for careful placement action.

Morale is a rubber band concept. It stretches a number of ways and overlaps several concepts. It can convey a sense of disillusionment, anger, or a sense of impotence in affecting either learning or change. It can be thought of as a quality of an individual's attitude or it can be identified as a characteristic of the performance of a group. There can be good morale and bad morale; it can range from despair to disappointment or some indication of the opposite of both. It can show up in dysfunctional behavior within organizations and can be related to a wide range of accomplishments or a lack of them. In addition, and of some consequence, is the possibility that low morale and high alienation are conditions that many teachers consider normal, predictable, and something that one needs to live with.

We are using the term "morale" here to connote the perception on the part of teachers that their condition within the organization of the school is one of alienation. And by that we primarily mean feelings of powerlessness and self-estrangement (Seeman 1959). Poor morale is highly correlated with leaving the profession, which in turn is associated with a number of alienation conditions, sending many teachers scurrying from the urban classroom.

The average career these days for teaching in general is eleven years; in the urban secondary school 50 percent of the teachers leave within five years (Stevens 2001; Hanushek et al. 2003).

In Paul's teacher-education program students were encouraged to read the work of Paulo Freire. The Freirian notion of helping students learn by empowering them to see and control the forces that diminished them was inspiring (Freire 1973). But what was the actual utility of that understanding on the part of the new teacher once he entered the urban classroom? In Paul's view this was an inapplicable idea because the students had no sense of themselves as exploited victims—or alienated for that matter. It was just the nature of the beast called schooling. Nor could they see any obvious connection between their education and what they could do with it by way of liberation. Unlike Freire's peasants who could understand that they would have more control over their life if they could read, Paul's students can't see any practical application in their daily lives of being able to solve algebraic problems. This apparently is the first step, getting students to see why their school lives seem so unrewarding and recognize they have an important investment in becoming educated.

Paul's hope, based on his idealism in this area, and this of course involves his search for acceptance by his students (he no longer hopes for love) is that he is there for them, working in their best interest, even if they have no idea what their best interest is.

Paul has learned, to his dismay although not to his surprise, that many students would rather be in the guidance room writing essays than having to do math in his room. They seem to hate math so much they have decided this is a permanent attitude, that they will never learn it or want to learn it. It appears they are not open to the possibility of Paul, or any math teacher, showing them some reasons to enjoy the subject. At this point he is losing his faith that, if they don't like the subject, they can be made to do it anyhow, as a path to later success. Delayed gratification doesn't seem to be a strong motivator in his school. The issue of what might motivate unmotivated students in urban schools has been a topic of considerable interest and importance in the academic as well as the schooling community (National Research Council 2004), but Paul has not yet been able to apply their solutions to his teaching. We suspect the reason for this is most solutions coming from academic researchers do not take into account that most institutions the size and complexity of urban secondary schools do not have the freedom or flexibility to experiment with innovative strategies.

If he had thought about it, Paul could have expected a certain number of "problem" students to be transferred out because it is a district policy (probably unwritten), probably a policy in many school districts, to recycle kids the district has given up on, until they're old enough to drop out. This does not sit well with Paul's social justice training and consciousness, but what's a first year teacher to do. On the other hand, he hadn't yet, until Pablo, given much thought to the transferring of students who were making real progress in his class, to another school where there won't be as many distractions of class routines by contentious students. Paul's conclusion, at this point, is that as much as he wants his students to succeed here, he is still happy for them if they find a way to increase their opportunities by going elsewhere.

CHAPTER FIVE

~

Collegiality and Social Class

In this chapter Paul will introduce his colleagues. All I know about Paul's colleagues is what he has told me but that was enough for me to make some comparison with my own colleagues back in the late fifties and early sixties. First of all it was important to both of us to have the support of our fellow teachers and to speak with them regularly. Unfortunately, the topic was and is usually the same: the problems we have with students and the dumb and sometimes funny things they say and do. It is good to hear from the trials of our colleagues that we're not the only ones who don't have the magic formula for classroom management.

Without his colleagues, Paul believes this year would already have compromised his well-being. Without the strong community in his math department, teaching would have been a lonely and, in some ways, a fruitless endeavor. I should also make note of the fact that community support in both our cases was a buffer against the alienation we both would have suffered in the face of an unsupportive principal and administrative staff who had no interest in our point of view. Where new teachers need perspective and class management suggestions badly, the need for collegiality is greater.

There is also the social factor that is important in a couple of ways. The most important way of course is the matter of seeing each other as complete human beings. After a drink or two on Friday after school, Paul's experience and mine were identical. There was the joy of collegiality, to see our fellow teachers as men and women who can have fun as well as act like professionals once we hit the school grounds. In my day the male teachers were required to wear suits and ties and the women were asked to wear dresses and hose, which made the informality of our social gatherings all the more relaxing. Paul does have some restraints but the dress code for teachers is much more relaxed. That may not be just a superficial change.

Another value I have always attached to getting to know my colleagues was to spend time with people I would not have normally associated with. Many of my colleagues were World War II veterans who enjoyed relating their war stories to those of us who were too young for service. Teaching for these men, at least those I got to know, was a step up in class-consciousness as well as social class itself. They were African American, Anglo, and Latino alike, mostly sons of working-class parents and were the first in their families to go to college. The GI Bill had created a mass exodus for children of industrial or farm laborers into the middle class. Paul has had similar encounters with the social mobility factor, but in his case it was more likely to be female based with Latinas and male linked with Filipinos.

A career in teaching has, until recent days, been an upward mobility strategy for children of the working classes. My experience of thirty some years working in teacher education provided me with the opportunity to observe children of minority groups in the process of increasing their life opportunities. The one thing I'm certain about is that this mobility phenomenon is accompanied by a far greater emphasis on long-term career goals for the average graduate of a teacher-education program than was the case in my day. Surveys we conducted in the early years of my teacher-training days (1965 to 1980) revealed that fewer than 20 percent of our graduates were in the classroom four years down the road.

Another thing Paul and I have in common is our strong suspicion about the actual value of the amount of testing we were and are required to do. In fifty years no one has been able to shift the value of testing from the school's needs to the students. There has, for many years, been an "accountability" justification and there still is as we witness the rationale for the No Child Left Behind legislation, but this has almost never resulted in a restructuring of the big schools that don't pass the mustard.

Tests have always been used to give teachers a basis for grading or to give the school a record that can be compared to other schools in the district. Paul will talk about testing, which he finds both excessive and not always a benefit to his particular goals. Except for the fact that it was one time when students were usually silent and occupied, I never found the amount of testing we did in my schools productive. If tests were used diagnostically and there was follow-up to the results based upon individualizing instruction, I would take a different view. The idea of using tests to establish one's accountability as a teacher or to motivate students to study is, to my way of thinking, vastly overrated in the urban secondary school. What it accomplishes, as much as anything else, is keeping the curriculum focused on standardized outcomes where the whole class can be tested simultaneously, thereby depressing opportunities for individualizing instruction. It also becomes the criteria by which teachers are evaluated rather than more important qualities like the ability to relate to students and to gear instruction to individual levels of understanding.

I did give tests as required by my administrators but for many of my students I knew it was a complete waste of time since students who had no interest in learning the subject matter were seldom concerned about how they would do on the test. This is exactly Paul's experience today. Why have we learned so little about testing in fifty years? The answer is because we find testing to be an efficient way to evaluate a large number of students simultaneously and in the urban school it demonstrates that teaching and testing students as if they're all at the same level of understanding is a sure way to produce a whole lot of failures, which we have. And as a final point on the subject of testing, it is one of the best ways to convince a student of his worthlessness. For most unmotivated students there is nothing like a consistent pattern of Fs on tests to convince a student school is not for him or her.

Like Paul I was sensitive to a considerable degree about social-class differences between students at my schools and others within the various districts. One area where it shows up is when teams from a more affluent part of the city or county come to compete in team sports like football and basketball. There is definitely an increased level of hostility, which is bad enough when teams compete, but it is made worse when social-class differences compound the feelings based on competition alone. In my day when my school's team competed with other district schools it was often a matter of a white team vs. a black team. Nowadays the mostly white schools have teams made up primarily of minority players.

When I first went into teaching I was assigned to inner-city schools because that's where the openings were for teachers, and I have to admit I felt a sense of inferiority to teachers in more affluent schools. This was something that grew on me from the first, whereas with Paul, at the Palm Springs conference, it was a surprise. My association with working in minority-dominated schools rubbed off on my psyche at first in ways it didn't after the first couple of years when I began to see my kind of teaching as vastly more challenging and rewarding than teaching students who would have achieved without a teacher. Paul, on the other hand, set out to work in an urban school since that's where he saw the challenge of teaching, not because that was where the jobs were, a very much more mature and socially conscious decision than I made.

Paul is beginning to see just how arbitrary financial allocations can be but it is never, in his experience, a question of allocating resources frivolously. There's always some need. It's a matter of the priority of one need over another. The main thing he has learned here is that budget priorities are not his business, nor are they any teacher's for that matter. Nothing has changed in the monolithic public high school in this area in the half century between my experience and Paul's. Teachers are just not in the loop where decisions about resource allocations are made, except in the rare secondary school where shared decision-making models of governance are in effect.

Finally, by way of introducing some of the content Paul is about to present, I should mention that one of my most memorable associations about urban teaching is the presence of humor in the classroom. My students and Paul's students were and are funny, many to degrees that interfere with their study habits. No classroom in the urban school, I would surmise, is devoid of very funny students, and for teachers who appreciate good humor as much as Paul and I do, there are bound to be as many laughs as there are tears. Unfortunately, classroom humor often does get out of hand and students need to be reigned in so the teacher who needs a laugh now and then and knows the students need one too, needs to find a way to keep students from letting go of the classroom lesson. Now, back to Paul and his world.

My Colleagues

I think it's important to point out that my students are not all there is to my urban school experience. After a couple of months, I've come to identify the adults in my school that help me see that my teaching life is not a solitary experience. Without these people I would rot away at the dry-erase board, isolated within my classroom. Certain people, some experienced teachers, some of my program colleagues, some administrators, some staff personnel, my graduate program field supervisors, are involved in my teaching day, in helping with decision making, my structuring the ways I deal with certain problems, or just listening while I vent my frustrations (and I have many). Without this, many tears would have been shed and my emotional state shaken.

The woman who teaches math in the room next to mine, Claire, whom I have already mentioned, continues to be a godsend for a new teacher. She let me know that whenever a student is out of control, I can send him or her over and she'll return the prodigal when he or she has cooled down. She doesn't imply that she's a better disciplinarian by the offer, but rather the notion that students often need a change of pace; they have to detach from the context that provoked their misbehavior.

Generally, Claire's interaction with students is thoroughly comfortable and genuine. She's seen all the problems I've had and many more and she communicates the sense that I'm not here to solve all the problems I see around me, but I better get accustomed to them because they never stop. I don't know how successfully I will be able to internalize this advice because I do see it as my job to solve many of the problems I see in my classroom, most of which have nothing to do with mathematics. A few of us first-year teachers see Claire as a "double agent." She connects well with the experienced teachers and the administration and then passes on to us what they think and say about us.

My department chair, Anthony, a Filipino man in his early thirties, was a student himself at Olympia High and doesn't let students forget it. If he made it to college and beyond so can they. He doesn't want to hear any complaints or excuses about their disadvantaged resources or difficult home lives if they're used as explanations for not doing their work. If they need to talk and share their pain, he's a good listener. Anthony is a funny, warm, friendly, and tough guy. He chews out students with a vengeance that makes them sit up straight with their mouths open, and they respond to him. Along with Claire, Anthony is a major receptacle for my discards of the day, kids I need to temporarily remove from the classroom if I'm going to have half a chance to teach. Students want to be on Anthony's good side because there's a lot to be gained by that. Many students tell me they are afraid of him. He makes them work harder than most other math teachers. Many of my students who are transferred to his class beg for me to take them back. I take this as an insult, but at the moment I have more pressing things with which to concern myself.

George is another math teacher, also Filipino, also from our UCLA program a few years back. He's a top-notch teacher with a major league sense of humor about the trials and tribulations of an urban high school teacher that perhaps surpasses mine. He keeps me laughing, and is, far and away, the funniest teacher in the school. I want to grow up to be like him, good and funny. There's little question that seeing urban schooling through a comical lens will keep me sane as I confront its many stressors.

Celia is a colleague in the math department, a young Korean woman with whom I like to talk, mainly because she can be so positive in the face of all the negatives. She always seems to be enjoying her work, despite many of the everyday tribulations. The thing about Celia, who is very youthful and sweet, is that she's not at all tough like one would imagine a teacher would have to be to survive here. She does more than survive; she has fun. She's the most creative of the math teachers in terms of the activities she brings to the classroom. She's also started a class for SAT preparation. Sometimes I think some of the activities she does are a little too corny to be effective, but she seems to make them work.

Leslie, my friend from my program, who has been teaching in the experimental program, a school within a school concept, seems to have the same range of discipline problems I do. Even though, presumably, her students are "creamed." That is, they are the students whose parents have requested that their children participate in this program. We share our stress stories regularly. Leslie cries more than I do, but some days do bring me to tears. She is still far from being hardened by the way some students relate to her. Leslie is white, in her early twenties and went to the high school across the freeway that is the symbol of privilege to many of the students in our school and one of our main competitors on the sports field. Our students know it as a rich white kids' school. Leslie very rarely tells any of her students where she went to high school. We remain good friends and helpful colleagues.

My favorite staff person is the head of the data-processing center, a woman named Lucia. Lucia sits behind her computer most of the day every day and I think she likes the little interruptions we teachers give her when we need a change of pace ourselves. Lucia, aside from her computer duties, is often called upon to help out in the area of translation, particularly to translate for irritated parents when an official translator can't be found. Lucia has a gift for calming agitated parents. She is in her early thirties, Latina, married, funny, and supportive of all teachers who come to her for assistance. I stop in from time to time just to chat and she fills me in on some of the mysterious forces operating behind the closed doors of the administrative wing.

Those are my significant colleagues. I expect I'll be developing more as time passes. I'd like to interact more with teachers from other disciplines but I don't see a way of making that happen right now.

November 1: The Obligatory Friday Test

Today, in my last class on Friday, my only advanced class, I consider, given the students' pleas, not giving the Friday assessment test I usually give. My motivation for the Friday test is that it is something of a tradition, a folk wisdom that holds one should give tests on Friday because the students are anticipating the weekend and are consequently bound to be frisky. While their minds are shifting to the prospects of weekend fun, the school culture has developed its own strategy to reel them back to the pragmatic world in front of them. It's not easy for them to stay focused and I suspect it's a reason why many students don't do well on the test. I also suspect it's one reason why there are more absences on Friday than other days of the week. The test, as well as the fact our students like longer weekends, account for the fact there are more truancies on Fridays and Mondays than on the other three school days. Personally, I find the test useful in that it keeps me abreast of individual student progress as well as helps me modify the next week's lesson plan.

I tell my last period class that if they can act like it's a school day and not a weekend trailer party, I won't give the test. They all agree to do their work and they do and I don't give the test. I'm wondering if this strategy will work with my other classes, since they are not as conscientious as this class. I may try it.

November 4: Social Class on the Gridiron

Being a loyal and enthusiastic supporter of everything I'm associated with, since I don't get into winning and losing too much, I attended my first Olympia High football game, which happened to be against the upper-middle-class "rich white kids" school on the ocean side of the freeway. Unfortunately, football is not the main sport of most of the Latino students at this school. They prefer soccer and they have an excellent team. Actually, they won the state championship the previous year. But they are outmatched on the football field in this sport and don't do very well. I've attended the game with my friend Leslie who has decided—wisely I think—not to join the other school's alumni band that is playing between halves, even though she was an avid band member when she attended the school we're playing and had been invited to participate.

November 8: Down and Out in Palm Springs

This past weekend I attended a National Council for the Teaching of Mathematics (NCTM), the largest mathematics teachers' organization in the country, conference in Palm Springs. After finishing my grading around midnight on Thursday, I got in my car and drove to Palm Springs, about one hundred miles east of LA. I was sharing a hotel room with a teacher from my UCLA program, Eugene, who teaches in my district. He and two of his female colleagues were waiting for me to arrive so we could sample the bar scene. I arrived around 3 A.M. due to heavy drizzle and sandstorms on the freeway. When I arrived, I realized my colleagues had already spent the evening sampling the bar scene at the hotel where we were staying. They now wanted to sample the city's after-hours scene. I was relegated to the roll of designated driver since I was the only sober one. Nobody seemed to care that I had just driven for three tough hours. All I could think was: what would the administration that had financed this trip think about how we spent our time and what would our students, who believed we were middle-aged and boring, think of this spectacle?

It rained hard most of the weekend and the sky was somber and before long my mood began to catch up with it. There were, as far as I could tell, a lot of teachers there who taught advanced placement math classes in middle- and upper-middle-class high schools. It was primarily a conference that focused on the best ways of teaching mathematics and not much on how we might deal with students who have absolutely no interest in learning mathematics. The two concepts were treated as distinct.

I found myself placed in a discussion group where I was the only one from my type of school, where more of our Introduction to Algebra students fail a math class than pass one. I had a strong sense that my concerns were not the concerns of most of the others in the group. It was not that I considered the more academic aspects of math education unimportant; I do have a love for the subject matter and a deep interest in ways of teaching it. Much of my disappointment derived from being in work groups where my opinions didn't seem to carry much weight. I thought that this had to do either with my youth and lack of experience or because I was a teacher in a poor "ghetto" school where academic issues don't take as much of a priority.

November 15: Keep It Private

Today I confront a female student, Angelina, who is spending much of the class time gabbing with a classmate, about her nonstop talking to the girl in the seat next to her. The confrontation leads to a back-and-forth dialogue between Angelina and myself. She doesn't miss a beat turning from her friend to me. Her tongue is greased and she has an argument at the tip of her tongue. Her justification for her talking is the person with whom she'd been talking, in the seat next to her, is a close friend, with whom she can never talk during the week because she has to go to work right after school. They have different lunch periods, and there are several other obstacles to maintaining their friendship that are private and I wouldn't understand. I counter this argument with my opinion that school is a place where one can learn something as well as nourish one's friendships, but not always at the same time. I believe I have created an environment that allows some students to spend all their time on friendships and fail and other students to do their work and pass. This is not my intention and I'll give this problem a lot of thought. I tell her I am definitely partial to students maintaining friendships, but at different times of the day outside my classroom.

Angelina continues to argue and I tell her if she does not cease and desist I intend to call her parents. She responds that she doesn't care. All this is done in front of her classmates. I realize that arguing with me is something she needs to do in front of her classmates, but I tell her calling her parents now is something I need to do.

That night I call her parents and Angelina answers the phone. Once she realizes I am the one calling, she begins apologizing for her behavior. She asks that I change her seat so she won't talk to the friend, but she can't be seen as requesting it. Angelina and I conspire for her to talk in class and when that occurs I will change her seat. The following day Angelina has her seat changed and is totally cooperative, working hard at her new desk.

November 20:
A Laugh a Day Keeps the Craziness Away

I think by now I see that humor in my classroom is fortunately unavoidable. Kids are funny and I believe in laughter as benevolent as long as it's not hurtful. Smart kids, regardless of their academic standing, are particularly funny. I've discovered that a good laugh on a bad day is very welcome. The laugh of the day this day comes from our friend Antonio, whom I introduced earlier as the boy who tried to stomp on a bird with his shoes. He also has a probation officer who has made my life easier. Sufficient time has also passed for him to forgive me for tactlessly confronting him in front of the entire class, a habit I have been trying hard to unlearn when I address classroom management problems.

Antonio has been doing better in class the past few weeks. He has a reputation around school as a member of a "tagging crew," so today, after he finishes a quiz early and because of his improved behavior in class, I decide to reward him by giving him an activity he will enjoy, knowing his penchant for getting into trouble in his free time. I give Antonio a couple of dry-erase markers and tell him he can use them on my board while the other students are finishing their tests.

Antonio seems pleased at first, but after awhile decides the markers aren't suitable for maintaining his reputation as a major league "tagger." So he turns from the board to me and says, "Hey man, these markers suck, you got any spray paint?"

November 21: Aha!—The Explanation Surfaces

Robert, my "weird" student, whom I requested to be evaluated by a student study team (SST), was still awaiting evaluation. An SST is a group of people (e.g., school psychologist, teacher, administrator, health professional, and sometimes a parent) who are assigned to a particular student whose educational progress is not progressing. They are often students whose behavior in the classroom is excessively disruptive. The SST meets regularly to assess the students. It makes recommendations for interventions in the classroom or for services outside the classroom.

Robert's only passing grades after two years at Olympia High are in art and PE, but he would be happy to know 156 other Olympia students had worse grade point averages. He is a leading candidate for the "leave him alone and before you know it, he'll be old enough to leave." This is the no-treatment treatment and is the perspective espoused by most of my senior colleagues. One colleague told me I seemed "obsessed" with this battle to save Robert. I think this is a flagrant misuse of a very powerful word. An "obsession" as I take it is usually used to connote a sickness. At worst I think he might have used the term "naïve." I'll readily admit to naïveté. This teacher does not believe Robert has special education needs and does believe I am needlessly wasting my time and energy. It's hard for a first-year teacher to swallow this point of view since, when we came out of our teacher-education program, we came with the belief that every child's educational needs could and should be accommodated. My view is that special education could make a difference for Robert. I'm not opposed to inclusion of students with disabilities, but a special-education designation would qualify Robert for special assistance to help him be successful in either the special- or general-education classroom. None of that seems to be in the cards for Robert. It is a joke that no one is even evaluating him. I bug his counselor every week or so and she assures me she is on it. On one occasion, in a fit of frustration, she admits she has been too busy to deal with any of her special-education students, let alone keep up with the student study team requests. I tell her I understand her being busy. I hope my tone conveys a note of sarcasm. I do understand, however, that counselors are grossly overworked. That fact, unfortunately, does little to help Robert.

I find out today that some information has surfaced to turn people around regarding what needs to be done for Robert. It turns out that several years earlier Robert was in an automobile accident at which time he suffered a traumatic brain injury. Now my request to have him evaluated for special-education services is seen to have merit. Why it took so many years for this information to find its way into Robert's records is mystifying. One of the characteristics of the urban school, I suppose, is there are unlikely to be knowledgeable advocates in the home. It is not something that could have happened in my suburban school where parents and advocates would never allow the bureaucracy to cheat kids out of an appropriate educational experience if they could help it.

November 22: A Gratifying Contact with Parents

I spent the evening calling the parents of students who are getting high marks in my classes. No member of the faculty ever suggested to me that this was a good thing to do. It was also not mentioned in my teacher-education program. Ninety percent of the input I've received since joining the faculty has focused on strategies for dealing with discipline problems and students who have trouble learning the math content, not on little things that could be done to help achieving students feel good about their achievements.

At first the parents I call act concerned, as if the call must have something to do with their child getting into trouble for one reason or another. When I tell them no, I was calling to tell them how well their children were doing, they have a hard time normalizing. They've never received this kind of call before. I hear some parents, both mothers and fathers, choking back tears. The responses from the parents warm my heart and assure me that making these calls would become a regular feature of my teaching practice.

November 22: Humor in the Dislocation of the Context of Language

I'm teaching probability using dice, trying to get students to understand the concept of sample space, when I ask the question, "OK, I just rolled a two, what else could I have rolled?"

One of my students, Rodney, calls out, "A ball!" It's too bad creativity was not one of his IEP goals.

Same day, another giggle. I hold up the textbook that the students should be using and suggest they think of it as the class bible. Dejaun raises his hand and tells me he prefers the King James Version because he doesn't understand any of the stuff in my bible. The truth is he's beginning to understand more than he knows, but it's still funny.

I've been thinking lately that one of the toughest jobs in a school like mine is convincing students who don't have a lot of confidence in their knowledge or ability that they are capable. In the high school I attended the problem was just the opposite: many students assumed they knew a lot more than they were given credit for.

I'm thankful that my students are funny. They also seem to appreciate my brand of humor. Without humor, I think for me, it would be impossible to teach in the face of many of the negatives that one experiences in an urban school. Examples of these negatives that most perturb me are the misuse of aides in classes with English learners, the endless number of problems that accrue from poor special-education identifications, and the high failure rates of students in the lowest level math classes. Without my kids the invidious system would eat me whole. I never thought I would say it, but THANK GOD FOR THE STUDENTS.

November 25: Arrested Development

Dejaun comes into class late today. In addition to a regular hall pass he has an excuse note from the Los Angeles Juvenile Court. After completing the lesson, I walk to his desk to find out what's going on. I sit in the unoccupied chair next to him. This seems to relax him. He tells me that last night he and a couple of his homeboys had been hanging out and the cops busted them. I inquire as to why they'd been busted. I can see he is very reluctant to talk. I tell him I'm not working undercover. He laughs but that's as far as we get, just that he had been somewhere he wasn't supposed to be and had taken something he wasn't supposed to take.

After class he came up to my desk and I sense he wants to talk some more. I'd been thinking he was probably charged with something like petty theft, not the best thing for a seventeen-year-old urban African American boy, but I'm still of the opinion he can overcome it.

I ask him what the charge is. He reluctantly tells me he's being charged with three felony counts of robbery. He told me the DA is trying to have him tried as an adult.

I know very little about the workings of the criminal justice system. I'd served on a jury in a civil suit in an affluent neighborhood four years ago. I also have seen the original version of *Twelve Angry Men*, but that's it. I'd never been charged with a crime. I once appeared in court to contest a traffic ticket. I have no experience that will help me guide Dejaun through this debacle. I decide I'd be of more service if I just listen. I tell him I don't know the process or procedures and ask if he'd explain them to me. He tells me he knows nothing other than what he's being charged with. He will find out if he's being tried as an adult at his court appearance in one week. I tell him I'd be happy to write him a shining letter of recommendation for the court appearance and ask if he has any questions. He tells me no, he thinks he knows what he has to do. He'll take his hair out of cornrows and cut it after school. He also tells me he will show up in court "in my finest suit." I'm wondering how many suits he owns. I only own one myself and I doubt if I owned any when I was in high school. I ask him if he thinks it was strange he has to alter his daily appearance for court. He responded, "No. I'll play their game when I have to and I'd be stupid not to know that now I have to."

November 26: A Conflict of Loyalties

On this day I am approached by the head of the English Language Learning Department and requested to tell visitors from the California State Department of Education who are coming to evaluate the program that she is not being given sufficient time to supervise this program. Nor is she given enough aides to cover those classes where there are few English speakers and teachers, like me, who only speak English. Any low-performing school like Olympia dreads a visit from state representatives. I know that the principal has taken time and aides away from the English language program and allocated them to special-education needs and the needs of a testing program by which second-language students can elevate their English proficiency status. These aides also are used to administer most on-campus tests, an apparently necessary practice. I am reluctant to criticize how Dr. Williams is using his resources, but it does seem the ELL department is getting the short end of an already very small stick. Dr. Williams is engaging in a deplorable practice and before the end of the day I speak to the representatives from the state.

November 27: The Wonders of Human Reproduction

One female student in my Introduction to Algebra class runs out of the room in the middle of the lesson, screaming that she has to throw up. She stumbles down the aisle and I'm hoping she makes it to the bathroom. The boys in the class laugh. I ask them why they are laughing and they say it's obvious, like it happens every day. It appears I've discovered another taken-for-granted fact of urban high school life: teenage pregnancy. It wouldn't have been my first thought when I saw a female student about to throw up, but it probably will be from now on. I decide to keep it light and I tell them, "It's ok to be pregnant in class, it's just not ok to get pregnant in class." They laugh and we can return to math. At least I can; I'm never sure when they're with me.

November 27: The Test Make-up Offer Falls Flat

I ask several of my students who were absent for the weekly assessment why they didn't come after school to take the make-up. From a range of excuses I have to conclude they'd rather take a failing grade than come after school. I strongly detect a "why bother?" in their expressions. It's difficult to remain invested in the academic lives of students who do everything in their power to not take advantage of my accommodations.

Analysis

Paul spends at least an hour after school every day debriefing the events of his school day with one or another of his colleagues. He is looking to see where he might improve but mainly he sees where others have the same problems and concerns. This is reassuring in a way. Sometimes it seems like a complaining session but still, the issues he confronts do gain clarity through his interaction with others. He's figured that talking about problem situations, if it's not just complaining, can lead to important insights.

His colleagues in the math department, particularly Claire and George, have helped him to understand a very important thing, that the rates of student failure are consistent across teachers, even the most experienced. His failure then is not necessarily his failure and shouldn't be taken personally, which does give him an important perspective. At the same time—and probably more important than his own sense of failure—is the idea that perhaps it isn't the students' failure either. Paul is beginning to sense that he shouldn't be blaming the victims. And they are victims, victims of the school's and society's inability to help them overcome the limitations of their socioeconomic conditions.

Recently there was an article on research in the area of classroom management in *Education Week* (November 6, 2005), a newspaper for persons in all areas of education that is read by many teachers. The thrust of the piece is that, although a lot of inquiry goes on in the area of classroom management, by way of academic research, it doesn't seem to be getting into the hands of teachers who need help in this area.

There is probably any number of reasons that the scholarly pieces on classroom management don't seem to make much of a difference and aren't read but we're guessing teachers as a group don't trust the knowledge of academics when it comes to their own classrooms. They assume academics are ivy-towered theorists who don't really have a grasp of the subtleties of the urban high school classroom. They don't have a grasp because they don't deal with the problems on a daily basis. They may also believe the problems of many of the students who disrupt the classroom have their roots in their early life experiences.

The journal article also discussed findings that many of the problems of classroom management are formulated in the children who disrupt the class well before they enter the high school and in many cases, before they even attend school. Somewhere, probably in the home or neighborhood, many children develop the need to act aggressively, to react with uncontrollable temper, to ignore or challenge authority. If this is the case, then surely efforts at managing children's behavior has to begin somewhere long before high school. Studies of the impact of childhood behavior on later behavior seem to indicate that early problems are a strong predictor of later problems, particularly in children of lower socioeconomic status (Lahey, Loeber, Burke, and Applegate 2005). This is the population we're dealing with here. The point is there are studied ways of treating these problems in childhood (Friend 2008) so as to reduce the dysfunctional consequences that lead to disruptive students.

Some academics in teacher education we have talked to about this issue suspect that the students they have taught about strategies of classroom management seem to be able to describe these strategies on tests and interviews but once in the classroom they resort to their own intuitions. The ability to translate the tools of a training program to the real work situation is one criteria of professionalism. There is clearly a need to connect the two if we are going to uplift the professional status of the teacher.

Unavoidably, a football game at Olympia High has taken on a number of ethnic and socioeconomic ramifications: Leslie's discomfort with her own class origins, Latino preference for soccer, and Paul's sense, which seems to stay with him, that many of the other schools offer students a much greater access to the American opportunity system than his does. This, of course, is not an issue that exists primarily on the athletic field. Social class differences in everything from home resources to school resources shape student opportunities and teachers in the urban school. Social justice teaching demands an ongoing alertness to the effect invidious social differences have on students' schoolwork. Alertness to developing strategies for creating a level playing field for students in low-performing schools is a social justice teacher's obligation. Unfortunately, Paul, who does have that "alertness," can't yet see the handle for creating that level playing field.

A short note about the Palm Springs conference: There was very little in this particular conference that focused on Paul's problems in the classroom. He has since been to other similar conferences where his concerns were better taken into account. His assumption, leaving Palm Springs, was that the idea that teaching math is the same everywhere is widely held. But it isn't the same. It is much more complicated, being confounded by very different levels of student knowledge as well as very different levels of motivation to learn. It is Paul's sense that at this early stage in his career he does not know how to teach algebra to many of his students. Many of his students have difficulty with multiplication and division. Though there are models of how this can be done (Lehrer and Lesh 2003; Lehrer, Kobiela, and Weinberg 2007), he is required to use the state standards: district-mandated curriculum, district-mandated textbook, and the department pacing guide. Paul, at this early stage in his career, is forced to chose between what he believes will help students effectively learn and what will help him effectively keep his job by adhering to the demands of the administration

Unfortunately this is more than a conflict of conscience; without learning or at least passing algebra, a high school diploma is impossible for his students. How likely is it that middle-class parents of elementary school students will let their children come out of school not being able to divide or multiply. Certainly many of the parents of Paul's students don't themselves have the ability to help their children improve their math skills.

It is becoming the habit of teacher-education programs in elite universities like UCLA, Stanford, and Teacher's College to place their graduates in urban schools. The pride Paul felt by both his identification with a top program and his commitment to social justice in urban schools was tested in Palm Springs. He felt devalued by other teachers because of the reputation of his school as a low-achieving and disruptive ghetto environment where teachers had to spend most of the time dealing with discipline problems. As if it was his fault. Paul wondered, and still wonders, if these teachers at middle-class suburban schools had any sense that many of the teachers in the inner city were as competent as they were and were teaching there by choice.

Most of us remember teachers who were able to run with the humor that spontaneously erupted in our classrooms. Humor has been shown to be an effective component of classroom teaching (Rareshide 1993). And we know that teachers who were amenable to it were liked for their humanity. We know that most students enjoy a laugh during the long and often boring day in the classroom. Yet we also suspect that in the urban high school classroom teachers are often afraid to engage students in humor because they aren't sure students won't take it farther than the teacher would like to see it go. But the subject of humor isn't only relevant to the matter of classroom discipline or a teacher's anxiety that it might get out of hand. Humor is a capacity very related to a student's intelligence and as Gardner (1993) has shown, students show their intelligence in many different ways. This association between intelligence and humor was established long before the work of Gardner, who developed a typology of intelligences into which the characteristic of humor skills fit (Hauck and Thomas 1972). It seems to us, one way to expand the achievement rates in inner-city high schools is to expand the number of ways students can demonstrate ability. That will hardly be possible in Paul's current situation or any like it since the current marks of achievement are scores on standardized tests. This means only certain kinds of knowledge demonstrated in certain kinds of ways are valued. It is both uni-dimensional and universalistic. The alternatives we are suggesting are multidimensional and particularistic. These alternatives allow for individual student attention on particular tasks where unique intelligence can be put to work toward a student's attaining success in his or her studies as well as other areas of life.

We couldn't see ourselves ending the conclusion to chapter 5 without paying some attention to Dejaun. The mess in which Dejaun allowed himself to become entangled could have consequences that will follow him through his life: every time he fills out a job application, if and when he applies for student support, if he ever tries to take out a loan to start a business, etc. He has frequently discussed with Paul his interest in starting a chain of barbershops. It is difficult to start a business with a criminal record. Paul never got the specifics of the criminal activity. He didn't really want to know. He only hopes this smooth-talking boy can manage to get himself out of this one without destroying his future.

CHAPTER SIX

~

Loosening Up and Seeing the Social Problems

Something extraordinary yet predictable happens to people who stop thinking about and worrying about themselves. They begin to notice others with greater acuity and can tune into them. Self-absorption in a teacher obstructs his vision, and yet, from the moment a student-teacher steps into a classroom to the end of his tenure period, he is aware he is engaged in a performance and needs to provide a good accounting of himself to the evaluator, the supervisor, the master teacher, the principal. There was nothing I resented more than being evaluated as an English teacher by an ex-PE teacher who had become a principal, whose priorities for the student's classroom behavior were considerably different than mine. My three principals were focused almost exclusively on how quietly the students were working and it made no difference to any of them what they were working on or if they were getting anything out of it. The question of content value and how it impacted their struggles were never part of the evaluation. Paul is experiencing the same thing many years later.

The issue is, as I see it, evaluators never consider the importance of finding out what a teacher is trying to do and why. It is always—from the administrators' point of view—what I want him to do and never mind the why. It isn't negotiable.

Sooner or later, I suspect, teachers do deal with their nerves and self-consciousness, and make peace with their shaky egos. The more relaxed with the students they become the more interest in and concern with them they can exhibit.

When teachers are able to give their undivided attention to the students and their difficulties achieving they soon discover that for the student it's often a question of limitations. What most urban high school students lack, unless they attend parochial schools, is social capital (Coleman, Hoffer, and Kilgore 1982). Just a brief consideration of the reality of broad differences in social capital between urban- and nonurban-school students should suffice to diminish the attitude on the part of many that the urban students are totally responsible for their failure.

I have, from my earliest days of looking at schools and schooling as a professional investment, been sensitive to the dynamic of what some researchers have come to call the "hidden curriculum" (Apple 1979). The hidden curriculum is what students actually learn in school as part of their socialization as students. They learn, for example, to compete for grades and they learn how to look and act in ways that make a favorable impression on the teachers so as to guarantee favorable report cards. They learn that the grade is more important than what they learned.

Another thing that students learn—which was as true in my day in the classroom as in Paul's—is that you are not trusted. School is a power hierarchy and students are not trusted to share any of the power. Anyone who has ever attended a school can tell you the many ways in which this distrust is communicated. In the urban school the case to be made for distrust is even stronger. There are barred fences around the schools, students need official passes to traverse the campus, teachers and guards patrol the grounds, teachers are not permitted to leave students alone in a classroom, as well as many others. The argument from the school's perspective is while most students are trustworthy the rules are there for those who don't deserve to be trusted. Therefore, all must be treated the way untrustworthy students "need" to be treated.

Another troubling concern of Paul's that I can relate to from my own experiences is the matter of a disconnection between the newer teachers and the more experienced ones. The urban secondary-school teacher who has been working in the school for five years or more seems to both of us to be a cadre of individualists who are not particularly looking for community. Perhaps that is inevitable in schools where community doesn't appear to have much of a chance to develop since the authority structure is monolithic and top down exclusively. If a teacher is going to stick around an urban school for any length of time he is likely to have made his individual peace with the enterprise. It might be interesting to study what those individual adaptations really amount to.

A very significant issue, in both our minds, which any past or present teacher of urban-school students can relate to, is discovering a very bright student in a "remedial" class. The assumption must be if he or she isn't cooperating with the norms of the school, then he or she must be a slow learner. The continuing uninterrupted process of associating disruptive behavior with learning ability may not always exist in all urban schools but it does in many and has for a very long time.

Turning back to Paul's encounters with the various systems of the urban school, we commence with a topic of which we are both strongly supportive, the need for humor in the classroom.

December 2: Relaxing and Joking

I'm loosening up, beginning to find my zone of compatible humor. It's the point at which entertaining the students doesn't detract from their respect of me or from the material to be covered that day. My colleagues tell me they can hear in my voice the troubled intensity associated with daily problems beginning to diminish. I've taken an "it goes with the territory" tone rather than one that expresses dismay about what kind of territory I'm dealing with.

I'm joking with my students more every day. I depreciate their adolescent lifestyle. I criticize how they spend their time, the way they dress, and how they wear their hair. They love it; it's all in fun. The students seem to enjoy being made fun of. At times I have to make certain that this isn't undermining my ability to teach them. I joke about superficial aspects of their lives and not their achievement or ability. My father tells me that little has changed in this area. It's one of the things he remembers best about teaching in an urban school.

I'm not sure I'm right about how much humor I should encourage. I know many students relate well to me when I kid them about their adolescent style, but I'm also aware that many of them have very fragile egos and the last thing I would want to do is add to that fragility. Another thought I've had is that I could be further alienating them from the dominant culture.

The way I figure it is, if my comments downplay my students' priorities they must think they're doing something right. I suppose I'm kind of a negative role model, especially since I'm white and a stranger to the culture. Today one student asked me if they had to have homework again tonight. I told them, "Of course. It's the only thing that gives meaning to your life." Most laugh. Probably most don't really get it but they enjoy being told that whatever they do unrelated to school is a waste of their time.

The truth is I want to be liked and I've always known I can be funny. I once considered a career as a stand-up comic. Life would be great if the kind of teacher I want to be is the kind they want here, but it isn't likely. But it's possible.

December 3: The Veterans and the Novices

I sense the senior teachers don't see any need for viewing our school as a community. It's one of the many ideas we carried from our social justice orientation and probably one more idea the more senior teachers see as part of our naïve idealism. It's a recurrent difference of opinion that separates us, the new so-called idealists, from the rest. Today eight senior teachers are absent and all the new teachers are called upon to cover teacherless classes during our preparation periods. Thinking we have no choice and wanting to play our part in helping with a community problem, we all take the assignments, even though we neophytes need the prep periods more than anyone. Later I would learn that the senior teachers, for the most part, refuse these requests to cover classes during their preparation periods as they have the right to do.

Now, my problem today is that I'd planned to run off some copies of an assignment, but have no prep period in which to do it. I'm giving this assignment to my next period class and with eight teachers giving up their prep periods I can't find anyone to run them off for me. So I chose a senior honor student in whom I have complete trust and give her the keys to the copy room and ask her to run off the copies for me. She goes off to do that for me while I go off to cover a class.

Unfortunately, one of the older teachers, a woman who has a reputation as a martinet, had entered the copy room and raised hell with my student, took my copy-room key from her, then composed a letter to me conveying grave disapproval, reminding me that students are never to be allowed access to the copy room. When I receive it I experience a disturbing mixture of feelings. My first feeling is one of anxiety. My thought is, ok, I screwed up and violated a school rule. Am I in trouble? My second feeling is anger. What I'm thinking about telling her, while I'm eating my lunch is, "If I knew you were free this period, since you hadn't taken a subbing assignment, I would have had you run off my copies."

I don't ever tell her though. I'm too new and am afraid to stir the water or burn any bridges, even if they could use a good torching.

Another of the same nature soon follows this encounter. Because we're still covering for teachers who are out sick, I find I've been assigned to sub for an English class where the regular teacher has left no assignments for the class. I had no idea I'd be subbing in this class, and since the regular teacher hadn't provided me with material to cover I decided to engage the students in a lively discussion of the meaning of success and the role this school plays in providing access to success. I pose questions like: Are all people capable of being successful? Would someone who attends this school have the same chance of being successful as students who attend Beverly Hills High School? I even briefly explore their opinion of the role race and ethnicity play in being successful. The talk is loud and spirited and the students are attentive and interested, and there is some yelling out. I suspect the noise level is high, but I'm too involved to be aware of that. I'm actually enjoying this discussion and I do think it's something the students need.

In short order one of the security guards comes in and asks me if I need help. He tells me the veteran teacher next door (a veteran who I have learned is discourteous to students and teachers alike) had reported there was excessive noise coming from my room. (Later in the year when I was subbing on the other side of her room she sent a student in with a note requesting that I either quiet my students or provide her with headache medication. I sent the student back with two Advil from my bag; that was my bridge-burning phase.)

I've learned that many of the senior teachers live in their own worlds and I know I have to watch out for that kind of adaptation. I still don't understand why veteran teachers choose to alienate themselves from the younger teachers. They make cynical nonproductive comments at faculty meetings and it seems all they have to chat about during informal gatherings is who is giving them a hard time and how. Almost no one seriously wants to engage in a discussion about the whys. Of course, the why of a student's misbehavior will always be a mystery as long as school is not a place where serious individual counseling takes place, and I don't see that happening any time soon.

I would imagine most of the senior faculty would argue the faculty meetings are nonproductive. I think it's a bit of a catch-22. One veteran math teacher has abandoned the textbook that the department has agreed on. He teaches his Introduction to Algebra students out of an Algebra I text. This material is too difficult for Introduction to Algebra students. I asked him how his students do with his challenging curriculum. He says that there is no mistake about it, those who pass his class will never have any difficulty in any math class. I think the difficulty is that only thirteen students passed his three Introduction to Algebra classes. That's a 12 percent passing rate in his Introduction to Algebra classes. None of his actions can be checked because the tenure system and the union have his back, that is, they protect him against sanctions. We new teachers are very much fueled by our enthusiasm. We are willing to throw ourselves into virtually any project. The veteran teachers, except for a few that still have the energy and enthusiasm of newcomers, serve the role of naysayers.

December 4: Talking About Weed

All the security guards are wearing pins modeled after the comic strip "CROCK" which say, "SMOKING IS A CROCK." One student asks me why all the guards are wearing them today. I tell them that smoking is hazardous to one's health. A student calls out, "Not if you're smoking weed!" Another chimes in, "Out of a bong!" Suddenly everybody is awake and wanting to contribute to the discussion. It's amazing how easily students can get distracted by almost anything that isn't their work.

Well, I take a risk, trusting my own judgment, and open it up and there seems to be a lot of good reasons for taking it further, but I'm too damn insecure to do this. I tell the class that is now unified and attentive and wants to talk about the pros and cons and healthiest ways of dealing with drugs that they have to settle down and go on with the pre-algebra lesson, but I do add that we can discuss the topic of recreational drugs and I will be happy to share my knowledge, if anyone wants to come after school. Nobody shows, of course, so I wonder if I should have let the discussion happen while it was hot. I suppose I didn't because I always have in mind how much math I'm expected to cover to meet the standards. We are on a tight schedule where the number of pages we cover per week is closely monitored.

December 5: An Accomplice in the Gang Wars

One of my students informs me that another of my students, a boy by the name of Carmello, is in serious danger, that there are boys on campus who are looking for him. From the tone of the message I assume they intend to do Carmello grave bodily harm if they find him. He tells me that if Carmello shows up, I should tell him to be careful today. There are many possible reasons, I'm thinking, someone might have a group of students looking for him with the intent to inflict street punishment or justice or whatever. It could be a matter of something he did that was offensive to someone else and that person's homeboys are looking to even the score.

Carmello could have been a member of any group from a tagging crew to a gang. Tagging crews are groups of individuals who claim particular territory as their own by tagging the spot with anything from markers to spray paint. I have already become familiar with many of the different local tagging crews through the graffiti that appears daily in my classroom. Tagging crews come into conflict with other tagging crews over territorial rights. Perhaps Carmello tagged on somebody else's turf for one reason or another. This could have been enough to turn another entire crew against him. Or, and this is the most serious possibility, Carmello could be a member of a gang and a gang conflict could be waiting to happen.

Two days earlier a student had lost his front teeth after being beaten about the neck and face with a crowbar in one of these incidents. There is definitely a lot to worry about if you need to stray from your turf. Carmello has been identified as gifted and talented but I have seen no signs of either. Fortunately my ambivalence about how I should deal with this is resolved by the fact that Carmello doesn't show up today and I don't have to become involved. I suppose I would have said something to him if he had appeared but I do wonder why anyone would think a teacher would serve as a messenger in a gang matter. I think about all the roles I have assumed in addition to educator: surrogate parent, counselor, friend, and apparently now lookout. I don't know if this means students trust me or just realize I'm not an effective teacher, but have proven more affective in these other care-giver roles.

December 6: Arrested Development

Dejaun had been absent the previous day because of his court appearance. All of the students in my fifth period today are antsy. We are all anxious—including me—about what will be the outcome of his second court appearance. My fifth period is beginning to seem like a family. The entire class appears to care about each other's well-being. In my family analogy, Dejaun would definitely be considered the Godfather. We want to know if the Don has beaten the rap in court. I know what he was charged with is bad, but I want him released because he is my kid. The court has to realize that he's more than his stupidest mistake. He is a smart kid who is beginning to learn, probably for the first time, that he is capable of doing well in school. I realize I have a very biased and very vested interest in this boy.

Dejaun shows up to class today, characteristically a couple minutes late. This is an acceptable practice for him because I believe I'm reaching him in more important areas than promptness. You can't teach a student who is not attending class. I have to get him there and only then can I begin to slowly cajole him into buying more and more into the system, without him feeling he is losing his sense of control. Feeling in control is extremely important to Dejaun.

I tell the students that I will give Dejaun a forum to speak when we have completed the lesson. We begin reviewing properties of the various polygons they had been introduced to through an activity the previous day. I can tell I am not into the lesson. I look at my students. Many of them are trying to get Dejaun to tell them what happened. He is angrily telling them that I have given him time at the end of class and to "listen to the fucking lesson." My students don't live in a vacuum and I feel that there is nothing preventing me from taking a break today, a day when clearly nobody's mind is on math anyway (me included).

Dejaun begins speaking from his seat. He tells the class he is being tried as a minor for robbery and gang activities. There are three felony counts against him. The DA is trying to secure jail time and have one strike placed against him. He said that both the DA and the public defender made their cases and the judge will make his ruling on the ninth of the month. After this I sit down next to him and ask him if he's doing alright. "Yeah," he says. This is a kid who would say he was doing fine if he hopped into an emergency room with his severed leg in his hand. I ask him if he's nervous. He responds, "What's there to be nervous about? I did this, now I got to pay the consequences." I ask him if he's nervous about the possibility of jail time. He tells me that jail is one of his possibilities and if he has to serve time, he'll serve time. "None of this is going to break me." "But it would be a hell of a lot easier if you didn't," I say. He puts the conversation to rest, "Yeah, but I do. I'm going to walk in that courtroom in six days and be judged." I smile and say, "Remember to wear that suit." He returns my smile, but is noticeably irritated by the whole situation. I don't have a response. This is out of my league. The bell rings.

December 10: Dejaun's Sentencing

Dejaun returns to class after his sentencing. He comes to give his final update. Donna, a strikingly attractive, petite Africam American student, cries as he enters the classroom. It is as if someone had just yelled, "Dead man walking." She refers to him by his gang name as she continues to cry it out through her tears. Apparently she has advanced knowledge of his sentencing. He glances at her, pauses a second, and then walks to his desk. I figure that since this class is ahead of the other Introduction to Algebra classes I can allow part of another day to be spent on Dejaun. I don't think the principal would approve, but I'm very touched. I notice then that I've been brought to the verge of tears myself. I had no idea I had become that emotionally involved in this boy and his success in and out of my classroom.

I tell him with his success in my class and his history class he will be graduating at the end of the year. I tell him a high school diploma will give him access to a lot of opportunities. I'm about to start discussing what he's planning on doing after he graduates when he angrily interrupts me. "I'm not going to fucking graduate." He's being expelled from the school and is being sent to a work camp, ten credits short of graduation. He could have gotten those credits by passing my class and his history class. I'd checked with his counselor to make sure of this. Now he's telling us it's his last day at the school.

After Dejaun turns eighteen, and after five months at the work camp, he can and probably will be retried as an adult with a possibility of his being imprisoned. The best possible scenario in his mind and in mine as well involves an eighteen-year-old high school "dropout" with a criminal record for robbery and gang-related activities, with a strike on his record, trying to make a life for himself.

"What the fuck can I do?" he says. "I'm seventeen and already have a strike on my record."

December 10: Antonio's Problem

Antonio, my passive-aggressive, strong-willed, bird-stomping student, is a smart young man who should be in a more advanced class but has been relegated to the slow learner group due to his disruptive classroom behavior. It isn't clear to me why they don't have a special class for especially smart disruptive students. I think it's a terrific idea but I'm not sure this doesn't contradict my opinion of tracking, although I have to say tracking looks less and less invidious the more I teach. It seems to me that schools could develop a way for systems of tracking to be a bit more nuanced that is for unique combinations of learning statuses, like smart but uninterested. There are certainly enough students like Antonio around to make a class. At least you might find a way to keep boredom from causing many of the problems of classroom management.

The truth is Antonio is bored stiff in my class and I've had to kick him out several times for being excessively disruptive. Today I feel I have the luxury of the time to deal with Antonio on a one-to-one basis and so I let him know that I know the material we are covering in class is too basic for him, but I have to go slowly because the other students in the class are not up to his level yet. I will give him some independent projects. Antonio is happy and when I provide him with the individual projects his classroom behavior improves considerably.

December 11: Alberto Discovers the
Metric System in His Protractor

Alberto is one of my favorite students, at least this month. He is far from a good student but he's a sweet kid. I find myself to be very volatile in my affection for certain kinds of students. One of the reasons I care about Alberto is because he seems to be a chronic victim. I'm a big fan of the underdog. Alberto is a short, Mexican American boy, classic Indian features, plump, silly, sometimes funny. The "tougher" boys pick on him constantly. He doesn't have a "macho" thing, pretending to be tough like most of the other boys do. As a student he doesn't do very well although he seems to be trying. The problem is Alberto doesn't get abstract concepts. He gloms onto concrete representations. He mistakenly refers to his protractor as the metric system. He amuses me, but I wish I could figure out how to get him to think in terms of things representing things rather than being them.

Alberto confides in me, waits for me first thing every morning with his bicycle pump. He tells me he needs the pump because somebody is slashing the tires of a lot of kids who ride bikes to school. He has to repair them and pump them up every day. I allow him to store his pump in my room. I doubt if this is a recommended practice.

A couple days later Alberto confides in me that he and some other bike riders caught the slasher in the act and beat the crap out of him. I know it is a capital crime to fight in school and I'm obligated to report all incidents within my knowledge, but I don't want to betray Alberto's trust in me. I feel if I were he I would have handled it in the same manner. I report the action to the associate principal (AP) in charge of discipline but state it as a hypothetical, to see what the punishment would be for beating up somebody who has been slashing your tires. The AP tells me he'd have to suspend the boy for five days even though he thinks the slasher got what he deserved.

I walk away and we're both smiling at the pretense of the hypothetical. What I've discovered is that nobody wants to punish kids if they can find a reason not to. Sometimes I agree with this practice and sometimes strongly disagree when I feel extreme violations have been committed. These are cases where I believe the absence of strong sanctions for some behavior, for example in the weak stand the school took in response to my being threatened by Jason, undermines a teacher's ability to control the behavior of some students.

December 12: Dejaun Again

A few days later I'm surprised and pleased to see Dejaun in class rather than somewhere lost in the juvenile justice system. I don't know what to think except maybe he struck some kind of deal. I imagine for a moment that the world is just. Or at least what I consider just. One of the students in the class calls out, "Hey man, you break out?" It seems any student who is arrested has immediate notoriety throughout the school. Dejaun informs me about the procedure, that there's a time lapse between the time you're sentenced to a detention camp as a minor and the time you have to report.

During my conversation with Dejaun, I detect the heavy, unmistakable odor of marijuana. It is not subtle. He reeks. I ask him if I could talk to him outside. I get right to the point, "Why do you reek of weed?" Dejaun shrugs and tells me that everybody knows he smokes weed, from the principal on down. I know this to be the truth. I tell him I can't allow someone in his condition in my classroom and ask him to go somewhere else. He replies, "Wherever I go, security will find me, and take me back here. This is where I'm supposed to be." I know this is most likely true. Finally, I tell him to sit in my room and put his head down, which he does and quickly falls asleep.

I have no sense yet how to deal with similar issues should they recur. I have just effectively condoned the use of marijuana at school. I later ask around among the experienced teachers I trust how they deal with students who are high in class. There is some consensus that the best thing to do is report it as a suspicion, since this leaves it to the administration to deal with it if they choose. I am later told, as I frequently am in a wide range of discipline matters, that the discipline office has enough to deal with by way of blatant violations of rules, that suspicions have a low priority. I'm happy to hear this since Dejaun has enough trouble on his plate. Not long after, Dejaun disappears from the school scene and is just a memory, but for me a positive one on the whole. I will continue to feel positive about what I think he gained from being in my classroom.

December 14: A Digression—Cheap at the Price

Today a good student, Pedro, offers to sell me a Cartier diamond watch to give to my girlfriend for Christmas for only thirty bucks. I tell him I don't have a girlfriend at the moment. He suggests my mother. I tell him I'm in the market for a man's Rolex and I'd be willing to pay thirty-five. He says he doesn't have a Rolex right now, but he should have one in by lunch. He says he'll stop by my room later in the day and, after a brief hesitation, asks me if I'm sure I only want one.

December 14: An Interesting Paradox

I've started figuring my student grades for the end of semester report cards and I'm beginning to notice an unexpected trend. It seems that the students in the sheltered Introduction to Algebra class, despite the fact that the class is twice as large as each of my other three Introduction to Algebra classes, and that most of the students speak very little English, are achieving better than the others in all categories: homework, tests, and notebook.

December 16: Tupac Lives!

There seems to be a general consensus in my Introduction to Algebra classes that the rapper Tupac Shakur, who we can assume is dead since that's how the media reported it, has faked his murder to avoid being the object of gang violence and is currently living in an obscure location recording his next album. I assume students pay attention to media as well as listen to their friends and dismiss the things they don't believe. I don't see this willingness to believe conspiracy theories as much in my Algebra II class. There seems to be a distinct relationship between achievement level and the tendency to believe in far-fetched theories.

December 17: Homophobia in the Classroom

Leslie, my friend and colleague from my teacher-education cohort, has attempted to get her students in her classes to look at their homophobia. I suspect that any attempt to broach this subject leaves one open to the belief on the part of the students that you must be gay. I'm afraid that Leslie might be undermining her academic goals by opening up a controversial issue unrelated to math. At the same time I think that countering homophobic attitudes should be an important educational goal. One of my former students from my student-teaching days here at Olympia admitted to me that she was bisexual and told me that both female homosexuality as well as homophobia were common in the school.

What I do know, since I see and hear it every day, is that accusing someone of being gay, or a fag, or a queer is a very popular put-down. And for the most part the expressions don't really have to bear any resemblance to the state of the other's sexual orientation. I don't know how much time I'd devote to the topic if it came up in my class but I do know I would like to give the topic as much time as it would take to make the point that depreciating one's sexual orientation is as inappropriate as degrading racial remarks. This is something the students would definitely relate to, but I'm hesitant to get into anything like that because I suspect my efforts would be fruitless. The simple act of teaching is difficult enough at this point for me; I will wait a bit before I begin to assail homophobia.

December 18: Why Do We Have to Learn X?

I've never been taught how best to handle those inevitable "why do we have to learn this?" questions. My assumption is that if they don't see the value in it I must not be doing a good enough job teaching it. Today, I'm trying to get students to explore different triangle congruency conjectures when the question arises. So how do I explain to them the importance in their lives of ascertaining criteria for determining whether one triangle is congruent to another? I'm feeling a little playful so I tell them, "Maybe someday you'll be walking down the street with your homeboys when a triangle walks up to you and shoots your homey in the face. He goes down. He's dead. The triangle hightails it out of there. When the police come by they're going to want to know information that will guarantee they catch the right triangle. If you haven't been paying attention to the work we've been doing, you won't be able to identify that critical information. The police will have nothing to go on and your homeboy will have died in vain."

Antonio calls out, "Paul, what drug are you on?" The truth is I have no idea how what I am teaching them is important. I will need to think about this because if I have no reason to care about this material how can I expect my students to care?

December 18: A Couple of Tough Ones

One of my female students is missing many of my classes. She tells me there's no father in the home, her mother is sick, and there are three younger siblings to look after. She knows she isn't doing well in the course and now I know why. She is not unique but what can I do about it? I tell her I understand and I'll be happy to provide make-up work for her to do at home, but I doubt she'll have the time, freedom, or resources to do much there.

The same day Tino asks me for a little money to get something to eat. I tell him if money is tight in his family he can apply for the free lunch program. He tells me that he knows he can do that but if he does it could get his family in trouble. The vast majority of the students in the ELL program do not apply for the free lunch program because either they or their families are undocumented. Tino tells me there are many kids in the school who are not in the ELL program who are in the same boat as well. Though there is a school policy requiring that no teacher under any circumstance give money to students, my friend Celia tells me that she will lend money on occasion to students she trusts. I give Tino a little money for lunch and tell him to keep it between us and not to make a habit of it. I wish we just had a free lunch policy in the cafeteria that students wouldn't have to sign up for. How can hungry kids concentrate on their lessons?

December 19: A Refreshing Finale to the Year

I am happy to report that for the first time in my teaching career a student came up to me and asked to borrow a book. It was a book on Che Guevara that a professor at UCLA had written and had given me. One copy had already been stolen. I loaned the book to the boy who was someone who had never given me any reason to distrust him. He would spend considerable time in my class the following semester reading that as well as many other books instead of paying attention, but it didn't matter since he got As on all the tests anyhow. Actually, I was so taken by the request I probably would have loaned it to any student even if I didn't know him. Merry Christmas!

Paul's Over the Holiday Reflections

The Markers—One of the thoughts that troubled me over the holidays, given that it's the first time I've been able to catch my breath, is how we use the "markers" of achievement. Markers are those indicators of achievement that schools use: grades on tests, attendance records, getting things down on paper, being quiet, "bell to bell" working at your seat. My thinking is that in the middle-class high school like the one I went to, we knew what all the markers were and how they added up. We knew that if we ditched a class we'd have to forge an authentic-looking excuse note from our parent. My students now don't mind having unexcused absences on their records and many of them don't know or care how all the indicators of being a good student add up. When I ask them why they don't write their own excuse notes for their absences, they tell me because they have to wait too long in the attendance line to get absence slips. I've learned since I've been at Olympia, one of the main functions of keeping attendance records is to use the record of frequently delinquent and absent students as part of the evidence package that will justify kicking a student out of school.

I'm pretty sure most of my students learn more and better than the grades on their report cards indicate. They just don't pay close enough attention to the "markers."

Critical Pedagogy—I've learned just how little my exposure to radical pedagogical ideas in the literature I was asked to read in the teacher-education program has been translatable to things I can do in my classroom. It's difficult to engage a student to dialectically examine the conditions of his social environment when he's passed out stoned, listening to his Walkman in the back of the class, or truant from school. I enjoy and gain great insight from the articles we read. I do know, or think I know, who the bad guys are, with whom hegemony rests, that Paulo Freire had some success, but I do believe I have to develop significantly as a classroom teacher before I can transition from theory to any kind of practical practice.

Pot or Weed—I've learned that marijuana use and possession are not treated as serious school or legal infractions nearly as often as they would be in a middle-class school. I'm not really sure of that since there was a whole lot of it floating around in my middle-class high school. What I am sure of is that the middle-class students hide it well, because they know they have a lot to lose if they lose the legitimizing power of the school. Here at Olympia, too many students don't seem to care a whole lot about sanctions. I definitely don't sanction marijuana use among students with growing minds, but I have to admit I can understand the occasional use of marijuana by my students who believe that school offers them nothing but a thorough devaluation of their self-esteem. I am emphatically opposed to having multitudes of students come to school high because they cannot otherwise survive the boredom of schooling. Seemingly the use of weed would simply prolong the time of the boredom. Unless of course they suddenly see that math can be interesting.

I know that if I can't make my class interesting I will be contributing to the problem. Still, in a general way the reality is there, that it is a huge task to motivate students who have been working to de-motivate themselves since middle school—the time most drug use starts. With the amount of substantive drug use that goes on among my students, teaching has become a much more difficult task.

Analysis

Because students spend a lot of social time downgrading their friends, if you're willing to play their game it tells them you consider them worthy of your humor, like any friend would be. We see allowing humor in the class as a kind of recognition, a caring, even when the remarks are derogatory. The more general point is that Paul is trying to relate to his students through their enjoyment of humor. Who doesn't enjoy humor and what student would rather be graphing quadratic equations than laughing?

No matter how close a teacher allows himself to get to a student, and teachers will run a broad gamut on this question, we don't want to lose the class to the street. But that doesn't mean some part of the street can't be allowed into the class. Paul's decision is to use his own wit to achieve closeness with some students, but never to tread on their self-esteem.

All we can really say about the relationship between the new teachers and the experienced ones is that it's usually a crapshoot. From what we have both observed, many schools may be staffed by a majority of teachers who see their role as not extending beyond their own classroom. They have made their individual adaptations, made peace with it, and don't want to be bothered beyond the demands of their own students.

Unfortunately the urban school doesn't retain most of its teachers long enough to build a community of those who stay and care. We've already referenced earlier some surveys of why teachers leave the urban high school. For a great many teachers it is simply not their cup of tea. It isn't the world they know, they don't get the respect they'd like, and they don't see much in the way of positive results from their efforts.

One of the most problematic characteristics of the urban school is the difficulty of creating an atmosphere of trust in an environment where you suspect a great many students will take advantage of it. No doubt the urban school is likely to be a place where widespread rule violations are predictable and this notion has to be taken into account. But we suspect that demonstrating trust in a student is a key ingredient in an effort to show them, many of whom are devalued in the home or on the street, that there is a place that values them and that place is the school. Having the same rules for everyone might seem more efficient for some administrators but it also serves to disempower both teachers and students. The consequence is that the majority of students are denied opportunities to assume responsibility in an effort to control the behavior of a minority.

To what extent do teachers want to become involved in the problems of students that seem to have their roots in the many problems of the neighborhood? This would include problems of teenage pregnancy, drugs, gangs, parental abuse, misdemeanor and felony cases, out of home foster placements, and problems of physical and mental health. There's no question that all of these factors can and do affect a student's ability to make the best of a high school education. So there is certainly a relevant connection. Irrespective of this connection in general, between the hours of eight and three, teachers do become surrogate parents. So, as Paul sees it, when a student's ability to learn in his class is compromised by some condition growing out of a home or community problem, he does think he needs to become involved. How deeply involved he can't know at this point. He does know that some teachers refuse to be involved at all and others take the problem right into the home to discuss with parents what can be done to make it easier for the student to succeed in school.

In Paul's first year he has seen many students who have experience in the juvenile justice system. He feels he has seen comparatively minor infractions. One of his peers in the program had a student who was arrested and charged with murder associated with a gang shooting.

Paul has spent a lot of time thinking about and worrying about Dejaun. Dejaun is an exceptionally bright student. Perhaps he will make it one way or another but at the moment Paul knows Dejaun's prospects are not good. Paul endeavored to the best of his ability to engage this student intellectually through mathematics while he had the chance. He also created a positive relationship in Dejaun's life. Paul knows that must count for something.

The majority of Paul's students are Latino; many have recently arrived from Latin America, mostly Mexico. The absence of services to deal with personal problems of Latino students has been looked at by a number of investigators. There is strong evidence to support the fact that there are inequalities in Latino communities as to the availability of mental health services (Kouyoumdjian, Zamboanga, and Hansen 2003). The stresses of immigrating and adapting to the United States are considerable, even traumatic, which would lead in many cases to post-traumatic disorders and depression (Burnam, Hough, Karno, Escobar, and Telles 1987; Cervantes, Salgado de Snyder, and Padilla 1989). The fact that many poor Latinos do not have health insurance is certainly another factor (Campbell 1999). The problems that exist in some Latino families impact the student's adaptation to school. Paul is still trying to figure out what, if anything, he can do, or is he, as a middle-class Caucasian, too removed to even try?

The point Paul makes about tracking is well taken. Teachers in difficult schools know that some form of tracking makes their lives easier. Paul came out of his teacher-education program believing strongly that tracking was one of the invidious forces in restricting efforts to make schools places where social justice is possible (Oakes 1985). However, as a teacher, he sees that tracking can relieve him of some classroom management problems. He is quite aware there are ways around tracking that do not establish invidious distinctions and unequal opportunities but he doesn't see how he has the independence to restructure his curriculum such that he can cater to the needs of students at different levels of understanding. Paul has been spending much of his limited time trying to differentiate instruction for different ability students in the same class. The issue isn't just one of tracking or de-tracking without making other necessary curricular and pedagogical changes.

In an educational climate that seems to focus more on test scores than the nuances of mathematical understandings, Paul seems to be barking up the wrong tree, in worrying about a student's ability to discern the difference between a concept and its representation, being able to generalize beyond the particular, and constructing informal proofs. He suspects many of the other students have similar problems, which is why variables (i.e., x's and y's) are not sensible to them. These are levels of abstraction to which students have not been exposed. To take some time out to push the envelope on what mathematical practice really is would require a different conceptualization of mathematics education. The standards Paul must follow don't allow sufficient flexibility in his assigned program to teach in a way he really believes students learn. Is Paul truly tied to these administrative mandates in the manner he believes? Irrespective, he currently perceives the administration as ultimate authority.

The issue of homophobia among high school students is not as much an issue of sex as it is of civil rights. Gay and lesbian students do suffer from stigmas placed upon them by their fellow students and there does not seem to be much in the way of an institutionwide policy or program in most schools to deal with it. Sears (1991) and Walters and Hayes (1998), aside from documenting the extensive nature of school homophobia, provide a list of what they believe to be effective programs for combating this attitude. But lack of successful programs and material for instruction is not the reason why programs are not initiated in high schools. Paul senses there's an attitude that pervades almost everything related to what teachers should stay away from, that these students ("urban failures") would go crazy and cause the teacher considerable anguish with respect to classroom management should he stray from the standard curriculum.

The fact that, in Paul's school, most of the students are Catholic Latinos partly explains not only why homophobia exists in his classroom and around the school, but also why programs to counter it are not initiated. School administrators are not known as people who choose principle above the pragmatics of not upsetting parents (Fontaine 1997). Nor, Paul suspects, would it advance his cause with the principal to confront the issue. An effective program would probably require a whole course of sensitivity training, not a few remarks from a teacher that comes between ratios and proportions.

What accounts for the fact non-English speakers are doing better than those who do speak the language? Does it say something about recent immigrants, mostly from Mexico, and those who have had time to become acculturated in the urban community regarding attitudes toward educational achievement and respect for teachers? It's hard to know. Paul has a hunch that the respect factor is more operative in this class so we're left with an empirical question if we want to generalize. Are attitudes toward education more positive among recently arrived immigrants or is what Paul is observing temporary or even a function of the fact all the other students in Intro are doing worse?

Paul is going to have to spend more time and thought on the issue of why students should study math. He continues to highlight the work on mathematical learning by Lesh and Lehrer (2003) because for him it provides a rich analysis of what is essential to the practice of mathematics teaching in order to maximize student learning. It provides a coherent picture of what practices are essential to the discipline as well as student learning of the discipline. There is other similar research for teachers to draw upon in developing their classroom environment. Paul does intend to devote time to explore this literature and participate in much professional development over the summer, but in the meantime what is to become of his students?

In many school districts throughout the country, like Los Angeles, a high school diploma requires the passage of at least one course in algebra. It would seem the administration would have given some thought to the very large number of students who fall by the wayside because algebra is too high a hurdle for them.

CHAPTER SEVEN

~

The New Year

In this chapter Paul will be encountering a range of events that are different from most events already discussed in their particulars, but not necessarily in their sociological roots. It is rarely the case that the same kind of dynamics would be observed in either middle-class public suburban or private schools. The roots we are talking about here are in such areas as student motivation, teacher disrespect, dropouts, transience, student violence, underachievement, home support, homework practices, and what seems like an infinite variety of classroom management difficulties.

It is not surprising to me that the same particulars as well as the same sociological roots are still operating some fifty years after I entered the urban-school classroom. I am compelled to ask myself, "Why am I not surprised?" Well think about it. While we are pleased and sometimes elated at how many ethnic and racial minorities have advanced educationally and economically, we forget to focus on how many haven't. The rates of minority students who haven't been able to graduate their high schools are still conspicuously large; the transience rates of poor minority families are still causing urban-school counselors headaches in trying to integrate new students and keep track of lost students, and teachers are still running from urban classrooms in droves because they can't or refuse to put up with the amount of disorganization and disrespect they encounter from their students. Having failed to discover the mechanism by which poor minority students can be deterred from fighting each other, we've allowed the problem to be compounded by the increase in the number of poor ethnic minorities that populate the urban school. It is too bad we didn't solve this problem of student violence before the gangs began to aggregate and the weapons of battle began to increase in their potential to injure and even kill.

Why am I not surprised Paul is encountering the same problems I did and worse? Because in all these years I've never seen society make the kind of commitment to education—and particularly to urban schools—it would take to really make a difference. Political leaders don't want to give anything more than lip service to what most of their citizens don't really care about. There are always higher priorities: the space program, the cold war, the hot wars, the drug wars, the war against terrorism, the war against undocumented immigrants, not to mention feeding the rich and denying the poor. Paul is beginning to be more preoccupied by ways to keep from being submerged in a sea of obstacles than he is by his hopes to make a difference.

January 6: Classroom and School Rules

It's probably appropriate that the first challenge of the new year for me is the age-old teacher problem of having to explain to students why they have to do what they have to do by way of general school deportment. I'm not talking about why they have to learn particular subject matter. I still don't have an answer for that question that would even satisfy me. I'm talking about everything else. Where they have to go, how they have to look, what work they have to do, when they can go to the bathroom, where they have to stand and sit, can they chew gum, when they have to raise their hands, etc. You wouldn't think a mid-year break would require students to learn the rules of school deportment over again, especially when they're in the second semester of a yearlong class.

Today I notice that one of the females in my class, Angelina, is out of the seat where she's been sitting ever since I changed her seat last semester. She tells me it's a new year so she's decided she needs a new seat. I tell her she can't just decide to move out of her assigned seat because she feels like it and she wants to know why she can't. I tell her I need to know where everybody is so I can keep track of who's here and who isn't. And besides, I tell her, it's to keep you from sitting next to someone you like to talk with which will get you in trouble.

In my mind I'm thinking, "I thought we already settled this." But I'm learning that contracts with students expire much sooner than I'd like, especially if I don't properly set up and maintain classroom behavior norms. Angelina tells me she already is sitting next to someone she likes to talk with and besides, she likes to talk to everybody. I am again regressing into inviting students to engage me in control struggles.

I'm feeling hard pressed to pull the "it's a rule" number out of my bag but I resist. I ask if anybody else feels they need a new seat for the new year. Of course most raise their hands so I tell them it's too much trouble for now but they're going to be assigned new work groups anyhow so that should take care of their need.

January 8: Students Get Depressed

Of course students get depressed, so I shouldn't be surprised when one of my students exhibits signs of depression. My emotions have certainly been uncharacteristically volatile since starting in this profession. Depression happens to many people, especially adolescents, either because of neurochemistry or because life is hard and justifiably depressing. My assumption is that most of my students who are depressed are so because of conditions that characterize their lives. There are so many possibilities where money is tight, parents are struggling, gangs are roaming, drugs and sex are available to adolescents, and violence and abuse are frequent in the home and the street.

The thing about the adolescent consciousness, as I understand it, is that they believe bad times will stay that way forever. These are probably the wisest words for adolescents in the Old Testament. I'm not particularly religious, but that message has definitely helped me to get through the last four months.

So, on the subject of depression, I've noticed that one of my A students, Ruth, has started to nose dive with respect to her grades. She'd been getting an A all year but recently her grades are dipping to Cs and below, so I decide to call her mother to see if I can find out what's going on and potentially help. Her mother confides in me that her daughter was raped two years before on her way home from middle school. She was only twelve years old. She's been prone to depressions off and on ever since. When this happens, when the depression hits her, she just doesn't seem to care about anything, especially her schoolwork that used to always be very important to her.

Wow, I think, that's intense and very disturbing and I'm too young and inexperienced to know what to do about it. I am not the resource this girl or this family needs and I don't know who that resource would be. I feel it's my role to find this girl and her family help because her mother entrusted me with this information. None of the other teachers seem to be playing the role of social worker, but I think that is precisely the reason it is my responsibility. I know her recent failing grades are the least of the problem now, but I am also painfully aware most colleges won't take her personal history into account. I probably, in the best of all possible training programs, should have been exposed to some answers but my sense is if there was anything our school could do about things like this I would have been informed.

I have since learned our school doesn't have the resources to help students with psychological or psychiatric problems that are likely to result from the poverty and crime that are endemic to this community.

January 10: I Feel Like a Missionary

After school today I call my father on my cell phone from my car. It's Friday afternoon and the freeway's a parking lot. I need to talk. My thinking about my life in the classroom has taken another turn for the worse and I'm eager to check it out with him.

I tell him I realized today that I feel like a missionary, that I'm unilaterally imposing an education upon kids who don't want it, don't see the need or use for it. I'm beginning to question my role in the classroom and whether I have the ability to fulfill that role. I'm coming from the outer city to the inner city and if they had a choice they wouldn't have me there. Some students like me enough, but I'm confused about my goals. I'm here to impose algebra on them. They certainly don't want my religion or me. They seem to be quite content with the life they have and don't spend a lot of time thinking about the life I think I'm there to help them attain. I have a student who wants to end up a bus diver like his mom. Do I have a right to tell him he should aspire for more?

My father asks me if I'm starting to believe that they're better off without me, without what I want for them. I have to admit that I don't, any more than the missionaries thought the natives were better off without Christ or salvation. The analogy is ringing really true.

He then asks me if I have more objective evidence about the value of a degree than the missionaries had about the afterlife. He asks if I'm troubled that my students don't look at the future the way I look at it for them. That is precisely the problem. The truth is I don't think many of my students do think about their future. When they do they think of it very differently from me. I hope some students are internalizing the values that higher education can give them opportunities they don't currently have. The way it feels is that all my attempts to make my classroom an enjoyable place where the students have most of the power and feel they are respected have basically failed. They still feel that something is being done to them rather than for them.

He asks me if I believe my students are really different from kids in middle-class schools. Do I think they also feel that forces outside themselves are controlling them?

It wasn't so long ago that I was one of those middle-class high school students and I don't remember ever thinking that high school wasn't something I wanted to get over with, even though I did well. But unlike most of my students now, I was quite willing to put up with anything I had to, to get the grades I needed to get into a good college. It was a rite of passage. Everyone I knew was playing the same game. I'm sure some of my students do enjoy learning and they particularly enjoy achieving, but even for them I don't think it has anything to do with going to college. Most of the ones I teach don't have any thoughts of going to college. They know the financial burden would be enormous and I don't think any of them have any models in their own family of someone who went to college and prospered. Where I went to high school the students had no trouble making the association between the success and affluence of their parents and their parents having a good education. Here most of the kids know somebody in their own family or in the community who has made a great deal of money without going to college or even graduating high school. Of course some isn't necessarily legal, but I don't think that bothers them.

My father agrees that my assessment of most of my students' aspirations is accurate but I must certainly believe that I am making a difference for some of them, maybe more than I think. I acknowledge that's how a lot of my colleagues look at it but I'm not ready to write off the majority. I hope I don't have too many of these crises of conscience. This cell phone call has cost me a lot of money.

January 13: Jason, My Nemesis, Shows Up

There he is, standing just outside my open doorway, surveying my class, probably looking for someone he knows. Probably looking to harass someone, anyone, would be more accurate. I don't know how long he's been standing there because he was not making any noise, but once he sees that I noticed him he starts talking trash to one of my students, and then another. Before long one of my female students, a Korean girl who is ordinarily not one to speak in class without being called on, turns around and starts talking trash back at him. She is not playing as he was; she is really angry. Then he walks away and shortly comes back and just stares at me.

I go to the telephone to call security and he takes off. I ask the girl if she is all right. She's shaking and says it is the most bothersome thing that has ever happened to her at this school. I'm sorry it happened but I compliment her on the way she stood up for herself and that makes her smile. I tell her and the class that he wouldn't be prowling the halls much longer. I can't imagine after my report on him that they won't ship him out. He already has more than three strikes.

I go later to the associate principal who said he is going to make Jason come back and apologize to the class, which would have been humbling (but never happened), but I still don't see why he's allowed to continue at the school at all. It seems nothing he does is ever serious enough to remove Jason permanently from the school. He's threatened me physically and bored a hole through his textbook with the end of the compass, the only thing he ever used it for.

I suppose I could keep my door closed but then students will constantly be opening it and that would create more of a distraction. Many students arrive late and leave the door open. Even students who aren't members of my class open the door and come in to hide from a security guard who's chasing them. I usually kick them out. Sometimes when my frustration is extremely high, I give my students a task to work on and go after students who should not be disturbing my class. I believe in working together to make the school run as effectively as possible, but I'm outraged that I feel driven to leave my class to track down students who disturb my class. It's times like that, when I'm running after a kid, I wonder what the hell I'm doing. They didn't train us to be sprinters in my teacher-education program. I still wonder what this police action I'm involved in has to do with my being a teacher. I believe that my reputation has now developed as a teacher who will leave his classroom to chase students. I'm undermining my own goals in this because now students from other classes disturb my class just to see if they can outrun me.

Apparently I don't have a reputation around school as a teacher who holds kids to a strict code of behavior. I suppose that's why kids try to harass me, disrupt my classes, steal my books and materials, and come into my classroom uninvited. I suppose I'll have to clamp down in a big way but it doesn't feel quite right to me. I don't want to run my classroom management like a fascist dictator, at least not yet.

January 16: Going Off to War

My father asked me today if the situation in Iraq is in the minds of any of my students, if the issue has surfaced in any way, if any family members of my students are being shipped out. I am well aware that wars, at least recent ones, are fought mainly by the children of the working classes, the ones who don't go to college, or the ones who believe the military will give them their only opportunity to go to college, provided they don't die first.

True to the sociological regularities it turns out that many of my students have brothers and sisters who are being shipped out on a daily basis. Actually many of my students have talked to me about their feelings, that they feel scared, or worried, but no one ever expresses a sense that there's something unfair about it. Which I am sure is what my father was getting at. One of my students, as part of an assignment having to do with convex polygonal forms, brings in a framed picture of her brother in uniform, who had just left this week for the Middle East.

Of all the consequences of receiving a second-class education, the going off to war pattern is the most egregious. And yet the victims of this instance of social injustice and those who will be the victims do not think it is particularly unfair. I don't get it.

January 20: A Grading Dilemma

I'm in the process of doing my semester grades and as I finish with each class I show the results to my father. In my first period class, out of eighteen remaining students (some have dropped out, others were kicked out), ten are getting fails. My father looks over my roll book at the individual grades and he notices that some students are getting Fs even though they have passed every test. He's bothered. I tell him they never turn in their homework, or their notebooks. I know he knows I suffer for every F I give out so I justify myself by explaining that the grades will motivate them, that there is some long-run payoff. I tell him that my main goal in this school is to help low-achieving students develop work habits that will give them a chance to take the courses that will lead to access to college. They are all smart enough to pass my easy tests in this basic course, but it is the habits of achievement that they are not developing. They are not paying attention to the markers. It's ironic that I, someone who believes these markers of success have nothing to do with actual mathematical understanding or achievement, am responsible for instilling these values in a population who has spent their previous eight years of schooling indifferent to them.

He tells me he can see my way of thinking, but on the other hand there is the notion of rewarding students for what they do, to show them that whatever they have achieved will be rewarded. He suggests that failing them sends a message that not even doing well on tests pays off. The truth is, in the long run they will never do well without being diligent about their homework and study habits. This is the design of schooling. And without this discipline they'll never be able to master the difficult material that is taught in the higher-level math courses.

He reminds me that that is what he tells me when we play tennis together, that I never practice so I never play as well as I would like, but I still enjoy playing because I think it's a lot of fun. He asks me why I don't practice and I tell him because tennis isn't that important to me. He asks me how important do I think pre-algebra is to my students. I'm not sure exactly what follows from this but it makes a point with me. I either will have to find a way to make kids feel what I'm teaching them is important or make the homework assignments enjoyable enough that students will want to do them. He suggests that maybe I can give my tests that they do well on as homework and make homework the class activity. I'll think about it; the details will have to be worked out. I think maybe I'll start practicing my tennis a bit more as well.

January 21: Another Mystery

Here's something I can't quite fathom. I'm designing the final exam for several of my classes and many of the problems involve the application of formulas. I tell them before every test they can program the formulas needed for the test in their calculators. In my high school this was done as a matter of course; in every class this was the first thing we asked, can we program the formulas in our calculators. If the teacher said no, we couldn't, we did it anyway. None of my current students has ever asked me about doing this and I've been recommending they do it all year, but very few students ever do. They also never take their checked-out school calculators for their assignments. To them these few things that could significantly advantage them in my class don't seem worth the time.

January 25: Free Speech

I've known that one day some smart kid would ask me a question about free speech, since teachers are always telling kids that there are some things they can't say in class, like cursing even though cursing at home and in the neighborhood is common fare. "So how come I can't cuss you out?" a boy asks me, "don't I get to have free speech?"

"Sure, you do" I tell him, "and I am equally free to kick you out of this classroom."

The students laugh. I'm sure I haven't done justice to the abstract principle of free speech but it's the answer the kids can relate to.

January 27: On the Subject of Looking Good

I have nothing against my students looking their best and I know very well that adolescents consider their looks more important than their education, but my classroom is about math. I've never seen so many combs and brushes and eyeliners and make-up anywhere outside a beauty supply store. They can find their hairbrushes a lot quicker than they can find their math notebooks. I don't understand why they can't do all their grooming between classes outside or in the bathrooms. That's what the girls did in my high school. But here grooming in their seats trumps all classroom rules and regulations. And taking a brush away from a girl is like taking away her sanity. They go ballistic.

Laticia, an African American girl, is an average student who is not usually a problem, but today I've asked her three times to put her brush back in her purse. Each time she refused, having as an excuse that today was a bad-hair day and her hair was looking too nappy to tolerate. It is clear to me she is not going to back down and would rather be kicked out of class than put away her brush. I decide rather than kick her out of class, I'll put in a call to her mother right then and there and maybe resolve this standoff peacefully.

It works, to my surprise. Whatever Laticia's mother said to her, the brush is put away and Laticia goes into a quiet funk as we go on with our lesson. I still find it quite amazing that some problems of classroom management can be dealt with by having a phone on my desk. Of course, there is the greater likelihood that in our school a parent will not be home or I will be unable to carry on a conversation in Spanish (which I readily admit is my fault).

January 28: Parental Interference

I have another student whose mother does not seem to be as concerned about her daughter's academic progress as is Laticia's mom. Donna, a marginal student, is taking her final exam. Her success on the final is the difference between Donna passing or failing the course. The students are in the middle of taking the final when I receive a phone call. The call is from the head of the attendance office requesting that Donna be sent to the office, because her mother is waiting for her and Donna's mother is giving attitude. I tell her Donna is taking her final exam and that it is very important for her to finish. The attendance officer responds that it is also important to accommodate the mother since she is in a rage about Donna missing a scheduled doctor's appointment. I comment to the vice principal in charge of attendance that she has to make the mother realize the import of the exam. She chuckles and then tells me to get the girl to the office and my insubordination in this matter will not be further tolerated. My concern for the girl's academics did not take priority to the school's pandering to the parents.

With respect to the mother, apparently this appointment takes priority over her daughter's final grade. I send Donna to the office and accommodate a seething mother and an unreasonable administrator. Donna, it turns out, does not do well enough on her incomplete final to pass the course.

January 30: A Gratifying Session

Today Dr. Williams comes to observe my sixth period Algebra II class toward the end of the period. The class has been working well for thirty minutes or so when a good student, Carrie, asks if I mind answering survey questions on what cleaning products I run out of most frequently. It is for a course she is taking that deals with domestic leadership skills, a course that many of our graduating seniors take to help them in the "real" world. Since it is late in the day and the students have been working well I choose to answer, at which point I see Dr. Williams enter the classroom. My first reaction is to tense up. My future at the school depends almost exclusively on his evaluation.

At this point, in a nice way, I suggest we drop the subject of Carrie's survey and turn to the next algebra problem. Amazingly, without missing a beat the students pick up on how important it is for the class and me to look good in front of the principal. They begin by asking relevant questions which I comfortably answer and I ask them questions which they answer and the rest of the period passes smoothly until the final bell. I've been told by Anthony that one of the principal's most important criteria in judging teachers is that their students are working and are engaged from bell to bell, even if they're not learning anything. I love these students, at least today.

January 31: Julio Takes the Rap

The student body president, Julio, is a student in my Algebra II class. Julio is Mexican American, the homecoming king, good looking, outgoing, very popular, and is on his way to being a neighborhood success story. And he knows it. Julio dresses very preppy, not like those who surround him. He is not a tagger, not a gangbanger.

Up until Thursday Julio had a C in my class despite his intelligence; he never turns in homework or notebook assignments. He recently failed a major test badly. He's a student who's always with me all the way as I work through a problem on the board. He should easily be getting an A in the class. Before he takes the final he tells me he couldn't study because he was in juvenile hall and didn't even think they would let him out in time to take the test.

I ask him what he did to end up in "juvie" and he responds he took the rap for one of his homeys who already had one strike against him. I tell him it was a risky thing to do, could ruin his future options, and add, "Julio, you're going to make it. Why would you risk your success?"

I can see the disappointment in Julio's face, since he thinks he'd done something noble, loyal, protecting his friends. Most kids I give personal advice to don't really care to hear it and only act interested. I don't know how long I'll keep that up. But I do feel with Julio I can have a real dialogue where he understands the point I'm trying to impress upon him.

My belief is that in this school the kids who make it to Algebra II are kids who are smart and have a shot at a promising future. I hate to see any of them blow their chances. I know that even among the Algebra II students, most of them don't have the study skills and don't want them particularly. I also know that here there are many students at lower math levels who could make it at any academic level or school, but they appear less intelligent because they never were exposed to demanding courses. I'm guessing that once students have been placed in my Introduction to Algebra class, less than 25 percent will ever even get to Algebra II, which is needed for admission to any of the state universities. The University of California schools require students to have been in honors math classes and it is unlikely that any of my Introduction to Algebra students will ever be in one honors class much less all of them.

Julio did well enough on the final to earn a C in the class but I don't know what damage to his future the arrest will do.

January 31: Fighting Rules Rule!

A girl on our academic decathlon team was walking in the hall when another girl came up to her and punched her in the face, rendering her, although she did not respond, the second party of a fight. The consequence of this was that she was suspended for five days, making her ineligible to compete and the team had to forfeit their participation.

I wonder if this had happened to one of our star soccer players would he have been made ineligible. Apparently, because the prospect of any fight is so potentially explosive in this environment, there is no mercy given in cases of fighting. Immediate suspension for all concerned takes place. Discipline takes precedence over any other school goals. The idea of safety needs models the real world for this population.

February 1:
What I Learned in My First Semester

I've decided that traditional education is not effective with most of these kids. Right, I know, I'm one semester into the game and making major pedagogical assumptions. Hubris, right. I can't help it. I can't see how any new teacher can help it. I'm pretty sure that lecturing at the board, having students work on problems at their seats, taking occasional questions from students, giving homework assignments out of the book or out of my head doesn't go very far toward motivating the kind of learning I'm looking for. I don't actually know what kind of learning I'm looking for, but I feel the only thing that works is situating the learning with the students; they have to take what's in the book and find ways of making it their own individual experience, where engaging in discourse with other students is critical. I don't really have any idea how to do that. I guess what I'm saying is that this first semester I learned more what doesn't work than what does and most of what doesn't work seems to be what the school is telling me to do.

I've learned how to keep the thought of danger out of my daily work. My school may be dangerous in some ways but you're so enmeshed in the struggle to find ways to get through to as many kids as possible that you're too exhausted to worry about threats to your personal safety.

I've learned that many of my efforts to befriend students and make them more responsible for their own learning haven't worked. Calling parents seems to make little difference with many students, detentions even less. On the other hand calling parents about how well their child is doing seems to keep the ball rolling in a positive direction. The parents appreciate it and so do the students.

I've learned that I must make peace with the realization that the majority of kids I teach in the Intro to Algebra class won't go on beyond high school and a majority won't even graduate. I need to consider this reality in planning my lessons but I don't yet know what changes I need to make.

I've learned that a lot of kids can fall through the cracks if no one is attentive to them. And for the most part, no one is, particularly to the low achievers. I suspect that once a student is labeled a low achiever he might as well fall off the planet as far as anyone at the school is concerned. Again the idea that keeps circulating from the more experienced teachers is, save your energy for the ones you know you can work with.

There is no one to blame really that I see on a daily basis. I see everyone working long and hard to keep the ship afloat. The magnitude of the battle we're undertaking in public urban education is plausibly unwinnable, but with the right effort I think there can be significant victories. I've had some of those victories. I've learned that much of teaching is like going to the gym. The process is hard and often not fun but the results are usually there if you stick to it. They must be there or I wouldn't feel so good about my future as a teacher.

The one major thing I've learned is just how difficult it is to do the job we're assigned to do with all the forces working against us. We teach too many students and the students have too much to deal with at home and on the streets. We don't have the resources we need to oversee the education of each individual student. My tentative conclusion at the moment is that there are too many failures but no one in particular is culpable. I sense the blame falls abstractly on all the missing people in these students lives: missing teachers, missing personnel workers, missing counselors, missing advocates, and often missing parents. I'm talking about those who should be there making a crucial difference.

Analysis

When students question a school rule they have been caught violating, it's not always easy to tell if they want to be excused or if they want to protest restrictions in general. Of course they know they can't win but it's completely understandable that victims of restraint would want to challenge those restraining structures at any possible opportunity. It would be unfair to students, however, to view all acts of resistance to authoritarian rules as resistance for its own sake. Very often there is a serious value difference between what students think is the right way to be treated and the way teachers view it. Authoritarian teachers—and we suspect the majority of teachers in the urban school feel they have to be authoritarian—do not view conflicts as anything more than a violation of school rules. One study looking at the issue concluded that in many cases students looked at confrontations between teachers and students as injustices. Knowledge of consequences did not seem to affect compliance. High school students want to be treated fairly and not as children by punitive adults (Sheets 2002).

We suspect in middle-class public and private schools students accept, and have accepted, what we are calling restraints, as necessary conditions for educating groups of students simultaneously. They may resist but probably not in ways that would jeopardize their future. It is also conceivable that middle-class students are allowed a wider range of freedoms in their classroom life due to the fact that they are not expected to cause problems. Such is not the normal assumption of the urban-classroom teacher for all the reasons these pages have conveyed. The bottom line is the flexibility of rules regarding student behavior increases to the degree expectations for deviant behavior decreases.

At this point Paul is troubled by what he takes to be the attitude of many of the teachers who have been there the longest. He was quick to jump to the conclusion that they didn't really like the students particularly, would easily quit on those they felt were unworthy of their efforts, and generally had very little expectation that most of them would ever amount to anything. Paul acknowledges that he needs to get to know some of these teachers better and to give them the benefit of the doubt.

It was, after one semester, Paul's feeling that some of those who liked students the least had the best control over them. He is on the verge of concluding that his assumption that the better students like a teacher, the more cooperative they will be, is fallacious. On some occasions Paul has asked some of the kids who are noisy in his class why they are quiet in other classes. A normal response is, "Because she's mean and she scares us." To what extent, then, is fear the major weapon in the arsenal of classroom control? This is true from the students' point of view but we suspect there's a lot more to it than that. Many students turn fear on its end and respond aggressively and contentiously. Often, they have worked out the fear factor in their home and in their neighborhood.

For many new teachers, we suspect, considering making fear a weapon in the search for student cooperation is a juncture point in the formation of a teaching style. Paul has decided he will not make a hasty decision to make "fear" the foundation of his approach to classroom management.

Paul's sudden awareness of Ruth's easily explainable depression tells us a good deal about the role of the school in the area of mental health. Apparently there isn't any role for the school. Or at best it's marginal. Many would argue this shouldn't be a role for the school, that the school deals with academic matters and other agencies attend to psychological problems. It shouldn't be that simple. There have been some attempts to place mental health services on school campuses, primarily in elementary schools, which does make sense since high school student problems do begin early and some may be nipped in the bud. The so-called one-stop school movement is a promising thrust in the direction we are suggesting. Also referred to in the academic literature as "full-service schools" efforts are underway in a number of states both to conceptualize as well as incorporate a range of services, including mental health resources, into individual community schools (Dryfoos and Maguire 2002).

While we know that some students, particularly those with the kinds of psychological problems that lead students to become part of the special-education system, are referred for psychological services, students who do well enough and don't cause problems in the public schools are not noticed except when they buckle under the pressure and fail to achieve at their normal level, and sometimes not even then. Paul had to discover the root of the problem with Ruth through a serious phone call with a parent. But even after they are noticed, as Paul did with Ruth, where does he go from there? Where does Ruth go if resources are not readily available in her community? It is one thing to understand the connection between a student's traumatic experience and the consequences for his or her schoolwork, but few teachers have the kind of training required to deal with the problem of depression without some kind of professional resource.

One study of mental health problems among urban adolescents focused on the exposure to violence that these students see in their community. Rape, of course, is one obvious example. Ruth is certainly a conspicuous victim, all the more so because it cut short for her a successful educational experience. Any consideration of the fact of depression in an urban adolescent student suggests that a history of the experience of violence in their lives should be examined (Pastore, Fisher, and Friendman 1996).

Many students in urban schools are acting out their personal problems in and out of the classroom. Paul sees an intense degree of anger, even ferocity in the faces of many of his students when he confronts them or when students confront each other.

While we do believe that the conditions that cause students to become depressed and lose interest in school will pass for many of them in all communities, we suspect they will pass much quicker in suburbia where students have greater resources (parents, money, therapists, psychopharmacologists) to deal with troubling issues.

Is it unreasonable to think of urban-school teaching as missionary work as Paul has? Many teachers in urban schools, especially new teachers, probably do feel they have something of a mission in front of them. And many, like the missionaries of old, have left their comfortable homeland to voyage across the city to a foreign world. Maybe the analogy for many middle-class teachers who travel to the inner city in the cause of helping the underclass student does fit. Perhaps the source of much of the frustration these teachers experience is based upon their inability to get students to adopt their work values, the qualities of mind and work they believe are necessary for social success.

Perhaps one source of the frustration that many middle-class teachers feel, at least initially, is how different their experiences are from the Hollywood model of the middle-class urban-school teacher in films and TV series who go into the ghetto or barrio and turn things around for some students who are otherwise doomed to fail. The most obvious models of these themes in film and TV are *Blackboard Jungle* and its myriad clones and a string of successful TV series such as *Welcome Back Kotter* and *Boston Public* (Bulman 2002).

An important issue that most teachers need to come to grips with is the unfortunate disjuncture between the classroom-management skills of the teacher and the overall practice of the administration. When career "troublemakers" are allowed to harass teachers at their leisure and teachers are not in a position to determine the consequence or even have a say in it, the result is frustration in the moment and gradual accumulating alienation in general. It is in situations like this that the size of the school and the number of discipline problems that the school has to absorb seem to play a part. Teachers in inner-city schools know the constraints of what can be done with perpetual discipline problems and they do learn to accept and live with them, but for a first-year teacher like Paul, it's a very frustrating experience.

It is a fact of life for Paul's students that many members of their community and family go into the military because they don't have the opportunity or the background to go to college. This is referred to in sociological jargon as "class-bias theory." Bias theory suggests in recent times (from Vietnam on) the men who have fought and died in war came from the lower socioeconomic strata of society. Studies of the Vietnam War support that theory (Wilson 1995; Gimble and Booth 1996). We suppose if it was a question of fairness and this notion was part of the consciousness of students, more people would be speaking out. But what would they say? And of more consequence to our concerns here, what would or should a teacher say? "If you don't buckle down and do your work you'll be more likely to drop out, go in the military, and be killed in a war." We suspect the idea is not far from the truth.

We were both wondering what might have been the effect, or the consequence, of Paul confronting them with the general fact that very few of the children of the middle classes went to Vietnam or Kosovo or are on their way to Iraq. Clearly we have a situation here that reeks of social injustice, so what should a social justice educator do about it in his or her classroom? We are wondering how many graduates of his social justice program are bringing this matter up in their classes as the United States begins sending poor men and women off to war in the Middle East.

We conclude this issue on a very troubling note. The students at Olympia High know they are not as well off as students in middle-class schools. They do make comparisons. But how does a teacher raise the question about the social consequences of being poor or working class? They feel these consequences every day when they come to Olympia High, but how would they or their parents feel about entering into a discussion about it? What would be the aim?

As for the issue of allowing students to indulge their obsessions with their looks, we have to grant that every adolescent subculture values appearance highly and we assume that appearing to be an enemy of that value for students is one of the worst stands a teacher can take. Yet the "time and place for everything" maxim doesn't go over well in the urban high school and it probably has a lot to do with how valuable students think school is—at least in comparison with how they look. The object lesson here, if the teacher wants to repose in the good graces of his students, is that the time-and-place idea has got to be something students understand and accept rather than something that is imposed upon them without explanation.

It is difficult to analyze the role of the principal in evaluating first-year teachers because we don't know what criteria are used, nor do we know how the prejudices of this administrator influence his judgment. We suspect a great deal. We would suggest that first-year teachers deserve some space in evolving as teachers, particularly in urban schools where classroom-management skills can be slow in evolving. In such circumstances we would believe that the evaluator's role in the first year or years needs to weigh heavily in the direction of helping and supporting rather than judging. It will become obvious to Paul, later in the year, that his present principal's major focus is judging teachers on the basis of how successful they are in keeping the students quiet and working in their seats.

The values of the subculture rule, as one might expect, and the costs for the urban high school student whose life on the street may be far more significant than his status in the school can be heavy. Paul chose to couple Julio's street dilemma with the problem of providing a bright student with a demanding enough math program to keep him interested. The academic challenge is hard enough but competing with the peer group for the student's attention and commitment to doing well in school is a losing proposition for students like Julio. The fact that good students in this neighborhood have a good probability of falling in with others who value education not at all is one more condition working against Paul's goals.

Much of what Paul has learned in the first semester he has learned for the first time. Much of what he will learn in the semesters to come is that the same things keep happening. New learning will not be so much about what the problems are but what, if anything, can be done to keep him from losing hope while attempting to overcome these problems.

CHAPTER EIGHT

~

Second Semester—
Old Patterns, New Insights

The new semester, or any new semester in the time cycle of a comprehensive public high school, cannot be expected to vary much from any particular old semester. Such is the nature of institutional life, particularly the life of an institution as conservative, bureaucratic, and linked to legislative funding as the school. The problems of the past are the problems of the present and probably, without major structural reform, the problems of the future. The beginning weeks of the new semester have exposed Paul to yet another series of fresh problematic issues that seem bottomless in the panoply of a new teacher's eye-opening experiences.

One of the major and most problematic activities of the new semester in many schools is the placement of students into their new classes. Paul is new to the complex process of student placement so at this point he is simply the passive subject of a mysterious process. Placement problems are particularly severe in the Introduction to Algebra A classes where there is about a 60 percent failure rate across the math department. Most replacements in the second semester take place by removing the students who failed Intro A in the first semester and fitting them into newly organized repeat Intro to Algebra A classes. One of the few exceptions to this pattern is to recommend high-achieving students from the Intro A class for placement in an Algebra 1A class instead of the traditional path to Intro B. This is perceived by most students to be a very challenging and probably difficult leap into deeper and muddier waters.

The only advice I was ever given in my days in the classroom by administrators that observed me and by my colleagues who heard my classes down the hall is "get tough and stop letting them take advantage of you." I never felt they were taking advantage of me. I was enjoying myself, after tenure anyhow. Before tenure I'd play the game of toughness and softness back and forth but I was never good at acting tough. To tell the truth, very early in the game I could see that acting tough was stressing me out so I stopped doing it until the next time I was warned.

The fact that social class consciousness was not an issue for me in my student days probably had a lot to do with the time in American economic history in which I was raised. Except for the very wealthy, who went to private schools and whom I never saw, I could make little social distinction between myself and my schoolmates. Until I decided to try to go to college I didn't focus much on those who were going and those who didn't, but I thought it was just preference. It's hard to believe, as sensitive as I have been for many years about class differences, this was not in my mind in high school. Very few students in my high school went to college. I myself didn't go until two years later when I began to feel the psychological effects of working in menial jobs. That's when the notion of social class set in.

For Paul, the idea of having his students graduate high school and go to college and seeing the reasons they probably won't plays hard on his thinking. That he might play a part in influencing a student to work hard so as to have a chance to raise himself up is all about his struggle and hopes and class consciousness. To listen to Paul talk sometimes you'd think his class identification was more a part of his identification with his school and students than his own life chances had been.

My insights into how little my lecturing to my students about how they were on the road to low-paying service jobs if they didn't buckle down led me to caution Paul about the hopelessness of that approach. If anything like class consciousness exists in them at this age, I suspect that kind of abstract lecturing, given their feelings of hopelessness about college anyway, pushes them even further into feelings of worthlessness. Again, nothing has changed. Most poor minority students in urban schools don't envision themselves in higher education, yet teachers continue to challenge them to be prescient about their future fortunes. I've often wondered if our motivation to have students performing well wasn't more to make our own work easier and seem more worthwhile. That may be cynical, but so what. No reason both teacher and student shouldn't benefit.

Regarding the issue of racial conflict and its aftermath, my own experience doesn't at all parallel Paul's. There were occasionally fights between black students and Mexican students and every once in a while a white student would get involved, but it never took on the proportion of race riot. What has to be dealt with in Paul's classroom and out of it when he's on duty in the lunchroom or the yard is what is seething under the surface in the minds of students. And not only in the consciousness of those who are likely to be involved in any violence, but in the fears of students frightened to be caught in the middle.

We begin here with an interesting encounter in which Paul is confronted with an example of the need some students have to feel good about themselves, even if it costs them a shot at a better future.

February 3: Please Don't Send Me Up!

One student in my Intro class, a freshman named Pedro, a sweet, cooperative boy, tells me at the end of the first semester that he does not want to accelerate into Algebra IA second semester, even though he's done very well the first semester and I am ready to advance him. Pedro's request, more of a plea, is based on how much he has enjoyed his achievement in my class, where he has received his first A ever in an academic subject. Pedro is looking forward to continued success with me. He is quite sure Algebra I will put an end to his achievement experience.

I know that fewer than 1 percent of students who begin their high school math career in Intro ever make it to a four-year college, given that the math requirements of the universities in my state (they can't afford to go anywhere else) are beyond their reach. The University of California suggests that students take calculus, which is an unlikely task for a student who begins in Introduction to Algebra, unless they go to summer school. For reasons I don't comprehend, students are not recommended to take summer-school classes unless they fail. Trying to get ahead is not encouraged here and the students don't leap at the opportunity.

It is not necessarily the case, however, that a student who begins in Intro to Algebra doesn't get to calculus. The chair of the math department, Anthony, began his studies at Olympia High in Introduction to Algebra. His success, as he tells it, was anything but easy. But Anthony is a rare exception. The difficulty of making it through the high school math program and going to a four-year college affects nonnative English speakers particularly, who are almost exclusively placed in Introduction to Algebra. If that's not structured racism then I don't understand the concept.

Pedro, who might improve his possibilities for further education, would rather stay in a virtually dead-end class where he experiences the rare feeling of achievement rather than have upward mobility in the math sequence where he thinks he will renew his familiar acquaintance with disappointment and failure.

It appears then that I'm put in the position of advancing Pedro against his wishes or retaining him to his ultimate disadvantage.

February 4:
George and Anthony Convince Me to Toughen Up

George and Anthony, my fellow math teachers, both Filipino, are about the same size physically, short and thin, but despite their size they seem to have fewer classroom-management problems than I do. They are not the kind of men that can scare the students physically into towing the line but they do have those rare qualities that influence students to pay attention. Both men have been teaching here about the same amount of time, around eight years. It seems to me like they're out of the same mold. They're both likeable guys whom I respect as teachers and classroom managers. And they both give me the same advice about discipline. Start out tough. They both told me earlier in the year not to expect to get much teaching done the first couple weeks of a semester. The first couple weeks are for making sure the students know and follow the classroom rules. I didn't completely take their advice at the time because I was new and had some ideas of my own about relating to students. As a result, I never did feel I achieved complete control of my classroom.

Coming out of a teacher-education program that did not teach much in the area of classroom management, I found it extremely difficult to deal effectively with the management problems in my Intro classes.

This semester I decided to take Anthony's and George's advice to heart and "toughen up." I've laid down the rules for my classes and I'm prepared to back them up rigidly. That is the part that is easy to say, but more difficult to put into practice. The students fight back, look for loopholes, inconsistency in disciplining and rule violations, and they argue on and on, which they would prefer to do rather than work on their math.

It's taken me a long—as well as painful—time trying to perfect the art of stopping student arguments the moment they start. I want to make students realize I am available to them if they have a serious complaint. I am in my classroom after class as well as after school. If students want to debate anything (appropriate), they know they are free to come in and let me know their problem. If, however, they argue with me during class time they now know they will see disciplinary action taken. In my observation and estimation, most students who argue in class rather than during appropriated times are looking to put on a show in front of their friends. I have allowed many of the shows to take place during my short time on the job. I am currently working hard to minimize any that could potentially take place in the future.

Students are neither afraid of me nor of any authority I supposedly wield. I've discovered that when I raise my voice to a student, the student raises his voice to me, so I know that's not the way to go.

I recently asked Anthony how long they could possibly fight me. He told me they would fight me as long as I allowed them to. George had a somewhat different way of thinking about it. George told me that I am the adult and they are children. He said our job is not only to teach content material, but appropriate value systems. He said there will be some students who will fight me for a semester, some a year, some their entire high school career. He told me that what I have not yet discovered is that every time we firmly place down boundaries we gain respect for ourselves and for the rules. He said as I teach longer, I will start to see more students who have graduated college come back to visit and to express gratitude for the discipline I instilled.

February 6: Class Consciousness

Having played too much tennis over the weekend, I am writing on the board when I feel the pain in my serving/board-writing arm. I drop my arm and wince. One Latino student, Jose, a muscular, athletic student in the front row, asks me what the matter is. I tell him I'd injured my arm over the weekend, hoping that will be an end to the boy's interest. However, Jose persists, asking me how I did it. I consider lying and telling him I injured it doing yard work or moving furniture or playing basketball, something I thought Jose would relate to, but, being curious how my upper-middle-class identity would influence my relationship with my students, I decide to tell him the truth, that I injured it playing tennis. I look at Jose, trying to see what his reaction is to my admitting to participating in such a bourgeois sport. The boy says something like, "Oh, you play tennis. I play football."

February 7: The Rapping Cell Phone

Penelope, the young Asian student who got me in trouble because I ignored the dress code, has blossomed into a very popular student. I'm afraid, along with her popularity, comes a more active social life and a less active student life. Today, I confiscate her cell phone and lock it in a cabinet. Phones going off during class, complicating the already prevailing disorder, is really too much. I'm not opposed to the cell phone revolution but I am against using them in class.

So, despite Penelope's protests that she absolutely needs to make a lot of calls during her lunch period, I demand that she bring it to me. I refer to it as a pedagogically motivated confiscation.

The next period, in the middle of a lesson that I think is going well, I hear a rap song playing from my cabinet. It's got a nice beat. The students, of course, make a big deal out of it, telling me they like my cell music. One boy tells me that he's going to confiscate it. I don't know what's coming next. Next year I may be competing with BlackBerrys and iPhones. It may come down to a battle between entertainment technology and engaging mathematics instruction.

February 11: The Failure of My Abstractions

I have a class full of students repeating Introduction to Algebra A, the kids who had failed it the previous semester. I don't know why the district policy insists that failing students and making them repeat a class is the way to go. Almost all of the students, according to my colleagues who have taught repeat classes for years, fail again. A few students are redeemed, but I suspect there are other ways to redeem them rather than make them take the class again.

I've planned to start with a pep talk so I start with something like the following: "Why are you all here in this class? Because you failed Intro A." Some students smile, others raise their hands proudly, others lower their heads. I then go on, by way of an "inspirational" talk, to acquaint them with the big picture that is both abstract and future oriented. I remind them that they are running out of options in their quest to graduate from high school and to qualify for college admission. There is always the temptation—at least I feel it—when working with unmotivated students, to press home the threat that they are building for themselves a dreary, economically marginal future. I talked for a while about low level of opportunity, service careers, and all the glittering generalities of the value of education, not only for a career, but also for the capacity of living a richer life. The students couldn't be less interested. A universal fog seeps into their eyes. I might as well have been lecturing on Newtonian vs. non-Newtonian fluid dynamics (which is actually quite interesting).

Then I opened it up for questions, and we started to get more concrete. The dialogue went something like this:

STUDENT A: Why do we need to go to college?
PAUL: Because college offers people great future opportunities. [My god I'm turning into my high school college counselor.] For example, on average, you have the opportunity to make more money.

STUDENT B: My uncle makes $90,000 a year and he never went to college,

PAUL: That's unusual.

STUDENT C: My cousin makes almost that much and he never graduated from high school.

[Is it possible that I have the only repeat Intro class with students whose un-educated relatives all make close to $100,000 a year?]

Many students call out how they know somebody like that too, many who are in their family.

STUDENT D: You went to college Mr. Paul, how much do you make?

PAUL: That's private.

[I pace the floor. This is a pedagogical technique used frequently when teachers don't know an answer or don't know if giving an answer is appropriate. The students come to the figure of about $45,000. I don't deny it, so it has effectively been confirmed. How did they know?]

STUDENT C: My brother didn't graduate from high school and he doesn't make that much, but he makes enough to get himself a cool car and buys all the clothes and CDs he wants.

PAUL: What about when he wants to raise a family? Does he live with roommates?

STUDENT C: No, he lives at home with us. If he has a wife she can move in with us, too.

PAUL: Wouldn't you rather have a place of your own?

STUDENT C: Why? At home you get taken care of. My mother's a good cook.

STUDENT A: What about Kobe? He didn't go to college and he makes millions.

PAUL: Well if you can play basketball like Kobe, you don't have to worry about doing well in Algebra. Besides Kobe was a good high school student.

STUDENT B: There's a lot more sports.

I'm thinking that maybe I need to start this class with a lesson in probability if they're thinking about going into professional athletics, but then I realize if they didn't pass Intro A, a lesson on probability has a low probability of success. Besides, will it make any difference even if they understand that it's a million to 1 that you can make it to the big show? Probably not. There has to be somebody, they would argue, why not me?

February 13: Vulgarity Unleashed

Thomas is a white student; the only one in my class. He is one of three male Caucasians in the school. Something I say to him or do causes him to lose it entirely. I may have been critical of what seemed to be his slacking off, but I've said similar things to most kids sometime during the course of a class period without drastic responses. He curses me out violently, using words I understood, unlike some of what I hear from the Latino students, which I have to let go because I'm ignorant of Spanish slang. So I begin filling out a referral to the guidance room, and as he's storming out of the room the curse words start coming faster and stronger and with more intensity.

At this point in my teaching career, I'm not usually in the practice of sending kids out of the classroom for cursing, unless they're cursing at me. I've struggled a bit with this issue. I know some teachers don't put up with any cursing in class but I take the view that cursing is so engrained in youth culture, perhaps more so in urban youth culture, that most of the time they don't even know they're doing it. But cursing out the teacher with a string of vile vulgarities is not something that slips out accidentally. So I order Thomas out of the class and give him the referral slip.

That evening I call Thomas's father who tells me he'd be happy to beat the crap out of him but the law doesn't allow it. Furthermore, he informs me that he can't wait until the boy is eighteen so he can kick him out of the house. He also informs me that when Thomas loses his temper he goes crazy. I can see this point since the first week and a half in class Thomas was perfectly fine. I also think he's an able student who just doesn't care about succeeding in school. Thomas's dad seems apathetic and I very quickly realize I will not be working with Thomas with his parents on my side. A student's parents are a giant resource for teachers in all settings but they are particularly essential in affecting the progress of students in inner-city schools. I'm now resigned to handling this very volatile but smart kid on my own. I have colleagues to talk to, but it's my classroom management that will ultimately stand the test.

Thomas's punishment, I learn the next day, meted out by the guidance office is that he has to write a note of apology and deliver it in front of the class. This he does and after that Thomas returns to his normal, quiet self for a short time; then he disappears from the class and isn't heard from for weeks. I do recognize that being the only white student in class and one of the few in the school may have caused Thomas certain social-psychological problems. The complexity of this is a little beyond my current understanding. It seems to me, for most of the students, race doesn't play much of a part in their interaction with one another in school.

February 14:
The Flip Off Mode of Polygonal Resistance

Today's lesson on polygons is successful although I had not accounted for student creativity carrying the lesson. My students love this assignment's artistic semblance. They are free to create any polygonal figure using toothpicks that appeals to them and list its relevant properties. This day's activity takes place on Valentine's Day. There are many Valentine's Day–influenced polygons. One of the pieces is a heart constructed as a thirty-six–sided concave polygon.

One group creates a twenty-three–sided shape depicting a hand with its middle finger extended. I imagine the group expects to be chided by me for this "vulgar" creation. I was happy that they have classified it correctly as a convex icosikaitrigon after doing some Internet research. I am satisfied that it is polygonal. I do not admonish them for the "inappropriateness" of their work. I inquire who they are flicking off; is it me, is it the school, is it the greater society? I don't get my answer that day. They, however, have successfully completed the assignment.

February 18:
Looks Like We Got a Faggot in the Class

It's my first encounter with blatant classroom homophobia. I wish I'd had some discussion in my training program about how to deal with homophobic students, particularly in a setting where most of the kids go to church and, as some of them have related to me, their priests emphatically impress upon them that homosexuality is a sin.

The way this starts is a new student, Fredrick, an average height, somewhat pudgy, African American student enters the classroom. His behavior resembles that of a nervous character after four strong cups of coffee. His mannerisms and speech are clearly effeminate and the students pick up on this immediately, one shouting out, "Hey look, we've got a faggot in our class!"

I ask the student who'd called out to see me after class. Arnulfo, the shouter, is a good student, generally does his work, and is usually cooperative. When he comes up after class it's pretty obvious he knows what I'm going to say, that it's inappropriate language in my classroom and shows disrespect for a fellow student, one who has done no one any harm. The issue for me is the importance of communicating this notion of respect but I'm not very clear how to do it, suspecting that Arnulfo is of the belief that being gay is a sin. What could I say, "Hate the sin but love the sinner"? But then I would be suggesting homosexuality is a sin. Then again I feel I'm up against his religious conviction if I go the route of insisting that homosexuality is not a sin. I also worry about students thinking that anyone who seems to be defending homosexuality, rather that the right to be homosexual, must be a homosexual. I think I need some advice here, but from whom?

I do push the notion of respect in my conversation with Arnulfo and let it lie there. I don't want to venture into a discussion of religious orthodoxy. At any rate he apologizes for calling out and leaves my room. I think he caught the spirit of my concern although I doubt he fathomed the logic of it, given his own belief.

February 19: The Individual versus The System

Today, in the lunchroom, one of my neighboring teachers with many years' experience complained to me that one of my students showed up in her class with a pass from me that I had intended as a bathroom pass. This same day, coincidentally, two lists were circulated from the administration, one with names of students who are not to be issued passes and the second with the names of kids who have been expelled who should not be anywhere on the campus. On occasion, I have a student in class whose name is on the expulsion list but who chooses to come to school or doesn't know he's been expelled. It appears that parents reenroll their expelled children all the time, not having been explained the full significance of an expulsion or having no other school in which to enroll them. There are other schools in the district, but parents may not know about them or may feel that other schools are too far from their neighborhood.

The point here is that I have a pass-awarding policy that I prefer to apply to my students independent of what the general policy is in the school. I democratically award each student four bathroom passes for the semester that they can use in whatever way they choose. If they choose to stop off and visit another teacher's class on the way to or from the bathroom instead of going to the bathroom, I don't see a problem, as long as they don't disrupt other classes. The point is they are given passes and can use them as they like but four is all they get. And if a student in my class has been expelled but is doing his work in my class, I think it's a shame to deny the kid the opportunity to learn something. I know, of course, that as soon as the student's presence is detected, he's gone. In the same way, while the general policy is to deny students the right to chew gum in class and to censor cursing, I feel that neither activity is worth policing since it takes up too big a chunk of teaching time. I have only fifty-three minutes to teach what I think is important and since cursing and chewing gum are integral to their youth culture, I'd prefer to let it slide and concentrate on teaching math.

February 21: The Race Riot and Its Aftermath

Today I'm exhausted and starting to nurse a cold. I've taught exhausted and with a cold or worse before, but this time I'm going to indulge my intuition that I need a day off. It's actually not all that rational since I can hardly get out of bed. I've only missed one day of school all semester so I decide to stay home, rest up, and recover from the worst symptoms of my cold. Still, I feel guilty about leaving my students to a substitute. I talked earlier about my feelings about subs. I think I need to get over that. I also need to get over the feeling that my students can't get along without me for a day. You can only do the best you can and a sick, exhausted teacher isn't much good in the classroom. So I get out of bed, phone in my lesson plans for the day, and then go back to bed and sleep until noon.

That Saturday I feel well enough to attend my UCLA class where I learn from the other teachers in my program that I missed a race riot. Now I feel even guiltier, as if the racial tensions would not have erupted if I were there. Of course I don't really believe that, but I still feel guiltier than I did before I heard about the riot. I'm pretty sure most of my colleagues at the school wish they had missed it and I'm also sure I'll become more comfortable with taking sick days as I become more of a veteran. To tell the truth I'm not sure my guilt has anything to do with letting anyone down but myself. I'm just sorry I missed it. I want all the experiences I can get.

The next day Dr. Williams meets with our faculty and staff to review the history of the Friday disturbance. One thing he is particularly good at is summarizing the history of things. The word "riot" in his summary is being downgraded to a "disturbance" even though it took seven security officers and fifteen police officers in riot gear to quell the disruption of school business. The sequence of events, as I derive them from the principal and a number of teachers, began early in the week. A fight broke out between two boys, one Latino, the other African American. This was quickly resolved, as far as the administrators and teachers were concerned. Most outbreaks are isolated events and don't have much in the way of follow-up since kids cool down while they serve their five-day suspensions. Later in the week, however, a SCROC (Southern California Regional Occupational Center, a program that offers practical courses like child care, cosmetology, animal care, etc.) bus carrying four African American students who were gang members was met at the school as the bus unloaded by a larger number of members of a Latino gang. The African American students were beaten rather severely with pipes and crowbars.

The next day, apparently, was "payback" during the lunch period. It started with a single fight between two boys and, as they were being escorted to the principal's office, there were a few glass bottles thrown at the teachers escorting the boys. One teacher was hit in the eye with a bottle. Fights broke out everywhere, even spilling into the teachers' cafeteria. The fighting was mostly between the two main ethnic groups but some of the fights were between students of the same ethnic group. No one has as yet come up with an explanation for that.

It was not an all-male confrontation by any means. Girls were in the middle of it, fighting both other girls and boys. Boys, according to witnesses, did not seem to take the girl fighters lightly. When the police officers arrived they started rounding up the fighters. Many students were suspended, some expelled, and some arrested. Work was immediately underway on how to avoid future recurrences. The principal scheduled a meeting with parents the following evening.

A few other events of interest transpired while the mess was being cleared up, things that the principal neglected to mention that I learned from the teachers. The first thing was that a bell was sounded as the fighting was becoming widespread, in hopes that this would signal the end of first lunch and everyone would immediately go to his or her fourth period class. Unfortunately teachers instead dismissed their students from class to go to their lunch period (second lunch). Students came pouring out of the rooms and went running toward the commotion to see what was going on. How could they not? Some of them joined in the fighting. Another thing we were misinformed about was that some of the cops had rifles in hand. This was never mentioned in the meeting. A third matter was the problem of communicating with the teachers in their classrooms. The school does not have an intercom system, but all rooms have phones. Secretaries were on the phones calling the teachers one by one. Several teachers received several calls. Some said they were told to hold their classes, others to dismiss their classes to the auditorium. Many were not contacted at all; these were the ones who dismissed their classes to the lunch area.

February 21: Expecting Student Misplacement

I'm already becoming immune to the continuing problem of student misplacements. I'm inching toward cynicism in this area. Today I walked into the placement counselor's office with a list of kids from my last semester's Intro A class, who failed that class but were promoted to my next class in the sequence (Intro B) anyhow. Since it is Friday I'm told the counseling office personnel will have a weekend to figure out that these students don't belong where they've been placed. So I assume that on Monday the corrections will have been made, give a day or two, but I'm not going to be surprised if they haven't been (and of course they weren't).

February 25: The Parent Meeting

I invite my father to attend the meeting to observe the principal, Dr. Williams, interacting with members of the community. The topic of course is the recent "disturbance" (race riot) and the parents' concern for the safety of their children.

The meeting starts promptly at 6:30 P.M. even though only a couple dozen parents are present. By 7:00 P.M. over a hundred parents are in their seats in the auditorium. The latecomers haven't missed too much since everything that is said has to be translated as a large majority of those in attendance are Latino and solely Spanish speaking. The principal goes over the history of the disturbance as he had with the staff and faculty. Then he spends the majority of his remaining time, before turning the meeting over to questions, going over the new measures that are being put in place to reduce the possibility of anything similar reoccurring. The corrections will be immediately put in place: the lockdown bell will tell all teachers to lock their doors and hold all students in class; there will be an increase in the presence of teacher-supervisors and law enforcement officers; drinks in glass bottles will no longer be sold; the lunch period will be cut short by five minutes to the state legal minimum (thirty minutes).

Then begins the question-and-answer period that becomes heated at times, complicated by the fact that everything has to be translated: the questions to the principal, the principal's answers, even the disputes between members of the audience.

Some of the major concerns of the parents, keeping in mind that most of the parents are not the parents of students involved in the fighting, are as follows:

1. Why weren't these measures you told us you were taking already in place? To this the only response is we thought the measures we had already taken would be adequate but now we will improve upon them. With each question of concern the principal asserts that his highest priority is keeping their children safe.
2. Why are there so many troublemakers in the school? Why can't they be sent to the continuation school right away? Many of the parents are upset that "delinquents" and gang members are given too many chances before they're kicked out. The principal reviews the procedures and insists we are getting rid of troublemakers quickly.

3. Many of the parents want to know how gang members who were not enrolled students are able to be on campus causing trouble. Apparently a number of those involved in the fighting were gang members who were not Olympia students. The principal reviews the procedures by which, once the morning bell sounds, those who did not have good reason for being there are prevented from being on campus. Apparently there had been no procedure in place to keep them from coming in before the start-of-school bell.

4. A young budding feminist said she came to this meeting to find out why a girls' soccer game was cancelled but the boys' basketball game wasn't. Apparently the soccer game was only a practice game and the basketball game was an official league play-off game. The same young woman wanted to know why a dance was also cancelled and the principal tells her because in his judgment it was just the kind of scene that tempts gang violence and he didn't want to risk endangering anyone.

February 28: Back to the Campus for Theory

Last night, as part of completing my program at UCLA, I attended a lecture at the university given by an African American scholar who had been raised in Compton (a low-income minority community with a meager economic base) and attended a high school similar to the ones I and my fellow credential-program teachers were teaching in. His remarks generally were focused on things he remembered that teachers used to do to get the students to feel that the teacher cared about them as people. "Break up your lesson. Tell them to relax. Ask them what interesting things are going on in their lives. Get to know them as human beings."

The next day I try to put his words into my practice. I break up the math lesson and ask them if anything interesting had happened to them recently. One boy, William, the African American boy of my IEP fiasco, put up his hand and said, "Well, last night I was hangin' out on the street with my homeys when a car with a bunch of Mexicans in it drove by and took four shots at us."

This is in a class filled with Latino students, mostly of Mexican origin. The lecturer hadn't told me what I should do next. He also hadn't told me that it might be a bit more complex. This assumption that I could easily delve into my students' lives with this fast-food recipe had perhaps not taken into account the full complexity of this probing dynamic.

February 28: FIGHT! FIGHT!

Two words we teachers dread and students respond to like a red flag to a bull is the signal that a fight is starting up. "Fight! Fight!" echoes down through the halls and is taken up by other students wherever they are until it becomes a chant. That's when I feel the knot in the pit of my stomach. It's a little like the feeling you get when you feel the first trembling of an earthquake. You don't know whether it's minor or if it's the BIG ONE.

A fight broke out today during the lunch period. Not my lunch period. What I was told was that a bunch of African American kids were beating up on a Latino kid. And for some strange reason none of the security guards seemed to be available to break it up. A couple of teachers finally had to. What was somewhat surprising was that more Latino kids didn't get involved, thereby raising the bar to the level of a race riot. I'm glad it didn't go that far but it's curious. The best spin I can put on it, to account for the fact that few Latino students became involved, was that it wasn't seen entirely as a race matter. I do wonder why the security guards didn't get involved though. There might be a fuss about that. Some teachers have suggested that it was a racial issue and since the security officers are predominantly black and the student being pummeled was Mexican, they looked the other way. I hope that isn't the case. I doubt that it is. I've seen a number of incidents where African American security officers have come down heavy on African American students who were causing trouble. I do hate it though when the first explanation offered is a racial one, but let's face it, race is a major force in the workings of a diversely populated urban high school. There isn't a day that goes by that I don't think at some level about racial differences in the school. Not that the thoughts are necessarily tied to any expectation of any kind of problem but it's impossible to be totally color-blind.

February 28: The Three Cultures

One of my female students, Laticia, an African American girl, is very cooperative in class. She doesn't stand out because she doesn't say much and she seems sweet. I expect her to pass the course. So, today I'm walking in the yard across campus and I see her walking next to her mother who is screaming at her using language that burns my ears. Her mother is throwing every curse word in the book at her.

Now if this girl utters any one of the words in my class I would have to discipline her. Is this socially just? Is it fair that the girl goes from one context where vulgarity apparently is normal, to one that punishes for the use of it? I'm not ready to draw any conclusions about that issue yet, but I do know I'm expected to sanction vulgarity. It's a bit of a contradiction to tell myself that I will both uphold as well as ignore specific administrative sanctions. I'm also aware that this is not an administration that likes to be ignored. I guess I'll just have to see how it goes, and try not to hear language that isn't intended for my ears.

Analysis

One solution to the dilemma of promoting Pedro, the boy who wanted not to be put in an advanced class, into a class he is afraid he will not do well in, in the best of possible school programs is to dump Intro to Algebra as a dead-end class, start all students in Algebra I, and then give them well-trained math teachers, low numbers, double blocks of time, aides (especially Spanish speaking), and technical resources. Because of No Child Left Behind (NCLB) mandates and accommodations schools are beginning to drop the Intro courses and concentrate on the materials pertinent to the NCLB testing program. This scenario for most comprehensive urban high schools would make Paul's decision with Pedro moot, but the dynamic of a student wanting to hold onto a rare good feeling about his schoolwork rather than increase his ultimate success possibilities is not moot. Paul's district was considering changing Introduction to Algebra into a two-year Algebra I class, beginning in the 2004–2005 school year. This is a practice being incorporated in urban school math programs throughout the country (Paul 2005). But it's unlikely the change in title will make much difference unless there's an accompanying change in the logistics surrounding the new course, such as the reforms we've suggested above, the ones that are not delivered by NCLB.

Classroom management in the Introduction to Algebra class is, basically, a struggle for control. We don't know if getting rid of the class will improve the lives of teachers since the likelihood of the new structure of math classes to imitate the old will leave teachers in the same old position, struggling to control an unruly class. Teachers who lose this struggle will not be likely to survive teaching in an urban school for very long. It is a dynamic analogous to parenting. Children need to know who is in charge. It is essential to their development. Yet if teaching is only about control, to what end are teachers struggling?

While teachers and researchers are working on control techniques every day, it is still our view that some teachers are not cut out for all manner of management techniques. It's a matter of both skills and personality. The urban schoolteacher has to have both and that, in the first year, is one of Paul's most important issues for reflection.

One of the problems Paul has continuously struggled with is what exactly is the nature of control? How much freedom can students be allowed without fracturing the control teachers need to retain? He sees a control struggle as an interaction between a student and a teacher that interrupts the lesson for a significant period of time. It's a back-and-forth duel that derails the flow of instruction. And in his mind, it isn't a simple matter of just silencing the voice of the student abruptly. Many teachers, he knows, would disagree with him and believe that disruptive students need to be abruptly silenced. Paul's thought at this point is to silence students for the moment but let them know that the disagreement can be revisited at the end of the lesson. He isn't totally sure he has the best solution for himself and the students yet but he's in the process of testing his assumptions as he grows in experience. He also knows, no cynicism intended, that many students in the urban school create disruptions and argue them for as long as they can because they find them far more interesting than the content of the class.

Paul was troubled by his awkward reaction to the question about how he'd injured his arm (February 6), about assuming that students would treat his being a tennis player as elitism. Then it occurred to him that in his high school, a public high school in an upper-middle-class community, there were many tennis courts on the school grounds. At his school now there are none. While it is true the Williams sisters, Serena and Venus, represent a model of class mobility through tennis, it doesn't help a lot if you grow up in a neighborhood and go to school in a place that has no courts.

Paul needs to accept that both he and the students already know there's a difference between how he experienced school and how they experience it. There is an obvious class awareness that he need not hide from. This is too disingenuous and disrespectful.

For the inner-city adolescent the cell phone, aside from being seen as a social necessity, is also a way of helping to deal with disruptions in the business of family stability. Paul's students are always on call to help with the care of younger siblings, communicate with adults regarding being picked up from school, and the need to be in contact with their after-school contacts regarding work. It is also, sad to say, a bit of comfort in the event that rumors of a race riot begin circulating.

On the subject of forcing students to repeat classes, there is considerable controversy. Most of the research seems to suggest there is little benefit to retention or repeating and that students who are made to repeat are harmed both psychologically and academically. Most studies on this phenomenon show similar results and conclude there has to be a better way (Holmes 1989; Heubert and Hauser 1999). Paul sees alternative possibilities around the act of retaining students since he believes if they are taught again the same material in the same way, they are not likely to get it or want to get it this time either. That should be obvious for most repeaters. His view is to create a whole new kind of repeat class where individual student weaknesses from the past semester are examined and diagnosed. Unfortunately curriculum logistics and budget restraints don't allow for any innovations of this sort. In addition, repeat classes are as overcrowded as the regular classes, which rules out much individual attention, and there is no effort being made to develop innovative material for repeat students based on their particular weaknesses. If Paul is expected to make these innovations, he should be given his course schedule earlier than the week before the beginning of instruction.

A number of conferences and national meetings on efforts to end the practice of social promotion are held regularly and reports on outcomes are available (Eisner 2000). Which suggests, of course, how important it is to make repeat classes different from those students have previously failed.

In the transition from elementary school to junior high where the problem is most serious, and then from junior to senior high where the whole history of the failure to learn culminates in failure and dropout, very little change is seen in most urban school districts.

Whether we're talking tennis or basketball, it's no secret that a very small percentage of high school athletes ever make it to the next level much less to the pros, where the money is. Actually only 1.6 percent of college athletes go on to play professionally. We can imagine the statistics for high school athletes. It is a message that sport's sociologist Harry Edwards (1973) has been communicating to minority athletes for half a century.

What Paul realizes is he's looking in the human faces of those that bring the sociological regularities he studied in college to life. For the boys a cool car, cool clothes, and the "off the hook" CDs were as far as they needed to look. It's unlikely the girls are any more ambitious and for many of them the prospect of motherhood is a way out of the identity problem and perhaps accompanying social conditions such as abuse, poverty, and school failure (Committee on Adolescence 1999). The fact seems to be that the way urban youth, for the most part, look at the world of work is almost exclusively in terms of outcomes, what they could buy. They do not seem to identify with a career at all (Chaves, Diemer, Blustein, Gallagher, DeVoy, Casares, et al. 2004).

When Lortie (1975) gave us his seminal exposé of the urban schoolteacher over thirty years ago, he was able to draw a distinct connection between teachers' attitudes toward students and whether or not they cursed in class.

Not coincidentally, the greater number of students who became anathema to the teacher because of their inability to control their language was African American. Things have changed in thirty years. Most teachers are no longer hypersensitive to the curse word in the classroom, and there is certainly greater sophistication about why students in the urban environment have a lexicon loaded with what are generally considered vulgarities, but there is still, within most urban schools, a principle that discourages cursing, although it appears to Paul that it is sanctioned differently by different teachers. What hasn't changed apparently, bringing Lortie up to date, is that the problem students—those who curse and fight and defy authority—in most urban schools around the country, according to teachers, are the African American students (Monroe 2005). Paul's sense of how he needs to deal with cursing is still ambiguous, but he is aware that once he develops a policy, he needs to be consistent. At the moment he is willing to differentiate between vulgarity that is inadvertent and vulgarity that is used in the context of a student displaying aggression or hostility toward him or other students.

What Paul is dealing with in the case of Thomas, the "dirty mouth" white boy, is probably beyond the scope of his powers as well as his understanding. We can imagine a number of explanations, all beyond the parameters of educational resources available to Thomas or to Paul. The school counselors frequently are not trained as therapists with the skill, the time, or the interest to intervene. Behavior that emanates from the actions of a student undergoing mental problems is lumped together with all deviant school behavior, as if they all result from the same cause. Therefore, it is assumed, they all are subject to the same sanctions. Regulating and enforcing a set of universal punitive responses is far more manageable, given budget and personnel limitations, than treating violations of school policy as idiosyncratic.

Homophobia runs deep at Olympia High School. The word "faggot" is a generic putdown, from both genders. The word "gay" is now used to connote stupidity, something that's "lame." Paul generally tries to let his students know where he stands on sensitive issues without pontificating, so when an act of homophobia erupts in front of him and the class, he feels he has to take a stand.

In most cases, since the Latino students are Catholic and attend church regularly, the stand regarding homosexuality is often simplified in the students' minds; homosexuality is a sin. Paul wonders if the school might not develop a teaching unit on dealing with the topic for the New Student Seminar class all freshmen are required to take.

With respect to Paul's being a team player and complying with uniform school policy, well, it's something he's dealing with. Carl's adaptation many years earlier was to try to find a mid-point between the rules or norms of the system and his own beliefs about the way some of the rules were counterproductive to his teaching. It's probable that if he weren't the only English teacher who could work with the problem students, the administration would have come down on him more forcefully than it ever did, but this too, many teachers know, is part of the game. If you want to tinker with the rules, be sure there are viable reasons why they wouldn't want to get rid of you.

The race riot, a.k.a. the "disturbance," was a break from the normal school day. This, of course, is a gross understatement. There were police officers with riot gear and rifles on the campus. Students were ordered into the nearest classrooms. Some classrooms accommodated more than seventy students. One teacher locked her door and finished up some grading while she ignored the brutality outside her classroom.

The riot brought home to Paul the complexity of student-control problems in the urban school, problems the principal deals with on a daily basis, as well as with others who work in the guidance office. The principal has every act of gang violence potentially involving an Olympia student memorized. He knows what gangs have provoked what fights and which gangs are likely to retaliate during the school day. Paul has overheard him give an order to an associate principal to transfer a student to the local continuation school because the day after this student had been brutally beaten with a baseball bat, he and his fellow gang members were expected to retaliate. Students are not sent from Paul's school to the local continuation school because of grades. They are sent because of "delinquent" behavior. It is just a lucky coincidence that many of those engaging in this behavior also happen to have low grades.

In Paul's opinion there is an awareness of race that the students seem to have as a fact of their lives as minorities, but it stays dormant most of the time and, as a rule, students interact well with one another regardless of race. But then there are the racial conflicts where students are forced to take sides. Paul feels strongly that most of those who feel compelled to fight on the side of their race mates would much rather it never came to that.

It is true that gang "warfare" can explain many of the reasons that riots happen. The kids say the riot occurred because gang members instinctually like to fight. Other ethnic groups are likely outlets for this need. It could be that a race riot that occurs now and then solidifies the gang's reason for existing.

We have to accept that gangs are part of the underbelly of the world of the urban school. It is something that every adolescent in the community has to come to grips with. It is something that, for Latinos particularly, can be explained by a number of factors, not the least of which is recent immigration. Racial segregation, discrimination, and isolation certainly contribute to gang membership (Carlie 2002). For many Latinos the gang serves as a refuge from the low esteem conferred by the school. Latino gangs have increased commensurate with their increasing population in the society. By 2000 they constituted 46 percent of all gang members in the country and the number is probably growing proportionate to the Latino population in the inner city (Carlie 2002). Rios's survey (2003) of communication problems between African Americans and Latinos is instructive. A cogent point she makes is that very little research has been done in this area since most ethnic studies make the comparison between minority and majority groups rather than between minorities. Hernandez (2007) citing research conducted by both North and Latin American researchers argues that the roots of the hostility and conflict between African Americans and Latinos in the United States are to be found in the African Americans' history in Latin America, where prejudice against dark-skinned people is centuries old. Much contemporary thought concludes that the conflict is economic, which it may be, but the history of interracial hostility may be important to acknowledge in any educational program attempting to alleviate the problem in schools.

Carl's main impressions of the parent meeting where the principal was pressed to reduce concerns about the violence in the school were: (1) The Latinas, mostly mothers holding babies, were generally willing to speak their minds and express their anxiety even when it was apparent they were not completely comfortable speaking in this kind of setting and situation; (2) There was a high level of respect for the principal, many parents acknowledging, based upon the times that their older children had attended Olympia High, that things were much more under control than they had been under former principals (in the ten years before Dr. Williams took over as principal at Olympia High the school had been under the direction of five different principals); (3) None of the Latino parents sat next to African American parents and it didn't appear they were listening to each other when they spoke.

What came through more than anything else in this meeting and in other meetings the principal held with the faculty was that he saw his main responsibility as principal as keeping a lid on the undercurrent of racial tensions in the school and managing discipline problems in general. Pedagogical goals were a distant second to behavior control goals although having a majority of students meet the "standards" was a frequently articulated objective even though everyone knew it was an unrealistic one.

We digress here for a brief summary of some ideas that are used to explain the racial tension that exists between Latino and African American students. At the basic theoretical level the two central notions underlying conflict between different racial or ethic groups are those of identity and realistic group interests. In terms of identity, African Americans are aware that Latinos speak a different language than they do, are being more and more populous in the Southwest in particular, and in general have skin that is less dark than their own.

Skin color not only counts across racial lines but also within them (Allen, Telles, and Hunter 2000). The relationship between skin color and academic and nonschool-related achievement that was found to exist in the African American community has been found to apply to Latinos as well (Gomez 2000). In both Latino and African American societies, lighter-skinned members of each group do better educationally and economically and find themselves more often in the advanced classes.

Both racial groups often occupy the same community and to the degree that gangs form turf on their streets, streets become dividing lines. Gang bangers carry those dividing lines onto the schoolyard and at times territorial collisions cause violent eruptions.

There is, in the minds of many observers of the problems of race relations in schools and communities, a feeling that the notion of a "presumed alliance" between minorities in the same socioeconomic condition is more a myth than a reality (Suarez 2004). Competition and distrust may be more the rule than the exception, in which case wouldn't it advance the case of social justice for minorities for the school to find a place to reinforce the alliance rather than focus entirely on guarding against the conflicts?

So why, we have to ask, don't the schools make a serious attempt to incorporate multicultural programs into the main stream of their curriculum? Researchers would probably make a more considerable contribution in some areas by investigating what isn't done rather than what is. New teachers in urban comprehensive high schools, it seems to us, are seldom given the freedom to affect the curriculum. Paul's peers from the training program distributed in a number of similar urban high schools share the same feelings.

Carl's career as a teacher educator and Paul's emerging cynicism about what his teacher-education program gave him in dealing with the myriad problems of urban school teaching leads us to the conclusion that this process has to be improved. In many cases in the history of student teaching there occurs a tension between what the schools want teachers to learn and what the teacher-educators want for them. In Paul's view a training program for urban schoolteachers needs to explore and practice approaches for dealing with racial tension.

Paul didn't feel that the security guards were particularly holding back during the most recent fight although a number of the Latino students did. He is aware that events of this type are always being filtered through the lens of race. This can't be avoided and shouldn't be taken as a criticism. The urban school with mixed minorities needs to accept this fact before it makes an effort to do something to deal with it. Multicultural perspectives need to be incorporated in the urban high school in some manner. Paul no longer believes, as his teacher-training program indoctrinated him to, that this must necessarily occur through mathematics instruction. Social justice can be achieved through effective education; education remains a viable pathway toward higher education and socioeconomic mobility.

CHAPTER NINE

~

Visions of Failure

By the time March rolls around it's becoming clear to Paul that his free pass on performance expectations has just about run out and he is expected to have learned what it takes to educate students who don't want to learn and don't mind letting him know it. What is not ambiguous is what they are expected to learn. That's in concrete. It's in the "standards."

In my day in the classroom we weren't so concrete about what the students were expected to know. The tests weren't standardized in any general way, although we were expected to give tests to show we had data to support failing students. Obsession with accountability, to be objectified in the form of standardized performance exams, is a relatively new phenomenon in the history of schooling. In the olden days teachers had much more freedom in what they taught and how they tested, but the creeping standardization of the material to be tested has always seemed to me to be a comment on how little we trust teachers. The more objective we've become, the less flexibility the teacher has to teach what he thinks is important. I have had the misfortune of hearing some of my academic colleagues who are fundamentalists in the domain of objectivity support their position on the grounds that teachers are not competent to set goals that will allow for accountability.

From what Paul has been able to observe there are very few teachers in his school who can motivate the low achievers to become high achievers. I would add the qualification "under the circumstances." I never remember a time when low achievers, by the time they'd reached high school, could be converted to high achievers in a mass production enterprise like secondary schooling. My principals and vice principals were pretty much unanimous in holding the view that school was like an assembly line. You move the students along who take an interest in learning and weed out, like defective products, those who don't. An efficient system of locomoting students through the comprehensive urban high school requires this assembly line consciousness. Individual teachers can fight the tendency and make a difference with some students, but it can hardly be thought of as a regularity.

This is the month that Paul will begin to seriously evaluate his own commitment for the first time: Is this the life I want? What are the benefits? Do I have the right stuff? Is it possible to have the impact on students that I want? Should I get out now if it's not right for me? It's a shaky time. It took me almost five years in the classroom to accept the fact that the system was too monolithic, too bureaucratized, too top down, and slowly becoming too objectified for my taste. I was never going to be as "strict" as the principal wanted me to be, nor was I ever going to be able to individualize instruction like I wanted.

Paul is going through a similar self-assessment several years earlier than it took me. I suspect it's because I was married with a couple of kids to support and he's a bachelor. He could walk away tomorrow and be all right. In those years, for me and many of the teachers I knew, it was a risk. Most of them stayed in the classroom and accepted the compromises. Today there are far more risk takers, or maybe in today's world it isn't quite the risk it was, but we know teachers leave the inner-city secondary schools in droves. It's an interesting phenomenon, this difference between then and now. I'm glad Paul knows he has an option well before I knew I did.

We begin Paul's March experience with the principal taking a position on Paul's management style.

March 3: Time to Get Strict

I've had a somewhat formal meeting with the principal, after a string of long visits by him to my classroom (mostly my "hell" class, of course). Every teacher has at least one hell period that they hope to hide from the administration. And of course that's the one he'll choose to visit every time. Several teachers have told me that these are the periods that you don't even endeavor to teach. You simply hope you can control everything sufficiently so everyone makes it out alive. So if I'm to be evaluated on my teaching, why doesn't he come to one of my classes where I can do some?

I was advised that I had to become stricter in the classroom. I don't know if it's in me. I'm not a strict person by nature. My teacher-education program taught me that good discipline comes from engaging lessons and building relationships with my students. I feel like I've got the principal on my left shoulder trying to talk me into behaviorist discipline and the UCLA advisors on my right talking about all the merits of social justice and good human relations.

I don't even like the word "strict." It seems to me "strict" is a word from another era. It's reminiscent of the hickory stick. He's telling me I have to become something I'm basically not, but I suppose I could become something I'm not if I just have to do it superficially. Just pretend that that's how I am. I have no problem being whatever he wants me to be if I don't feel morally compromised. I feel this is one of my values and beliefs vs. the system issues surfacing again. The system does not yield.

Maybe Dr. Williams is right, that given the situation we're faced with, "strict" is essential. Dr. Williams said that he wrote the words "Be Strict" on top of every lesson plan his first two years in the classroom because this didn't come naturally to him either. He also imparted to me that students were running around his classroom and throwing things at him on a daily basis. My classroom-management problems aren't quite that severe.

Being "strict" seems to be one more thing I'd have to incorporate in my role as teacher to which I'd never given a lot of thought. I'm required to be a security officer, an overseer of student ethics, a disciplinarian, and in addition cover the rigorous mathematical material at a furious pace. I may not write "Be Strict" on my lesson plans but I know I'll be keeping it in mind for the present.

March 4: Disturbing Results

I've had a chance to look over the results of the 2002 California Department of Education Academic Performance Index Report which has just come out. Bad news—my school has scored on the bottom rung statewide and next to the bottom of schools with similar demographics. This pathetic ranking causes me to wonder why, given my sense of the faculty as competent, and for the most part run by dedicated, hardworking administrators, the school hasn't done better than it has. I particularly wonder why a school with a large number of first-rate teachers and student teachers from my social justice teacher-education program hasn't been able to make more of a difference. Social justice is not being advanced with scores running at this level. The magnitude of the problem, taking the larger view, seems more than I can grasp. All assumptions of incompetent teachers and administrators dismissed, it doesn't add up. Not this level of performance. The only way of dealing with it in my mind is not to take the larger view and try to account for the school's disappointing performance as a whole, but to focus on one class at a time, and one day at a time.

March 6: I've Hit the Wall

I've concluded I've hit the wall. This means to me, to continue the marathon runner analogy, I've done too much sprinting and not enough pacing. I've been too immersed in dealing with every student's problem, as if I could solve them all, and I've spent too little time worrying about the cost to myself. The bottom line is, I've taken too much too personally. I assume I'm at least partly responsible for all student failures in all my classes. I know better. I know, for example, that when students argue with me in class they are, for the most part, limelighting. They don't want to come after school or even after class to discuss whatever it is that's bothering them. They want to do it right here, with me, with an audience of their classmates looking on. There are just too many power struggles. It is something I can't ignore; it has to be dealt with, but I don't have to take it personally.

The fact is I'm working too hard and barely sleeping. Not only do I have to finish teaching this year, but I have to finish my master's portfolio for UCLA. I'm becoming more and more irritable. The students that I went into this field to work with are now getting on my nerves. Teachers have ten sick days a year. Experienced teachers refer to them as "mental-health days." I think I'll need to use a few more mental-health days. It's something I hadn't counted on doing.

So, today one of my students, Frederick (my overly effeminate hellish student that provided me with the opportunity to fail to address homophobia wisely), gives me a different perspective on my encounters with misbehaving students. He tells me if I don't want my students clowning around then I picked the wrong profession. "Students clown around. That's what students do," he tells me authoritatively, as if I must be pretty dumb not to know this. The truth is I certainly clowned around when I was a high school student.

What I hear, and maybe it's just what I want to believe, is they don't "clown around" because they don't like me; rather, they do it because I let them, I give them room to behave the way they want to in class. The main thing many of them want to do is to "clown around." I take it being strict is to take the "clowning" out of them. Or rather, I'd prefer to say I need to limit the number of opportunities they have to "clown." I'm working hard to minimize the amount of time students can get away with clowning around.

In my middle-class high school classes many students "clowned around," but they always drew the line at what would jeopardize their grade point average. Students would often come to class high as well but they would usually come with their homework in hand. A student coming high to my class today would definitely not bring his homework. Most of our sober students seldom show up with their homework.

This encounter stayed with me for several days. I realized from that one comment that most of the students in my most difficult-to-manage class have never been in a class where the students aren't there to "clown around." I began thinking: what would it be like for these students to be in a classroom of students who were in class to learn, to do well, to "clown around" only as a last resort if the pressure to achieve was overwhelming? What I'm learning here is that students learn their roles from some kind of unspoken consensus about what they're in class to do, and they pick it up from each other and play their role for each other.

Students are unbelievably perceptive and can quickly gage what will be permissible in a particular class despite the rules posted on the wall. I have calculated that students spend about three weeks sizing a teacher up. Many new teachers assume that they have a good class during this period and let their guard down. I have learned that no matter how good they seem during these weeks, it is more than likely an illusion that most teachers at one time or another get drawn into.

I suspect students will do whatever they're given the freedom to do. This is a lot to think about but I need to sort it out if I'm going to break through this wall of behavior problems. Right now I need to spend more time with myself. I spend most of my day grading and see my roommates for two hours a day at the most before I go to sleep. I'm going to burn out if I keep up this pace, yet my buddy George told me that his social life disappeared during his first two years in the classroom. Is this a life I'm ready to accept?

March 6: Apples and Oranges

I'm afraid I depended too much on the metaphor that you can't mix apples and oranges to emphasize the point that you can't combine X's, Y's, or constants with each other. I like to make my lessons tangible and a little bit fun. So, in my attempt to concretize the abstract idea of combining different variables, I made the idea even more abstract and incited a food fight. I brought in a bunch of apples and oranges and put them at the students' tables to make my point. I found out very quickly that you can definitely mix apples and oranges if all you want to do is hit people in the face with them. A projectile's a projectile no matter what color it is or what it tastes like. For the thirty-seven students in my Intro B class, many who were placed there because they failed Algebra I, the apples and oranges are something to throw at each other. As often happens, things that start as fun end up as combative. A fight breaks out between Frederick, who is tall and thin, and a short husky Latino student, Emanual. I'm forced to pull Emanual off Frederick before he eliminates him. I have a student call security and they are taken away. I collect the apples and oranges and resolve to forget about analogies that involve potential weapons and perhaps gear my instruction around things related to disciplinary practice. I need to use analogies that have something to do with the concepts I'm trying to teach. I need to think of ways to represent these mathematical ideas without the use of manipulatives that can be used as weapons.

March 7: A Refreshingly Positive Moment

Twenty-five students have shown up after school to participate in the chess club that I've started with another teacher. All the students are there to have fun and improve their chess game, and they are all happily engaged in their games. Why can't all of my classes be like my chess club?

Of course, it's not a meaningful question under the circumstances. Members of the chess club are there voluntarily. As we say, the class is "creamed." Voluntarism is an interesting concept for schooling. I don't know if anything like it is logistically possible in the urban high school where motivation to succeed in school is far from universal. It's also, I find, an interesting phenomenon that there is to be no money coming from the administration for materials and certainly none for the teachers to spend extra time after school with students. I've had to buy the chess sets and boards myself. I'm just delighted that my expenses have not been laid out in vain.

March 10: Shattering Glass as a Management Strategy

Today my third period class is starting to get away from me. I'm working hard to bring them back from the weekend and I'm annoyed they're not focusing on what I'm trying to teach. We are reviewing for an important test and most of them need to do well to avoid failing the class. So I stop writing on the board and turn to them.

I begin to deliver a lecture that reveals I am angry and they had better listen. Most students are listening attentively. I have been told by George that it doesn't matter what you say during discipline-focused lectures as long as you make the point you are disappointed or angered and are clear about what is disappointing or angering you.

The first thing I notice while I'm delivering my "disappointment" speech is one of my female students, Janine, has her mirror out and is applying eye liner around her eyes. I call out her name brusquely. When she raises her face from the mirror she sees me staring at her and she knows she's caught. She coolly puts the liner back in her purse and hands the mirror out knowing it's as good as confiscated. I have a policy about confiscation and it's one I adhere to rigidly. I walk down to her table and take the mirror from her hand, then walk slowly back to my desk and slam the mirror down harshly. It shatters loudly. The class is stunned. Initially they chuckle, but when they realize what I actually did they are deathly silent. I walk back to my stool at the front of the room and, without missing a beat, continue what I was saying. At some point during my lecture I make a point of telling my students, "I'm willing to trade seven years of bad luck to help you pass this course."

For the rest of the period I have better attention from the class than I've had thus far this semester. At one point a student raises her hand to ask a question. I hear her friend whisper for her to put her hand down. She says, "Mr. Weinberg is calm now: don't go upset him with what you don't understand. He's crazy!" This isn't the effect I was hoping for.

In high school I had a trigonometry teacher who we all thought had schizophrenia. My idea of building a relationship with my students does not involve convincing them I am suffering from mental illness. I need to learn to control my temper. It's difficult with all the stresses of the job.

March 11: White Power

George, basically not a troublemaker, is half Latino, half white. His appearance is very Caucasian. He is the only white-looking student in the class. During the lesson, George sees one of the very few white students in the school passing by outside the open window. In a moment of spontaneous glee he raises his fist in the air and yells out the window, "WHITE POWER!"

I am speechless. I look at him and he has a broad smile on his face. Many of the other students are laughing. I say to him, "George, why don't you look around? That might not be the best thing to yell out."

He smiles and says, "It's cool."

March 17: The Noise isn't a Problem!

Today we're reviewing for a test and I decide to try a reward strategy. I put the students in small study groups and tell them the first group to come up with answers to questions would get candy. The groups seem motivated and their voices are raised and excited as they race and cooperate to get the answers. Not long after, a security officer comes in and tells the class to keep it down. I tell the security officer that it's ok, I don't mind the noise, they're doing group work.

The security officer acts like I've pulled rank and challenged her assessment of the situation. She leaves the room with a loud silence and the next few times I pass by her and say hello she doesn't acknowledge me. I don't think we have a policy here for dealing with different interpretations of what is or isn't a problem.

March 19: I'm from the Ghetto. I Talk Different

Moses is an African American football player who has never played in a game during his two years at Olympia because he has never been eligible due to his poor grades. He blames this on white racism, given that the coach is white. It doesn't matter that more than half the players who do play are African American. My opinion, after knowing Moses for a while, is that he has low grades because he does no work and talks about whatever he wants, whenever he wants, during class. He's in my repeat Intro A class. This implies that if the counselors made proper placements (not an obvious assumption) he has failed Intro A three times in a row, not including the possibility he failed it during summer school.

He says something to me I don't totally hear but I do hear the anger in his voice and the contempt he's expressing toward me, so I tell him he's going to be given a referral. He answers that he's from the ghetto and "We talk different than you and you didn't understand me." He continues to imply I'm being racist and silencing his voice because his voice isn't the way I speak. I'm wondering if it is a good idea for me to have introduced the concept of silencing one's voice and I'm willing, this one time, to accept his version that I didn't understand what he was saying. I don't believe him, but I don't want to belabor the point. I tell him and the class that if anyone thinks I'm misunderstanding them, I would appreciate it if, in the future you would let me know after class.

March 20: An Inadvertent Drug Bust

I'm starting my lesson on combining like terms with use of the distributive property at the dry erase board when I detect somebody aiming a laser pointer at me. I locate the spot in the class where it's coming from and I tell the two boys who are sitting in that location to bring it up and I'll return it after school. One of these students is spending his first day in my class and I'm almost certain it is the other one. Neither would admit to having it. I tell the class I'm calling security and the boys will be searched and if nothing is found, others will be searched. No one admits to having the pointer so I call security. They come in and search the backpacks of the two boys. In the backpack of the boy who is in the class for the first time they find a quarter-pound of marijuana, some pipes, and rolling papers. That is the first and last day he'll spend in my class. Security kindly takes him to the guidance office and the sheriff kindly escorts him to juvenile hall. They don't find the laser pointer, but by this point that seems moot.

After class a male student comes to my desk and tells me the boy with the weed had offered to sell him some earlier and if he had bought it, the other kid wouldn't be in so much trouble. It seems to me he's speaking out of relief and with very little concern for what happened to the other boy. To him it was a simple twist of fate. My students saw this as a typical event on a typical day. I was upset and slightly distracted for the remainder of the day.

March 21: Spring has Sprung—One for Me

Dr. Williams makes another surprise visit to my Algebra II class and luck is on my side. The students are actually paying attention, all of them— almost. The only one who isn't is daydreaming, but I let him be.

After a few minutes of regarding the class as a whole he goes over to one of my weaker students, one of my many Jesuses, I assume on purpose, and asks him what he's doing. Jesus says he's solving a math problem and Dr. Williams asks him how he's doing that. I have one ear out for Jesus's answer while I'm circulating around the room checking students' work. Jesus explains he is "solving systems of linear equations by using inverse matrices." He then went on to explain the process by which he was doing that. I was ecstatic: Jesus understood the material, was articulate in explaining a complex process, and left Dr. Williams scratching his head as he feigned understanding.

Dr. Williams tells him to keep up the good work and leaves, apparently baffled yet satisfied that I'm earning my pay. He leaves with the urgency of someone who feels out of place in an environment where everyone else present has a much deeper understanding of the topic under discussion than he does.

March 26: I'm in the Middle of a "Transient" Fight

Donald is an African American boy whose enthusiasm is only rivaled by his intellect. He is truly a bright student with potential for success. Unfortunately,

Donald is inflicted by a problematic home life, which is reflected by his school behavior. His parents are deceased and he and his slightly older brother are under the custody of his nineteen-year-old sister. His sister is rarely available to discuss Donald's school progress because she works more than forty hours a week and goes to community college. He's in a hard situation, but seems to have the resiliency to overcome it.

Donald loves to skate the line as far as rules are concerned. He is truant more than in school, has failed Algebra I and has been demoted to Intro B. I made a deal with him that if he maintained his A through March, and did not get into any trouble of any kind, I would promote him to Algebra IA, the class for which he was truly qualified. Historically, he gets As on all the tests he takes but is still absent frequently. When he is in class he's a complete nuisance, can't be quiet, or stay in his seat. Today he leaves his seat and comes to my desk without permission. I tell him to get back to his seat. He responds that if he goes back to his seat he'll get into a fight. I tell him to go back to his seat. The month is nearly over and he's too close to being promoted to Algebra IA to let it slip away.

He apparently was serious. He and another boy, Rosario, are swinging at each other as soon as I look up. I try to get between them but I'm getting hit. Claire, from next door, hears the ruckus and comes to help. She grabs Rosario and I hold Donald. A student calls for security and a security guard comes in and takes the two of them to the office where they are forthwith suspended for five days. Probably more serious for Donald was my decision not to recommend him for Algebra IA.

I tell the counselor who is in charge of placement that I won't take both students back into my class since this could potentially lead to future violence. This is what my UCLA advisors told me to say. The counselor tells me that I'll have to take them back, but not to worry about future outbreaks. They're not gang members so their fights are "transient." I've learned a new concept. I've deduced that the attitude of the administration is student fighting is a routine and usually random activity. Just suspend them for a few days and they'll forget about it. They'll even forget with whom they were fighting. "Urban kids get into fights, no long-term meaning. Once over, things will be all right." I suspect she is right but I still find it hard to believe, that today's mortal enemy can be tomorrow's buddy.

I'm trying to arrange a conference with Donald's sister because I suspect from what he says she has a positive effect on him. Once I talk to his sister and him about the fight in my classroom I'm hopeful he'll come around.

This may be the day I decide on my general principle for breaking up fights: stay out of it if both kids are bigger than you are.

March 28: Extra-casual Friday

I go to school today wearing shorts, tennis shoes, and a bright red T-shirt with a picture of Che Guevara on the front. One teacher asks me if I'm going on a "field trip." Another suggests none of my students will know who Che is. I respond, "Perhaps this will encourage them to ask."

My dad feels that it is pretty early in the game for me to be pushing the envelope in establishing myself as a radical pedagogue. Although he admits he never resisted pushing the envelope in his teaching days. Actually, I really don't know how radical I want to be. I don't see how I can be a radical teacher and strict at the same time. I also don't think I can be too radical before I have tenure.

My students it turns out think I look "cool." I'm quite aware that my principal does not think that students should think teachers "cool." I don't know what he bases his belief on. I'm not at all convinced he is right.

Analysis

Paul is beginning to define himself as a classroom teacher with a coherent belief structure and he is finding that these beliefs often conflict with standard practices of the school and, when he reverts to "strictness," of the UCLA teacher educators. He is trying to negotiate between operating in two very differently conceived systems. He suspects there are many worthy goals he can't help students attain while the principal breathes down his neck about more rigorous discipline strategies. The principal, not the UCLA theorists, is responsible for hiring and firing decisions. Paul is toying with the strategy that afflicts many beginning teachers, that when he achieves tenure he can be considerably more lax. But we wonder: once a teacher starts going down that road of compromise, can he ever find his way back?

Olympia High School has performed embarrassingly low on the API (Academic Performance Index). This score is determined by performance of students on three statewide tests. This is an index that compares the performance of the students in all California public schools. There is much talk and fear that the school will be taken over by the California State Department of Education. This would lead to numerous firings that would start at the top. Paul is losing confidence that Dr. Williams is the best kind of principal for this kind of high school, but he is almost certain that changing principals without changing the social and economic conditions of the community would not help bring up scores. Teachers, whom Paul believes are quite good, would have to endure constant intervention until they raised their API score.

Paul, as he expressed, is befuddled since he believes in the teachers; he believes in the values that were instilled in his teacher-education program. This we believe is something teacher educators in schools of education devoted to social justice causes need to deal with. What is being lost in Paul's struggle to survive in the classroom and ultimately prevail is his particular ideals, the ideals he took from his training and hoped to apply to his teaching. The idea of empowering students has lost its power as an idea. Giving students a "voice" in their learning experience is a goal that is being sorely tried by the consequences of his trying to get students on his side by allowing them to freely express their concerns.

The social justice precept embedded in his effort is to avoid silencing voices, in this case the voices of even the most disruptive students in the class. How this notion is meant to apply in the process of managing difficult classes is to Paul still ambiguous. Practically speaking there seems to be a thin line between allowing students a voice in their classroom and opening the gate to chaos. How, pragmatically, does one negotiate a student's desire to sound off, take center stage, show up the teacher, provoke laughter, and still maintain control and encourage respect for his efforts?

Social justice educators, we believe, need to caution their budding teachers who are about to face a classroom of students more interested in entertaining themselves and outgrowing their requirement to attend school, that there is a difference between encouraging students to express their feelings and concerns in a productive way and giving students license to undermine the integrity of the enterprise and in the process humiliate the teacher.

Paul's creation of a chess club for the first time in the history of the school was something that made him proud. In addition to playing chess, the class engaged in discussions of politics, pop culture, and virtually anything that was important to someone in high school. Paul felt it was a reprieve from his hard day's work and the students felt it was one from theirs. There was also no sign of racial/ethnic tension in the confines of the chess club. Students were unified in something they enjoyed.

There must be an important message here, a living, breathing example of what is possible even in a minority-dominated, low-income, comprehensive urban high school. We are both of the opinion that a whole curriculum could grow out of such an occasion where students of different races come voluntarily into a situation that leads to some of the best education that any of them have had in this school.

Just a brief word about George and "White Power." We have to admit we're at a loss to generalize anything sociological about George's declaration. We're quite sure he isn't trying to identify himself as a supporter of the Klan.

Our best guess is he wants to be funny. We might have the same problem as a black student in a school with only a few black students giving the black power yell. Maybe and maybe not. We suppose though there's security in numbers, either very many or very few. Or it could be there's a little extra security in some kids and the desire to make their peers laugh.

The intrusion of the security guard into his class and the apparent contention of authority with the teacher it represents goes to the heart of Paul's dilemma. What is the grounding principle of the classroom, learning or order? And what kind of order? In an environment that keys on indicators of disorder, the individual teacher's opinion is far from supreme. All of the structures of control are systemically in place, and if one teacher chooses to disregard policies intended to keep trouble from erupting, he's going to be overruled or, in many cases, criticized. In this particular case Paul has lost the regard of one of the security guards, which could come back to haunt him in the future. This is especially probable because the principal gathers much of his information about an individual teacher's classroom management from the security guards.

The more general point is Paul is convinced most effective mathematics activities involve student questions, conjectures, and argument. This type of student interaction requires structured "student noise" more than prescribed nonengaging activities. Paul is beginning to accumulate a repertoire of activities that will be similarly structured around student discourse despite what he knows to be the administration's preference. The traditional practice of lecturing, putting problems on the board, and assigning bookwork is not engaging for the students nor is it enjoyable for the teachers.

An important issue unrelated to how the teacher chooses to teach math is how much hostility toward mathematics is an offshoot of the dislike of white teachers by students of color. If this is in fact an issue, how does a teacher communicate to someone who, he suspects, harbors hostility to white teachers, that he's not a racist? On first consideration we would hope this would be communicated in the way the white teacher relates to all students of color, that is, equally and without prejudice. But might a student who has failed and been failed by white teachers over a high school career be hard pressed to interpret punishments handed out by the white teacher as free of prejudice?

Paul suspects this could potentially be one more dynamic a teacher must overcome in order to help students learn. On an individual basis teachers can get through to some students and overcome prejudice on both sides, but to convince an entire class that wants to object to almost everything the teacher says and does can be an imposing task. How much is their resentment of the teacher's race and class? We can't really know for all individual students, but Paul does believe many of the students he works with, particularly those who are achieving, don't seem to care much what color Paul is.

Paul's view now, whether students like him or not, is that he needs to help them learn how to study. This he sees as trumping the need for them to learn specific content in the context of the classroom. There are a number of techniques for achieving this such as giving students take-home tests. This does raise issues of cheating, but it ensures students do attend to the work, for the most part. It is essentially homework by a different name.

Paul's experience with Donald, the boy being cared for by an older sister who has no time to come to school, raises what we both consider to be Paul's most troubling state of affairs: a very smart student who can't stay out of trouble or in school long enough to use his native intelligence. According to both of us, and things haven't changed in fifty years, there have always been many students like Donald in urban schools—too many, a tragic waste of human talent. Many students like Donald, who lack home supervision, find it easy to ditch school. The research seems to indicate that dropping out and failing classes often begins with a pattern of not going to school or class, and students who were prone to skipping did so because they found school boring (Fallis and Opitow 2003). We suspect many middle-class students find school boring as well, but their focus is not on being interested but rather on being successful. We are not suggesting that interesting lessons are sufficient for Paul's students, but they are necessary.

CHAPTER TEN

~

April Flowers and Doubters

There is not much flowering that Paul can see coming from his watering of his students' minds. It is, for him and many of his first-year colleagues, a time of doubt. It is a time of big questions. Is it me? Is it the circumstance of low-income inner-city life? Is it the curriculum mandated by the district? Is it the execution of the program by the administration? Would things be different if teachers had more power, smaller classes, bigger budgets, and a different principal? Would I have been better with a more traditional hard-line teacher-education program? All good questions, none of which Paul has answers for this early in the game.

In thinking back to the first year of my urban teaching, I believe I was far less introspective than Paul. My own training never engaged me in questions of how things should be or might be in the public schools. How they were was a fait accompli and we were not encouraged to question the rules, the stratification system, the policies of the school board, the lack of financial support, the poor salaries, or the way we were assigned to teaching positions. Which were quite random, the inner city first. I suspect, actually strongly believe, that young people entering teaching today are far more liberated in what they feel they have a right to be concerned with and object to than in my day. The idea that if teaching doesn't seem right for me I can change careers was unthinkable in a time of desperate security needs. Being raised in the 1930s, 1940s, and 1950s kept our risk-taking behavior to a minimum. Paul is thinking career. I was thinking job.

As late as April some classes still don't have the proper books. The "not in Kansas" metaphor doesn't apply much any more. Dorothy's arrival in Oz was a matter of a fantasy trip to a fantasyland, not a question of a teacher going from an environment of opportunity to one of deprivation, from quality to inequality.

One thing that impacts all of the teachers at Olympia High, as the year draws to a close and scores are still down, is the fact that they are all working under the strain of being taken over by the state. The idea of students receiving a superior education in an urban public high school was no more intelligible in 1957 than it is in 2007. The idea that a state should be concerned about failing schools was not a working phenomenon in the minds of politicians who didn't care much about education anyhow. Recently, however, it does affect the thinking of both politicians and teachers in today's low-performing schools. The failure to improve student achievement scores, even though teachers are doing their best, will have consequences for how much extra work teachers will have to do, should they fall under the surveillance of "The State." Apparently the limitations of resources and the problems of size and the existence of gangs and racial economic differences will not be taken into account when making achievement comparisons. Most schools with the same demographics and resource limitations are not doing much better.

One thing I can vividly relate to from my own teaching experience is the suspicion that students with poor understanding could easily pass courses by demonstrating disciplined work habits, which led them to advanced classes and a high school diploma. I have no doubt that cooperative students faired better in grades I assigned than their test scores warranted. I didn't want to fail a student who was trying and was cooperative in class. Paul probably figured this out earlier in his teaching career than I did, which caused him to emphasize work habits and got him to stop worrying about why bright kids were doing so poorly. Ultimately these habits should improve achievement scores as well. They should definitely impress teachers.

One area in which there has been significant change for the worst has been in the area of fighting. When it comes to girls going at it hot and heavy I can't be much help since fighting in my day was almost exclusively a guy thing. Additionally, in my day the students fought "fair," keeping their punches above the belt and having nothing to do with guns or knives. Paul assures me that those rules are obsolete. They probably have been for some time.

Having taught in both the Philadelphia and Los Angeles school systems it was of interest to me to see how students reacted to bad weather in both places. Good students did not seem to be affected either place, but on a rainy day in Los Angeles where it hardly ever rains, students in the lowest-level classes stayed home in droves. There were not enough umbrellas in a family to go around. As some of Paul's vignettes indicate, this is still the case. In Philadelphia the weather didn't affect truancy. If a student didn't feel like going to school one day it didn't matter what the weather was. If anything—and this is just a distant memory—absentee rates were higher with the onset of nice weather.

One final comparison for this chapter would be my sense of how the fact of poverty, or living close to the bottom of the economic ladder, has remained a source of humor in the minority community across the decades. There are many ways to think about this interesting phenomenon, but I would prefer to leave it to minority scholars who understand those communities far better than I or Paul ever could. This phenomenon will be revisited again in the analysis section.

April 1: The Bear Roars Like a Lion

I went last night to see our school's production of *The Wizard of Oz*. I thought an April Fools joke was being played on us. There was Dorothy, Toto, the Scarecrow, the Tin Man, and a Bear. Unfortunately, the play production group did not have a lion costume or any money to buy one, but they did have a bear costume so the lion was dressed as a bear. Close enough. The bear still roared like a lion.

I observed that half the audience was made up of women holding babies, many of whom cried during the performance. In my three years in play production at my own high school, I never remember a baby crying or the unavailability of a costume. If my play production group needed anything, the money always seemed to appear and of course those parents who wanted to see the play could afford to hire babysitters.

Nonetheless the students did pretty well. If things ever get easier in my teaching, I'll probably volunteer to work with the play production group.

April 7: Girl Fight

Outside my room I see two girls, one African American and one Latina, starting to swing at each other. I look around for security but there's none around. I now subscribe to the belief it is only advisable to break up a fight if all participants are smaller than you. I figure I can handle a "girl fight" so I chose to become security for a day. Isn't that why I'm paid the "big bucks?"

I've broken up fights between guys before but never girls. I figure, given the immediate circumstance, it's no one or me. Before I know it, I'm in between the two young women holding one and fending off the other who is swinging wildly and catching me on the back now and then. These girls hit hard. The one I'm holding is reaching around me trying to land some punches herself. I take a couple of those too. Suddenly, I'm screaming at the one I'm not holding at the top of my voice to back off. To tell the truth I don't remember my exact words but apparently some of them were words a teacher shouldn't use to students. It's hard to remember exactly what you say when you're in the middle of something like this and you're not totally on top of the proper etiquette for breaking up fights between two or more female students. Eventually security shows up and the two girls are escorted to the office.

Later on in the day the mother of one of the girls, the one I screamed at, arrives at school, about the same time I'm walking near the main building. The daughter comes out from the administration building and confronts me, "Did you call me a fucking bitch?"

I tell her I would never say anything like that to a student, but I may have said something of the sort in the heat of the fight, believing students think you're serious if you're cursing at them. She tells me her mother is very upset that a teacher cursed at her. I asked if her mother was upset about her getting into a fight and she says a loud, sarcastic "NO!" Nor, it appears, is her mother particularly grateful that a teacher had put himself in harm's way to keep her daughter from getting hurt or hurting someone. This is adding up to a lose-lose situation. I'm beginning to suspect that many no-win situations are a teacher's destiny. No one in my teacher-education program ever advised me on how to break up fights. I can't imagine that they didn't know that a fight was a likely occurrence in an urban high school.

April 9: Paul's Observation on Intelligence and Hard Work

I probably think too much. I'm forever trying to make sense of the whole pedagogical enterprise and develop theories about what counts and what doesn't in helping kids succeed in school. This day, caught in normal bumper-to-bumper traffic on the freeway, I have an insight. I dial my dad and tell him about it. I tell him I just had the insight that the key to student success in my school is not ability but hard work. It was right there in front of me all the time.

I tell him about all the students I have who have considerable ability and are flunking my class. I also tell him about all the students who are hard workers, many of whom are not very good in math, but none of them are failing. I know a couple of students who are especially bright and bring novels to class to read and both of them are taking the class for the second time. One of the boys is marginally passing. He never studies or turns in homework but he has aced a couple of tests.

So what's to do? An observation of that depth has to be worth something.

April 10: Why Am I Still So Stressed?

My father asked me today why I'm so stressed. It's been a long time and the pressure seems to be increasing. It's very hard for me to report the details of my teaching day without infusing my descriptions with much of the effect I experienced at the time, and of course that troubles him as it would any parent (I assume everybody knows that for first-year teachers stress comes with the territory). Unfortunately this reality never intruded into our teacher-education curriculum. I don't think the concept of experiencing stress ever came up. I suppose because no one associated with the program had any idea what to do about it.

I think I have a pretty good grasp of what's causing all the stress but I don't know if that will help in reducing it. The problem for me is I'm not clear about how to deal with kids who are quite capable but don't care to achieve, but I keep trying to find ways. The kids I'm talking about have heard lectures from every teacher they've ever had about how they're not using their abilities and how they need a high school education to succeed in life and all the opportunities that will be open to them if they complete high school. I don't think that registers with them because they don't seem to care. So I don't give that lecture anymore and their not caring deprives me of the edge that my authority in the classroom should give me. This means that my discipline problems increase and my rate of achievement successes doesn't improve. Both of these conditions I find stressful.

Another factor that produces stress is that I continue to care and continue to believe that "not caring" students are salvageable. I suspect that teachers who do not experience stress are those that have stopped caring about those students who don't care. Unfortunately, my stress turns to anger toward the students for wasting their abilities and I am angry with myself both for not finding a way to help them achieve and for being angry with them for not achieving.

I know for a fact that almost every teacher in our school engages in a yelling session several times a week. Every time I walk across campus I hear some teacher reading students the riot act. I find myself yelling at students more often than I'd like and it should come as no surprise that yelling produces stress as well, in the yeller as well as the yellees.

April 14: Another School–Student Culture Clash

My general policy is there is no place for grooming in my classroom. This makes me a Neanderthal to my students. I am forever asking them to put away their brushes, mirrors, combs, and makeup. I have no doubt these activities distract immensely from what I consider more worthwhile classroom activities and I have no doubt my students feel just the opposite that schoolwork distracts from looking good. Or at least "cool," which is about the same thing.

My students know I am not part of their culture of cool dress by the clothes I wear and how I wear them. I wear collared shirts practically every day and I try to keep a crease in my pants. Sometimes I segue from asking them not to groom in class to a general lecture on consumerism and exploitation. I try to convince them that I have no problem with conflicting cultures of style but I do have problems with how they, as consumers, are manipulated. We have been having an ongoing conversation on this subject throughout the semester. This is the type of dialectical discourse my teacher-education program believes is important. I don't expect to win but I don't intend to outspend them to gain greater acceptance. I also don't want them grooming in class.

April 16: Rain, No Gain

Yesterday was a rainy day, a very rainy day. My Intro to Algebra classes were depleted. Almost no one from my Algebra II class, however, used the rain as an excuse for not coming to school. Today I ask a student from my Intro class, who was absent yesterday, why he wasn't in school. He tells me he didn't have an umbrella. Another student said she got so soaked she went home to dry off. A third told me he was afraid he'd be hit by lightning.

The attendance differences between my advanced and beginner classes strike me. My interpretation is the advanced students don't want to miss something that might be on the test and the beginners don't care much about that. I'd say that many of the stay-at-homes easily convince themselves they aren't going to get much out of the class even if they do attend. I doubt if they experience much of a dilemma weighing the relative values of attending versus not attending.

I worked hard yesterday in all my classes trying to get students to feel happy that they didn't take the day off. It has to be noted that a hard rain in LA is not only infrequent but when it does happen, many streets get flooded. Also it's true that it is hard to remember an umbrella. I was pretty wet myself when I arrived.

April 21: Bald-faced Lying

Kinsey, whom I haven't had occasion to mention earlier because she is normally cooperative, although normally absent, is giving me a hard time today. I have figured the probability of her attendance to be about 40 percent, or two days out of the week. The probability of her throwing a tantrum is about once a month. I have talked to her mother many times on the telephone and have had a conference with her. This has had little effect on Kinsey's behavior. It actually served to make her hate me more. Her mother believes her anger comes from the fact she dislikes her stepfather. I just exacerbate the problem. Kinsey's mother had strictly forbidden Kinsey from using her bedroom until she changed her behavior. She was forced to sleep on the living room couch while a younger sibling slept in her bed. Her mother did not drive her anywhere except to and from school. I could understand her frustration, but I also have a classroom full of kids to teach.

Today is one of those days when Kinsey is in a rare mood to give the teacher a hard time. For kids who don't cause trouble all the time I think of it as kind of a manic inspiration: ah today I'm going to mess with Mr. Weinberg.

I'm passing out papers and all the while she's chatting with me like I'm one of the kids in her peer group. I tell her to stop and she says she doesn't feel like it. I know this is only going to be the beginning of a behavior problem. I can see she isn't to be reasoned with today so I go back to my desk and start writing out a referral slip to send her to the guidance room. While I'm writing, she's yelling out, "What the fuck is he doin' up there?"

I hand her the referral and she reads it aloud. I tell her to go; she tells me she won't, because what I wrote is a lie. A teacher's only recourse when a student refuses to be sent out of the class is a referral. I tell her she's not to come back to class until I have a parent conference. She tells me she has no parents, that she's an orphan. That's a lie and she knows I know it. I've had a parent conference with her and her mother together. We told teachers lies in my high school too but never those we knew they would know were lies. I'm pretty sure my students who misbehave consistently and deny things they do even if they know I've seen them in the act don't care whether we teachers believe them or not.

The next day I have a conversation with Kinsey's mother. She tells me she will tell Kinsey that if she causes me one more bit of trouble she will come to school and sit in the back of my class. I allow Kinsey back in my class and it seems like nothing's changed. I'll have to get back to her mother.

April 25: Being Poor as Comedy

Here's a thing about being economically disadvantaged that surprised me at first but my father tells me it's as common in the urban school as high fences. It seems that kids from lower- or working-class families turn their economic condition against each other in the form of comedy put-downs. My father still remembers some of the funny things his students said to each other fifty years ago when he taught in an urban school. I'll mention just one to illustrate the phenomena: One boy says to another, "Man, your house is so small, when you put the key into the lock of the front door you break the back window."

There's not much to say about this practice that goes back a lot of years. It's a game that used to be called the "dozens" and some kids can go on with it for hours. If I were teaching English I'd find a way to convert the students' creativity in this area to creative writing, but I can't find anything in algebra to make use of this skill. The kids enjoy it and it doesn't do much harm since it's always, or almost always, taken in jest.

Anyhow my student Janine, the same girl who made the "white boy" comment and mirror culprit, is the class put-down expert and it usually takes the form I've been talking about. She picks a lot on her friend Mathilda whom she describes as pretending to be "punked out" because she can't afford to buy pants that don't have holes in them. Mathilda probably buys them new and tears the holes herself but I can't help laughing at Janine. Who am I to come between friends?

April 29: A Gratifying Turnaround

Juliette is half black and half white, one of the few mixed race students in the class. She's a haughty young lady who is frequently presenting me with a challenge of one sort or other. Today, notebook turn-in day, Juliette tells me she can't turn in her notebook. I ask her why and she tells me because she doesn't keep one; she says she doesn't need to. She tells me she has a great memory and gets As on all her tests because she understands the material. It's true she has gotten As on the last couple of tests so I tell her as long as she keeps getting them I'll let the absent notebook slide.

Juliette fails the next test badly. The following day, without my saying anything, she arrives in class with a new notebook.

Analysis

Very little needs to be said about the sad state of having what some call "extras" in the inner-city school (Augenblick and Anderson 1997). It would be unreasonable to expect costumes or sets for a play in a school that can't afford enough teachers to reduce class size. In parts of Los Angeles, where children of people in the film industry go to school, if the school needed a costume for a play, a father or mother could call wardrobe at Warner Bros. and the costume would arrive that day. Of course the comparison is meaningless for urban communities nationwide. If we consider the privilege of middle-class or private schools, we can make more salient the difference between the resources of these schools and those of urban schools. The same thing said about costumes applies to musical instruments, computers, calculators, art materials, tennis courts, college advisors, AP classes, and even books. The contrast between schools is stark.

It should not be surprising, in an egalitarian culture where females assume the right to equality, that girls on the high school campus assume the same right to fight as boys. And they fight for the same reasons: for respect, to defend against a slur, or because their hormones are raging out of control (Miller, Clayton, Miller, Bilyeu, Hunter, and Kraus 2000; Hemmings 2003). Breaking up a fight on the school grounds is an act no one particularly appreciates. Not the students, not teachers, not the administration. Though it is within a teacher's legal right to try to prevent students from pummeling each other into nonexistence, a teacher is not required to exercise that right.

Once all the dust has settled on these fights it often turns out the kids are pissed off because they weren't able to settle their "business," and the administration requires teachers to fill out lengthy paperwork. When the kids are marched down to the dean's office they come up with stories of how the teacher injured them physically and verbally. Students always seem to believe they have been treated unfairly, despite the fact they either provoked or were involved in a fight. Paul is genuinely distressed by the dilemma posed by the prospect of breaking up a "girl fight." He doesn't want to be involved because he has a lot to lose (e.g., students may claim sexual harassment), but he doesn't want them to injure each other.

Often the intelligence of a student is hard to gauge by their academic success, or failure, in urban schools. Paul has stated that he has numerous students who can easily discuss politics, literature, as well as numerous other topics, intelligently. And many of these students fail his class and most other classes as well. When looking at state standardized test scores for his students he was stupefied to find that some of the students that scored in the highest percentile statewide have failed his school's lowest level math classes. He also noticed many of his students scoring in the lowest percentiles on the standardized tests perform well academically. That is, receive good grades. What does this tell us about the impact of having to take classes on student success in an urban school?

Turning from the indicators of ability in school to the indicators of social success on campus, Paul's position on physical appearance and the use of class time to indulge in it speaks to a broader social concern than how well they do in class on any particular day. He wants students to understand they are victims of an exploitative, consumer society. The issue of the extent to which teachers should be at all involved with adolescent values regarding consumerism and exploitation is too ambiguous to be dealt with here. It is also probably futile.

The issue raised by Paul's interaction with Kinsey, the self-reported "orphan," was the extent and the way a teacher might use parents to modify a student's classroom behavior. In Kinsey's case, as in many cases of this nature, the problem in the classroom is aggravated by problems in the home and vice versa. There is little that any teacher can do about a troubling home condition unless the parents, stepparents, or foster parents choose to use the teacher in a positive way to ameliorate the home situation in the interest of improving the situation in school as well as the home. If only some mechanism was in place that would promote this kind of interaction between parents and teachers.

The expression "playing the dozens," as we've indicated, refers to a kind of game in which one person insults another person, usually by touching on some characteristic of the down and out urban lifestyle. It has, as one anonymous author puts it, "deep roots in the humor, personality, and social relationships of Black America." A representative example from this piece would be "your car is so old they stole the Club and left the car" (Lewis 2003).

Scores that students in the urban high school attain on tests are seldom as telling about their intelligence as the games they play to amuse themselves and each other on the yard or in the classroom. Playing the "dozens" is a perfect example of this. It's too bad their creativity can't be better channeled to their educational advantage. While Paul is correct that the games don't yield easily to mathematics instruction, any arena in which the student can transfer his or her skill in the informal culture of the peer group to the formal culture of the school may spill over in productive ways to general academic performance. In many ways achievement follows from self-worth and it seems like a legitimate strategy to search the adolescent culture for areas where self-worth outside the school can be parlayed into self-worth within the school.

What seems to have worked in the example of Paul's interaction with the sophisticated Juliette was the principle of allowing students to make their own rules in areas where they are successful, and of course hold them accountable if their own systems aren't helpful. Juliette tested a hypothesis about what she needs to do to succeed and failed but responded well to the outcome. This requires teachers to allow for myriad ways students can demonstrate achievement or understanding, but unfortunately in an over-crowded school with too many students breaking the rules and failing, too much individualism is deemed pragmatically unwieldy.

CHAPTER ELEVEN

~

Emersion

Paul is, to use an expression popularized by the media during the war in Iraq, "embedded" in the cultural world of his students. It took the best part of eight months for him to lose the awareness that what he's experiencing now is very different from everything he's experienced about school life in the past. And as his father, I would emphasize in his home life related to schooling as well. As parents, his mother and I couldn't help, by example and by instruction, but emphasize the value of education. By both being educators we couldn't help familiarizing him with the world of our work and the value we placed upon schooling. Most of his friends had parents with similar values regarding education and assumed some role in helping their children achieve. We all helped with homework, made sure our children had resources, oversaw the work of their teachers, edited their papers, attended school-related meetings regularly, pushed books in front of them, and made sure they learned how to work with computers.

Once Paul walked out of the university and into the high school classroom he had only one concept of the relationship between the home life and school life of the student. It's taken him eight months to reframe that relationship. He now knows his burden is far greater than that of his parents, or at least different from theirs. His consciousness has changed and with that change the differences he notes in how students think about school are no longer striking. Their behaviors are no longer surprising, which means they no longer stand out as interesting events in his discoveries about what makes up an urban school and what is expected of a teacher.

The problem of this evolution of his understanding for the progress of the book has been he hasn't been accumulating many anecdotes lately for us both to process. We know it's not because nothing of interest to the social justice theme of the work is occurring. Something relevant to that notion happens every day. Nor is it because Paul has lost his focus; it's more that he has become absorbed in his focus, that it's a rare instance now when something happens he doesn't expect. Or maybe a better way of expressing it is he expects just about anything and isn't hugely surprised any more by events. Encounters do not stand out because of their freshness and their impact upon him as they once did earlier in the year.

Instead of Paul calling me on almost a daily basis to relate an incident he's experienced, I now have to call him and probe him on his workday. And sure enough there is usually material that is very relevant to our mutual interest. The experience is more an "all in a day's work" kind of thing, even when the experience is not a repeat of anything that has happened in the past, or anything that we have reported. There is still the feature of idiosyncrasy about most events even if they no longer surprise him. So for the rest of the school year we've agreed that Paul needs to reaffirm his commitment to pay close attention to experiences that relate to the themes of the book and I need to do what I can to help him do that.

I would like to suggest a few comparisons to the themes of this chapter that seem to me illustrative of our theme that too many important structures of urban high school life haven't changed in half a century.

The most important thing, I believe, is the persistence of ritualistic, mass assembly-line teaching. All students, in general, have to learn the same things in the same way. This is in part a function of classrooms that are too large to accommodate individualized instruction (that concept by the way was alive and well and ignored as much in the fifties as it is today). A second function of assembly-line teaching is it is easier to control a large class when you can spot the student who isn't working at his seat if everybody is supposed to be doing the same thing. Administrators in large comprehensive high schools are focused on the teacher's role in classroom management, or discipline as it was called in my day.

I also wouldn't be surprised if class work assignments, where students ritualistically work on math problems at their seats (page 29, exercises 1–94), problems they don't know how to solve in the first place or feel they have any use for in the second, aren't any different (except in content) from useless exercises given to my English classes in 1959.

We begin with the consideration of a phenomenon that wasn't talked about much in my time, the matter of grade inflation. Grade inflation seems to be related to helping students overcome their disadvantages, which are related to invidious differences in educational resources and opportunities. That consciousness was not very prevalent in the fifties and sixties. We did give passing grades to cooperative students, but that was just because they were quiet and polite, not because they needed a hand up in the struggle for improved life chances.

May 1: Grades—To Inflate or not to Inflate

The issue for me today is when, if ever, do I inflate a grade for a senior who needs to pass to go to a college to which she's already been accepted. This kind of thing comes up often and will continue to come up. I need to arrive at a principle I can live with. Many of my students need to pass my course in order to graduate and I suppose I feel almost as strongly about that as I do about them going to college. At least it's a start on going to college some time in the future. Although I have to qualify that thought based on a number of conversations I've had with some of my students who have older brothers and sisters who did decide to go to the local community college, but most of them dropped out within a year and took a job.

As long as I'm teaching the Algebra II class, since these students are the most likely to be applying to colleges, I'm often going to have a student who, for some reason, is not passing a course he or she needs to go on to higher education. It seems to me there are a number of students who overachieve in the elementary math classes. Their transcripts look good at a certain point, but eventually, particularly in math where the content increases in difficulty, they run into material that hard work and attention exclusively can't get them through—at least not by themselves.

Genia, one of the girls in my Algebra II class, a Filipino student and a sweet, kindly person who spent most of the semester talking to her friends, has been accepted to a local state university. I have had her in class before and she's been hard working, helpful, and cooperative, but this semester she just doesn't understand the concepts—perhaps because she isn't listening often enough. I've given her extra tutoring after school but the tests just throw her and toward the end of the semester she has a failing grade.

She would be the first in her family to go to college and it troubles me greatly that I could be the one to hold her back. I don't know what I'm going to do. My department chair and some of my other colleagues would not hear of passing anyone who doesn't have the grades, but, on the other hand, another teacher I know went back and changed a grade she'd given a student two years earlier to help her get into college. George, who knows the girl and her math performance, told me she would not be successful in a college math class. The question is whether to fail her now or let her fail then. She could take Algebra II again at a community college. Nonetheless, I do need to evolve a principle regarding whether or not and on what basis I would raise a grade to help a student attend college. At least I'm clear enough now on the difference between getting into a college and succeeding once you're in.

A number of students I went to school with who never took much of an interest in school and didn't do well enough to get into a four-year college went on to a community college and turned things around for themselves. I suspect, for middle-class students, once they showed an interest in school the family resources would back them up. I don't know if that would happen very often in this school.

May 2: High Security Alert

A student working in the attendance office following unclear directions from the administration goes room to room with packets of notices about rumors of a major gang fight on campus planned for later in the day. Since I'm given thirty notices and directions to pass them out to all students I follow my orders. Following orders is one of the most impressive qualities in a new teacher, according to the administration. So who am I to stand in the way of this guideline? I personally thought it strange that I was told to give them to all students, since the heading was for faculty and staff.

Shortly afterward I receive a telephone call from Claire, who's been here long enough not to follow orders mindlessly, telling me to collect the notices immediately; they are not meant for the eyes of students. So I collect them, but the damage has been done. A number of the students are freaking out and are asking to use the phone to call parents to come get them. It is obvious there will be no math taught this period. I allow some of the most frightened girls to use the phone. Kinsey proves very useful. She calms the frightened students with her extensive knowledge of gang behavior and procedures, particular the two gangs that she knows to be involved in this potential confrontation. She takes one frightened girl to her desk and gives her a five-minute counseling session. The class is most comforted by the thought that the issuing of this notice would postpone any gang activity that was planned for that day.

Meanwhile the girl from the attendance office comes to take back the collected notices. I have four missing which I have to track down before I give them all back. Kinsey continues to inform us about gang habits. She seems to have a lot of knowledge about neighborhood gangs. She apparently has spent much time in their company. Ironically my biggest behavior problem and my worst student academically shows she possesses many skills that are not normally rewarded by the school. These are probably more valuable in her world. I don't think I can compete.

Fortunately there is no gang activity today. Maybe because of the alert, the gang members know that something is coming down because they are reading it in the notice and know that police would be on campus. The police are on campus and things are quiet. Nonetheless, a lot more parents show up to escort their children home than is normally the case.

May 5: What Does This Have To Do with Math?

It sometimes amazes me that some students don't get the idea that's it's ok for me to be talking about something besides math during the math period, particularly if I punish them for doing the same thing. It indicates to me there's something rigidly ingrained in the students' consciousness about what can be thought about in discrete classes. It's true I've had teachers who have berated students for doing any other schoolwork than that which is taught in their class. I feel there's something wrong segmenting thinking in this way, especially punishing students if their minds drift to other academic subject matter. I feel very strongly that digressions into other fields should be welcomed if the issues are relevant to the students. Of course, I'm not all that clear about just how far I can take the idea of allowing digressions and still keeping up with the time required to "meet the standards."

I'm not talking about the training of students for AP tests. I'm talking about students who won't be graduating to college level mathematics. My thinking at this point in my first year is that fifty-three minutes is too long for these students to just be listening to lectures and then doing scores of virtually identical math problems from the district mandated textbook (which is the administrative expectation), especially in the Intro class where students have neither the skills, an intrinsic interest in the subject, nor the concentration to stick with it for very long. I feel if a subject comes up that relates to students' understanding more school dynamics, or how to make sense of events in the world or in their own lives, it's ok to deal with it. I don't think my principal agrees.

Today a student in my last period class raised the question of why I yell at students more in this class than I did last semester in a first period class. Not an irrelevant question? I think about it and am glad to have this kind of feedback from students who have had me in different time slots. I tell them simply that stress accumulates during the day and during the week, and I ask them to think about their own moods as time goes on. There is some discussion about this and they all seem to understand, at least those who are listening do.

Just when I'm feeling that I've successfully dealt with an important idea (or at least an idea), one student, Moses, yells out, "What's all this got to do with math?"

Moses, a very unmotivated student, doesn't do math three minutes a day much less fifty-three and has turned in only two math assignments all year. I tell him, "OK Moses, we'll get back to math so you can get back to sleep."

The class laughs; so does Moses. I don't think he'll raise much of a complaint again should I decide to talk about something that keeps him awake.

May 8: I Did It All Myself

Richard, a good student in my Algebra II class, who is also a good basketball player and will be going to college on an athletic scholarship, asks me after school about my history as it pertained to who helped me do well in school. Richard drops in after school from time to time when he doesn't have basketball practice and likes to chat about personal matters. I really welcome that. I wish more students would.

So, today he wants to talk about me and who helped me do well in school. Here's a kid who never heard terms like "social" or "cultural capital" but intuitively knows what it refers to, and he knows he doesn't have it and suspects I did. I tell him as honestly as I can about how I was helped greatly by my parents, particularly my mother, until I could sail along on my own.

Richard's father has not been present in his life, he has three younger siblings, and his mother could be of no academic assistance. I ask him how he thought he did so well without any help. He thinks that is a strange question. As far as Richard is concerned he did it by himself because that is all he had, there wasn't another option, and he was damn proud. I also suspect being a top-notch athlete kept him in the gym and off the streets where he could get into trouble.

May 9: Wrong Place, Wrong Gang

Rosario was not in school this week. Rosario is a short Latino who talks tough about himself and his homeys and always hints at his gang membership. The idea of a gang, as I understand it from the kids in my school, is sometimes a very nebulous concept. Gangs are normally a group that fights and tags. Sometimes it refers to a group that engages in certain mischievous activities like tagging and stealing but doesn't fight. Other times gangs are thought of as a group that occupies a particular neighborhood or turf and defends it against "invaders." They are usually identifiable by their clothing, tattoos, etc. Some students suggest to other students as well as to me they are members of a gang but I am never sure exactly what that means, vis-à-vis their capacity for serious violence.

The story I was told by some of my students was Rosario was walking on a street claimed by a rival gang. Rosario was beaten up so badly he had to miss a whole week of school. His face was brutalized by brass knuckles and he was kicked in the face numerous times. Rosario had been dating a girl who lived in that area and he decided to take a chance on that day in order to see her. That was a chance he will long regret taking.

My dad asked me if school isn't something of neutral ground for gangs and I told him anything but. As far as gang activity is concerned, the expression I would use to describe the school is as retaliatory ground. If a kid takes a beating from another gang on Saturday or Sunday you can be pretty sure he will show up on Monday with his posse, many who don't even go to the school. I'm a little worried about the retaliation that Rosario is plotting. It won't be for a while though because he will be out for at least a week.

May 12: In God We Trust, on Sunday

I've discovered today, through a conversation with Kinsey, who is a strong believer in God, that she doesn't see a contradiction between being a religious person and engaging in bad behavior, even very bad behavior. In our school most students are Catholic and believe in God. But they apparently don't all see God as an obstacle to their baser instincts. Kinsey insists she doesn't do bad things that she thinks God would disapprove of, but she knows a lot of students who do on Saturday night and go to church on Sunday. They go to church every Sunday. I've been told that many of their mothers go four and five times a week. Kinsey has been behaving quite well since her mother threatened to sit in the back of the class and I feel I can have an open conversation with her.

Kinsey asks me if I believe in God. This is the first time in my teaching experience that anyone has raised a question about my religious beliefs. I have to admit that this is an eye-opening conversation. While I'm thinking about what to say about my own religious beliefs I can't help thinking about kids who commit serious offenses against people and property and go to church regularly. I want to push Kinsey on the subject of sin and what she thinks counts as one to her and the church but the ball is in my court. I tell her I have strong ties to the Jewish religion but I wouldn't consider myself a true believer in God. She nods and prepares to leave but before she does I ask her, "Do you think torturing teachers is a sin?"

She smiles, "A couple of Hail Mary's and a promise not to repeat it will take care of that."

May 13: Vulgarity in the Classroom

One of my volatile students, Thomas, who hasn't flipped out lately, is a mentally sharp but poor-achieving student. Thomas cursed in class today and I've learned to ignore most cursing when I'm pretty sure the students don't know they're cursing at the moment they're doing it. I'm more willing to let cursing slide if I'm pretty certain the student isn't cursing at me or for that matter another student.

This continues to be a tough area for me. On one hand, I don't like punishing students for things that come out of their mouth spontaneously and without malice toward others or me. On the other hand I do care that they learn to develop the controls they need to give themselves "cultural capital," that is, the qualities that the larger society respects and rewards. In my view they need all the "capital" they can accrue.

On this occasion, however, I decide to bounce off the church conversation I've had with Kinsey and tell the students, looking at Thomas, that I'd like them to think of my classroom as a holy place. "You wouldn't curse in church, would you?"

Thomas's response is, "Hey Mr. Paul, the only thing holy about this classroom is your undershorts."

I laugh and decide enough about religion and enough about vulgarity. I probably won't bring the subject of religion up again, even in jest, but who knows what the students will want to get into? Clearly at this point of my evolution as a teacher I haven't established my boundaries for what topics I will or won't entertain. And I'm far from clear about how to deal with vulgarity in my classroom.

May 15: Déjà Vu All Over Again

Unfortunately, I have a number of students who are repeating my Intro class from the last semester so I have to consider whether it's a good idea to use the same strategies or curriculum with them I used last semester. Since my goal is to interest them I wonder if it might be for most of them like seeing a movie you hated over again. At the same time, I know that a number of them won't remember the activities since they either ditched my class most of the time or didn't pay enough attention to recognize the exercises much less the topics. A few of them think they remember my probability exercises but aren't sure. It is kind of a déjà vu moment for many of them.

Antonio, however, remembers. He tells me he doesn't want the same activities since he had it last semester. I raise the possibility that if he'd paid attention he wouldn't have disliked them and might have passed the course.

Antonio grants that I have a point there. I tell him I'll try to change some of the material or at least some of the activities I had used to teach it. I decide not to change a particular probability exercise I like, but it is soon apparent that the students aren't that interested.

Then it occurs to me that most of my students are shooting craps when I enter the room every day and I also see them throwing dice outside against the building between and during classes, so instead of taking the dice away so I can begin my lesson I decided to use their interest in the odds involved in craps. I give them all dice and tell them I can predict how often they'll be able to throw a seven or eleven and would they like to see if I'm right. Most of them think it is a good idea and indicate an interest. I predict that over the course of a hundred throws they'll throw a seven or an eleven two out of every nine times. They are amazed when every group on the basis of one hundred throws comes close to the two out of nine prediction.

A couple of the students, of course, distrusting teachers, think I've given them loaded dice. Others suspect I'm using a kind of voodoo. A lot of the kids think they can beat the odds by shaking the dice a certain length of time (called "schooling" the dice), talking to the dice, pleading, looking at them in a certain way. I tell them to use their own dice and use any mystical strategy they like. The kids who own their own dice (many of them) throw a hundred rolls and again, it comes pretty close to the two out of nine ratio. Then I show them how I figure it out by looking at sample space, expected value, and the law of large numbers. They quickly see the same principle can be used to predict the frequency of throwing any number. They ask if they can start betting and I tell them not here.

May 16: The Handoff Game—I Usually Lose

My students have it figured out. I admire their skill at handing off something I'm trying to confiscate. They're like magicians. An object they shouldn't be playing with during class will vanish in a heartbeat. They're so fast at it they must know in advance just what route the to-be confiscated object will take. The things I confiscate the most are personal notes, dice, combs and brushes, GameBoys, iPods, laser pointers, etc.—that is, when I can get them before

188 ~ Chapter Eleven

they are handed off and disappear into the void. I just can't afford the time to search everybody.

I've had to learn to swallow my ego and not think of it as them beating me at some game, especially one they're so skilled at. I prefer to think of it as my classroom-management techniques in their early stages. Today I beat one boy at the handoff game, although it wasn't all that difficult to confiscate a guitar.

May 22: Sex and the Single Teacher

As I learned in the dice example, I'm always on the lookout for areas that will allow me to connect with my students, that is, for things that interest both of us. Something comes up today that feels a little more challenging than usual. When I walk into my Intro class, I find a packet of condoms sitting in the middle of my desk. My first thought is, don't be embarrassed, and turn it into an educational experience that meets the content standards. I can't think of a way off the top of my head. My mind goes quickly through the entire algebra textbook searching for some topic where it might work. I think of how I could teach them the condom's volume or surface area using calculus, but decide my Intro class is too mathematically unsophisticated and too apt to go crazy if I spend time fooling with a condom.

Maybe I should have been prepared with a way to handle something like this but it isn't anything we dealt with in my teacher-education program (how would Paulo Freire have handled this). It is obvious the whole class— or at least those in on it—are waiting for my reaction. I'm pretty sure everyone is in on it. My thought is, "Well at least my response should be funny." I read the cover of the package, said, "Oh, small size, I wonder who left this here," and threw it in the trash.

The students roar with laughter. It immediately occurs to me what far-reaching implications my comment might have had, given that I'm a beginning male teacher who is not under any circumstances permitted to relate to his students in a sexual manner. From my perspective my comment is not intending to be sexual with them but who knows how things are defined and communicated within the impersonal bureaucracy. I suspect my reaction will circulate through the halls and who knows where it will end.

May 27: I'm Just Kidding

The incident with the condom reminds me that not all students get my sense of humor. Camila, an average student who seems to like me, is in my first period class. Today she comes to my fourth period class as well, so I tell her although I'm deeply honored that she showed up again and how delighted I would be to have her 106 minutes rather than the normal 53, there are rules that say she can't attend just any class she wants any time she wants. "Besides," I tell her, "I feel bad that we're depriving your fourth period teacher the benefit of your presence."

Camila looks at me with her mouth open like she can't make any sense of what I'm telling her. She leaves the room shaking her head.

May 28: To Snitch or Not To Snitch

Yesterday Moses, the short, pudgy African American student who couldn't stop talking to save his life, reported that someone stole his watch. I tell him I'll call security, which I do and two of the boys Moses assumes are guilty are searched. Neither has the watch but they believe I am the one who singled them out to be searched, so they're angry with me. I didn't single them out and tell them so but you can't spend your day trying to get kids to believe in your innocence.

Shortly afterward I'm called outside the room to talk to a parent (which should not occur during class time because I have a classroom full of students to manage) and while I'm doing that, a book flies out the door toward me. It's a heavy book and if it hit me it could do some damage. But it doesn't, so when I return to the room I ask the class who threw the book. Nobody's talking. I tell them we'll stay in the room during the lunch period until someone confesses or tells me who did it, even if that takes us through lunch.

They don't believe I'll keep them in very long. I'm telling myself that I really don't care enough about the book to waste my own lunchtime. They remind me that it's their code of honor regarding snitching that keeps them from telling me anything. It is my code regarding authority that places me one step ahead of them. I can always win this kind of standoff but do I want to? In this particular case I do.

One boy threatens to walk out and I tell him that will get him suspended. I make my authoritative move and decide to call Dane, a security guard. Dane isn't very much smaller than Shaquille O'Neal and he has a commanding way about him. I also know that Dane is a very religious man and can probably put a spin on snitching under the right circumstances that can turn some heads around. It also seems to me a valuable lesson they can learn.

Dane comes in and as I'd hoped gives a valuable sermon on the merits of snitching. It turns out his brother was killed, the murderer was never found, and that Dane prays for just one person to give him the name of the killer. He then takes the kids out one by one and asks them who threw the book.

After he's interviewed the whole class he told me it was Moses who threw it and escorts him to the office. But before he goes he tells me he found out it was Moses from the first two kids but went through them all so Moses wouldn't know who snitched. Good thinking.

I have a genuine feeling that some of the students had a genuine allegiance to me and are happy that Dane gave them a religious justification for snitching on Moses.

May 28: A Blue Day

Some dismal statistics were circulated about our school today, along with notices regarding certain other matters. The statistics showed that only 188 students out of over 3,000 were on the honor roll, meaning they had maintained a grade point average of better than 3.0. Only 33 percent of our eleventh graders passed the CAHSEE (California High School Exit Exam). Less than 50 percent of the seniors will graduate. Teachers are told they must submit a written form to the counselors office if any senior is certain not to pass a course. If no form is submitted in advance, the student cannot receive an F.

All teachers received instructions at the beginning of the year to post the "Standards" so students will know exactly what is expected of them. However, the standards are written in language not easily understood by most students, even if they bothered to read them, which they won't. It was also suggested that hall passes should not be given unless absolutely necessary and that only official hall passes be given. I hesitate to use official hall passes because of the likelihood that students will steal them. This is a certainty, actually. It is also unnecessary since most students already have an ample supply.

In the notice it was also suggested we encourage all students to keep working each minute of every class until the end of the school year, regardless of how poorly they're doing. I find it very hard to encourage students to keep working when they are failing miserably, not only because there's no chance of them passing but also because my encouragement will fall on deaf ears 100 percent of the time. I could tell them that hard work is good in and of itself but who's going to believe that?

I don't have my heart in following this recommendation, but I do encourage students to work hard to show they can do it even if their grades are not passing. It seldom works and I come away feeling like I'm supposed to represent an ethos, a belief system that characterizes teachers. Notices from the office only serve to reinforce that ethos in case we're inclined in certain circumstances to let down our pose.

May 29:
The End of the Teacher-Education Program

Last night I attended the last class of my teacher-education program. One of the directors of the program, whom I had seen only once during my two years in the program, showed up and gave a survey to the students. One of the questions the survey asked was how long each of us expected to stay in teaching. It also wanted information on how helpful we thought the program was in preparing us for this past year of teaching. I wrote that I didn't think I got more than 30 percent of the knowledge I needed to survive in the classroom. I figured since it was a math-education program percentages would clearly express my sentiment. From previous discussion, I indicated most of the students from the program I've talked to, all in schools like mine, didn't feel there were solutions to the problems they faced on an ongoing daily basis, so the choice to stay in teaching was a matter of how much stress and aggravation they were willing to, or could, take. I was surprised to hear at least half of my group of twenty-four didn't expect to be in an urban classroom more than five years down the road.

May 30:
A Long-Standing Problem Seems Resolved

This is one story that has a happy ending. My spirits are always raised when I see that some teachers go out of their way to help a student who is on the verge of falling through those ugly cracks.

Marlene, an African American student who has been, at times, out of control, has been my biggest headache for much of the semester. She is not consistently a problem; much of the time she is a model student and is quite smart. Then, for no apparent reason I can fathom, she will go off the deep end, walking around the room in the middle of the class screaming and cursing at students in the class as well as me. It is a regular enough occurrence that I suspected some psychological or psychiatric problem is getting in her way. I have to call security; they are the only ones who can deal with her. But I know I can't leave it there. I try on several occasions to talk to her mother but she is never home, and although I have left several messages I never received a return call. There is no father in the home.

I know she is on the basketball team so I go down to the gym to talk with her coach who confirms the problem. She will be normal most of the time and then off she goes, "schizo" is the coach's expression. The coach, who is also African American, tells me she is going to look into it further and see what she can do.

Within two weeks I start to see a significant change. Marlene's "crazy" episodes come less and less frequently and then stop entirely. By the end of May she was a model student. I don't know exactly how the change came about and the coach is not inclined to provide information about a student's private life, but I strongly suspect medication. I'm not opposed to medication at all when it's indicated to deal with psychiatric problems, but I suspect that the problems most of our students are having are social.

Analysis

It's hard to know if Genia, who needs a little grade inflation to go to college, stopped understanding the material because she became too social or she became too social because she quit on the material. Either way, an understanding of the mathematics had moved just beyond her grasp. Unfortunately, the directionality of her collapse becomes moot since the teacher in the urban school has too many students to have the time to unravel causes and effects. Still, she needs to pass to go to college.

Neither of us are absolutist when it comes to most ethical issues. In this case we believe some students deserve a bigger hand up than others. Most teachers, we suspect, have an intuition about what students deserve special consideration. If the consequences of giving a student a slightly higher grade than he or she earned is important, as in the case that Paul described involving Genia, and if the student has shown work habits that deserve to be taken into account, then we most likely would reward the student with a better grade than she earned on the tests.

We suspect the urban high school teacher would be pushed in this domain of ethics more so than teachers in schools where students have a wealth of social and cultural capital to depend on.

To what extent, then, does the urban high school teacher need to take into account the disadvantages of his students? Perhaps the question might be better phrased, to what extent can the teacher avoid taking into account the child's socioeconomic condition? That question takes us into the realm of the teacher's background, which we took into account by having Paul reveal his background in the first chapter.

We can set the bar high but may need to give the hard-working student more help in reaching it than we might for students with more advantages, for example, private tutors, more free time without the need to work after school, and more access to resource materials and parents who help. Is this comparable to affirmative action, conceived as creating a more even playing field? Probably.

As to the option of seeing the junior college as a way out of dealing with the hard choice of grade inflation, a number of years ago a sociologist studying junior colleges arrived at the conclusion that they serve what he called a "cooling out" function. This referred to giving students the illusion of an open education system where they can earn credits toward going to a four-year college. But empirically this doesn't seem to happen. The older brothers and sisters of Paul's students seem to be reinforcing today the findings that Clark exposed forty-seven years ago (1960).

The matter of racial-based violence surfaced this month to the point where students are quite frightened. While it's true that the poor communication between the office and the teachers resulted in exacerbating the anxiety, the main concern we have is with the potential eruption of racial conflict. What can be done other than turning the school into a highly policed environment? As far as Paul knows there hasn't been any activity in the community to bring African American and Latino groups together to see if something might be done to assuage the potential of violence. This is an area where more work needs to be done. We need to understand more about the problems that pit Latino Americans against African Americans. A recent journalistic piece focuses on the perceived "invasion" of Latinos into domains previously occupied by African Americans. This would include neighborhood housing, jobs, and in one case in particular in LA, health care. For many years the Martin Luther King Hospital in LA was perceived by African Americans to be their special province; the hospital was built by them and for them. Currently, most of the hospital's patients are Latino. The population and ecological shifts in the American Southwest have made minorities, for the most part, rivals (Fletcher 1998). Yet this is only a small part of the whole story. What Paul observes is many African American and Latino students relating very well to each other. But when the fights start, the lines are drawn. This is where researchers should be looking.

When there are frequent occurrences of school violence, we have come to attribute it to a tragedy of logistical errors by the guidance and counseling offices. These are likely to occur again and are potentially dangerous to all involved. When grave logistical mistakes in the counseling office place rival gang members in the same class, this grave mistake can have disastrous consequences. Of course how are the counselors to know?

Kinsey, Paul's informant on the dynamics of gang life, has raised the question of the degree and nature of female participation in the gang world. Female gang involvement has been looked at by a number of social researchers.

There seem to be a number of reasons why females would and do become in-volved in gang activity. Chief among these are peer pressure, protection from other gangs, lack of family warmth and nurturing, access to excitement, and money-making activities (Walker-Barnes 2001).

There hasn't been any initiative on the school's part to work within the community on this problem that seriously affects the school and its members, most of whom are not party to the violence. Paul is not clear about why this doesn't happen. To what extent is the school responsible for affecting a co-operation consciousness in the community? Who specifically should be the one to initiate efforts? Dr. Williams assumes responsibility for reducing anx-iety among parents after the fact of violence, but there doesn't seem to be any plans for preventative measures.

Getting away from violence and onto what strikes us as a critical area of concern, we have to ask, what does "do it all yourself" mean in Richard's terms? Is it something we can reproduce, to have students take pride in over-coming obstacles, or is it too much to ask? What it means is that every night you have to decide whether or not to do your homework because nobody is telling you to. It means writing your essays without anybody checking them over. It means getting up early and coming to school regularly even though nobody's going to tell you that you have to get up or go. When Paul was in elementary school he won first prize in a DARE essay contest, but they re-fused to award him the prize because they assumed his parents must have helped him. Perhaps they did do some editing but it was his original work. This was probably true for most of the students who entered the contest. Most middle-class parents read and edit what students write. It's normal. That's the point here. What is normal in the middle-class school is that par-ents take an interest in and often help their children. Paul knows that some parents in his school do help and the results benefit the students. Education is a cooperative effort between teachers and parents. Nobody reads or edits Richard's work. He's a special kid. He deserves to be proud.

Teachers in the urban school have to accept that, for most of the students, they are the one and only educational resource in their lives, the parent sur-rogate, which is why teachers need to schedule class time for interesting proj-ects and not make them home projects. Many parents take that for granted, that during school time teachers are the sole resource. One of Paul's friends, Leslie, called a parent to tell her that her son was misbehaving and the par-ent responded, "That's not my problem. Between 8 o'clock and 3 o'clock he's your responsibility. I have enough trouble with him when he's not in school."

Unfortunately we have to return to the issue of violence against a young-ster. Not because of the violence per se but because of a more serious phenomenon that affects all students. We are talking about fear, fear of violent students in our midst. Rosario's misfortune of being on the wrong street at the wrong time speaks to this issue of students being reminded, afraid of the violence that might loom in the dark hallways, bathrooms, and schoolyard, for students who are unaffiliated with gangs as well as those who join gangs and then have to worry about the threat of rival gangs. What role can a teacher play to make a difference in this area? The only answer for most inner-city comprehensive high schools now, leaving teachers out of the equation, is more police-type surveillance (Weiner 2000). It would seem a community school with parents, teachers, administrators, and community agencies collaborating to ensure safety has the best chance, but this kind of arrangement requires leadership. Teachers have to understand that a student who is worried about who might jump him after school is not going to have a free mind to learn in the classroom.

The problem of violence in schools has been a high, if not the highest, priority of urban high school administrators for well over a decade. Better than 20 percent of students, in one survey of urban high schools in three states, reported witnessing acts of extreme violence in their schools (Children's Defense Fund 1994). Other studies suggest that minorities are overwhelmingly the victims as well as those who are punished the most, both physically and through expulsion (Fallis and Opotow 2003). However, according to one author based on his analysis of a number of studies of school violence, the number of violent acts in American high schools is decreasing. The author does suggest a number of strategies that he believes will reduce the incidents of violence even further, and these, primarily multicultural programs, should be looked at closely (Duhaney 2000).

The two things Paul's students most want to know about him is his religion and whether or not he has a girlfriend. There are a number of areas where open conversation with students is tempting but it is not usually clear which areas are definitely off limits. Socially conscious high school teachers would normally want students to be exposed to a wide range of information about social and political issues. It is pretty clear in Paul's school and probably most other urban high schools the principal, with the sensitivity of parents in mind, determines the parameters of what is acceptable.

The student culture in the urban school is, according to both our experiences, more powerfully influential with the students than in middle-class schools where the norms of the student group are less distinct from those of the teacher group. The fact that many of the poor kids from the school neighborhood around Olympia High identify proudly with the heavy crime areas of LA rather than project themselves into a middle-class lifestyle is an interesting phenomenon. We suspect many figures in African American popular culture (e.g., rap artists) are not posing for their album covers in Bel-Air, where they may own homes, but rather in the "hood." Apparently, as Paul picks it up from many of his students, to look poor and to look criminal is to look cool. Low slung, baggy jeans have their origin in prisons where there are limited sizes offered. Tupac Shakur used the construct of "thug life" as part of his representational style as well as identity to reify how he believed African Americans are perceived by the white dominant culture. This is more than fashion; it is identity.

There has always been a contest of sorts for the heart of the adolescent student between the student and the teacher cultures, even in the all-white, mostly middle-class high school studied by Gordon in the late 1940s (1957). The theme of the socioculture power of the peer group among adolescents was later advanced and developed by Coleman (1961) and it has never been clear how best to negotiate the differences, when the values of the two systems (school and peer group) conflict. Unfortunately, we can't help but conclude that students in urban schools are often forced to sacrifice their educational futures to fit in with their peers. Just one more of the "hows" that accounts for the way social justice is denied the inner-city student.

There seems to be an unspoken acknowledgement among teachers in Paul's school that students who fail a course once are likely to fail it again. It's hard to know if they fail again because teachers have already given up on them, because they've given up on themselves and the school, or there just isn't enough time or energy to conceive a whole new curriculum for students who did poorly the last time they took the course.

It's hard to know what the thinking is among educators about having kids retake courses they failed. Surely some must understand all students don't fail because they are not capable. When it comes to a simple class like Introduction to Algebra it doesn't take much by way of ability. They fail, Paul has concluded, because they don't care if they fail. It's a kind of freedom, isn't it? One would think that rather than replay the failed course over again there should be some effort to design the repeat course in such a way as to motivate student interest through use of theories of how students learn mathematics that have empirical evidence (diSessa 1991). The question yet to be answered is why these courses haven't originally been designed this way?

Certainly the numbers of students who fail courses in the inner-city school are going to be considerably greater than in middle-class or private schools. This should be assumed and remedial classes using appropriate strategies for students who don't get it the first way it was taught need to be reconceptualized. Remedial classes, as we think they are usually offered, are not going to change student attitudes about mathematics. As we noted earlier the evidence suggests that holding students back doesn't work. However, it may not be the students themselves that are the issue.

Perhaps summer school could be used to diagnose weaknesses and provide support but it's not always clear that summer school is used well or wisely. Paul has been told to discourage students who are passing from wanting to go to summer school to take additional classes they will need toward college. Unfortunately in Paul's school, the failure rate in repeat classes during the regular semester is as high as the original failure rate. We need to flag students and their weaknesses and focus on individual learning problems as well as collective teaching problems.

As to the event initiated by Paul's discovery of the condoms on his desk, we have no advice that we're totally comfortable with. True it is no longer a time when teachers are presumed to be as sexless as nuns. But it is still apparent that neither teachers nor students can talk about human sexuality without eliciting nervous giggles and salacious comments from students. In Carl's day in the classroom, he would have pretended the packet of condoms wasn't there. He'd have put a paper over it and gotten rid of it after class. Not only because sexuality was anathema to schooling in general but also because it was thought to be anathema to teachers. One no more thought of teachers as sexual beings than you would think of your parents having sex. But the adolescent culture in Paul's school is heavily infused with sexuality. They seem to be much more mature about it than the students in Paul's high school would have been. The girls are as quick to throw out four-letter epithets and sexual innuendoes as the boys. According to Paul it isn't that unusual for a student to show up pregnant. Paul's ease with the issue is indicative that he's willing to share their interests and their humor, or at least not be offended or afraid of it.

Phil Madison, a big, muscular white PE teacher in the school, is Dr. Williams's primary advisor on discipline matters. Many students think he was a former gang member and give him very little trouble, which is their version of respect. He has headed up the guidance room for the past two years but is about to go back to being a PE teacher. After school, Paul and a few of his colleagues went out for drinks with Phil and he gave them a different view of the snitching pattern at the school. He told the teachers, when he tells students that more students snitch at Olympia than at any other school where he has worked, the students then, relieved they aren't the only one's breaking the code, provide him with the desired information. In actuality he has never worked at any other schools.

Statistics that show minority students in low-income comprehensive high schools failing miserably are repeated year in and year out throughout the nation. Classes where teachers push the students to be working in their seats with no hope of passing or ultimately even graduating seem to be a mockery of schooling. What Paul senses in himself and Carl recognizes as ordinary is just how much of schooling, in schools like Paul's, is a student ritual, a pretense, and an expression used as a key term to characterize the enterprise of schooling, "a shuck" (Weinberg 1973). Teachers often go through the same motions in teaching introductory classes, because they assume no matter what they do the students just don't care. If this is true, then action to encourage them to care about and develop their practice should precede instruction, but what action? District-sponsored professional development sessions are almost entirely focused around mapping the mandated standards to the mandated textbook.

We know for sure that lectures on the consequences of failure or the long-term benefits of success ring hollow in the average urban adolescent's ear. Those who will succeed in school are those who come to school wanting to succeed, prepared to succeed. As for those who have given up before they start, it will take an exceptional teacher to turn them around, to find the hook. We would like to assume every student has one, but for most it is too difficult to locate when time constraints and class size make it impossible to get to know students well enough to connect the dots. The lecture and then assign bookwork model also doesn't help us toward this goal.

Overall, the view of most of Paul's class of first-year teachers was that they were ill-prepared for what they had to deal with, but most were unclear about how much preparation for what they have faced is possible in a teacher-education program. Many felt that some attention, at least, could have been given to this issue, even if the directors of the program didn't have the answers their candidates were looking for.

After the last university class, Paul ruminated on a question that was never asked. Did his instructors really believe that they were preparing the students to solve the problems they would encounter in the urban classroom? Did the math trainers really believe that students who could barely add or subtract after eight years of schooling, and didn't care one bit about school, could be taught algebra? And if they did believe it when was the last time they did hard time in an urban high school math classroom?

CHAPTER TWELVE

~

They Smell Summer

There's an edginess growing in most of Paul's classes, particularly the Intro classes where more than half the students are failing and many aren't even showing up to class anymore. Summer fever is common in most schools in most places but in the urban school, which has been a year-long trudge for most students, the appearance of June signals a time when students who have had nothing but failure experiences in school all year can regain some of their self-esteem on the street.

Summer fever signals to many students who are failing that there is too little time to turn things around. Not that most of them would or could but at least they could think they might. Unfortunately for these students the mathematics has passed them by and it is too difficult for them to start trying to make up lost ground. What I remember best looking over the faces of students who had failed my lower level English classes were the faces of students about to repeat the drudgery of grammar rituals in summer school where the lessons were not only as boring as the past year but conducted in uncomfortable heat.

I have no quarrel with anyone who would suggest that learning grammar does not have to be drudgery, anymore than doing a long series of algebraic computations or long-division problems need to be drudgery, but I will say it's my experience that teachers working in grammar books—like those working with math texts—with lower-level students in urban classrooms, then and now, use the books as a way to keep students busy and quiet. This is, and has been, a consequence of most of the things that are wrong with urban schools:

tracking, overcrowding, stressed teachers, noncaring students, limited resources, and, in too many cases, the absence of parental involvement. My
own experience, like Paul's, is seeing only the parents of students who are doing well on back-to-school night.

A second way the approach of summer works against a tranquil classroom
is many of the students, even those who are passing, have their minds focused
on what they are going to do in the summer or have burnt out early and are
unable to run the last mile of the marathon. Also, for many students who
have had little money available to buy the latest fashions or the latest CDs,
summer is a time they can work and put some cash in their pockets.

At any rate, June is a difficult month for teachers for the reasons expressed
above but also because the teacher needs to look to his own goals, especially
in a school that overemphasizes standards-based instruction. And he must
prepare the students for their finals, and for seniors, the California High
School Exit Exam (CAHSEE).

Some of the experiences Paul talks about in the chapter dealing with closing down for the summer do ring some bells in my memory. The experience
of finding there is a student who needs to be rescued by teacher interventions
is familiar. There was more than one teacher I asked to raise a grade for one
of my homeroom favorites, not only because I liked him or her, but rather because I was convinced the student's personal problems at home really caused
the student to drop by the wayside with respect to his or her studies. In one
case I remember quite well a young man whose eyesight was marginal but
who had never been diagnosed, who was failing or on the border. I made sure
every test he took was readable and sometimes proctored it myself. I never
figured out why after nine or ten years in school no one had taken the trouble to make accommodations and from the one phone call I'd made to the
parents, I concluded they just didn't care. I'm sure there has been some improvement in this area by now.

The fact that the urban school is a place where prospective good students
fall through the cracks created by large-scale educational bureaucracies is no
less a problem today than it was in my day. How could one not conclude
there is something about large comprehensive urban high school systems that
continues to work against the welfare of many if not most urban minority students? If we started with the focus on the nature of these urban monoliths,
we might be able to evolve a teacher-education model that would alert future
teachers to ways of countering the effects of anonymity and running an assembly-line operation.

One important thing I think my experience and Paul's have in common
is that students, except for those who were bitter and angry with everybody,

tended to like us. Even those we had to fail, I had a distinct advantage in my last school that gave me the flexibility to loosen the controls and deal with student personal issues. The advantage I spoke about earlier was that I was the sole English teacher with tenure who had no trouble with those considered unteachable and disruptive. Because of the administration's view of my students, I was pretty much left free to do anything with them I wanted as long as I accepted them in my classes and kept them from tearing the place down. Paul unfortunately does not have that kind of freedom, but enough of his caring comes through that students react to him positively. And as will be seen in this chapter in the case of Angel, he takes unjust treatment of students personally.

June 2: An Angel Crying—Three in a Row

A young biracial Latina–African American girl named Angel in my Algebra II class has failed my last two tests and now it looks like she isn't going to pass the course. When she sees her grade on the test I've returned today she starts to cry. The time has come for everyone to go home, including me. The class leaves when the bell rings and Angel stays in her seat, head down, continuing to cry. I tell her she can take all the time she needs to pull herself together. I then walk around putting my room together after the long day.

Finally she lifts her face, still plastered to her desk by her tears. I go over and ask her what's so wrong. She hands me a piece of paper, an unofficial transcript. She tells me as I'm looking it over that she needs my class to graduate. I make a mental note that it isn't the math class she needs but the units it carries. She could have signed up to be a teacher's aide or enrolled in any other class she was certain to pass.

I talk to her about it not being the end of the world; she can go to summer school or complete the requirement in a community college. I also tell her that there is still some chance to pass the course if she passes the final, but I can bet one hundred to one that won't happen. She just doesn't understand the material. It's one of those cases where students can get through Algebra I with hard work and good work habits, but in the higher-level math classes the material is difficult. Hard work and good work habits won't suffice if the underlying understanding isn't there.

I tell my father about the situation and he tells me it isn't cosmologically wise to fail an Angel. I tell him it's too late for that kind of thinking since I've already failed three Jesuses.

Anyhow, I find myself caught on the horns of something of a dilemma. I'm trying to view this through the lens of social justice. I'm so damn eager for these kids to beat the odds and have a better future than they expect that I become distressed when one of my students like Angel, potentially the first in her family to graduate high school, doesn't make it. So I again raise the question to my father and to myself: when, if ever, do you pass a student who doesn't have the grades? In this case the student has been totally cooperative, turns in her homework, and never causes trouble.

My dad tells me that, as an English teacher, the problem wasn't so difficult since the grades on essays and compositions and book reports he evaluated were more subjective. You can read more good into something than it really contains, but in my subject it's all in the numbers. Although I can give a student a little more partial credit even when answers are wrong but the thinking is in the ballpark. This hasn't happened in Angel's case. The material is way over her head. She even comes after school for tutoring but she is so far behind it doesn't help much. I'll talk to some of my colleagues to see how they resolve similar cases.

June 3: Angel Redeemed

It turns out all of my anguishing over what grade to give Angel was moot. But it is still an issue worth having contemplated since it will come up again, and I'd like to know what side of the issue I'll come down on.

The way the issue turned out to be moot for Angel is a story in itself. Sort of a horror story, the kind of thing that happens, I suspect, in a school where numerous logistical problems fall all over each other. Problems such as overcrowding, language differences, kids ditching, and coming and going and being kicked out, enrolling and leaving mid-semester, can't help but stretch our resources. When there is so much to deal with, some logistical problems are bound to show up and some kids will fall through the cracks because of them. As to who falls through the cracks, well that's more complex. Almost by definition, the ones I care most about, the ones who have the most to lose are the ones who fall through the cracks most frequently. Angel is a typical example.

Because I am troubled by Angel's situation and before I push my ethics to the brink in deciding to pass or fail her, I go to her counselor to be sure Angel is telling me the truth, that she does indeed need the course to graduate. Her counselor looks at her transcript and assures me that it is correct. Angel does need to pass the course to graduate. She asks me if I could see it in my heart to give her a D–. I look over her transcript and take it back to my room to look over carefully. Lo and behold, it turns out the counselor has miscounted her credits; Angel has enough credits to graduate without passing my course. I run back to the counselor, get her to check my calculations (we're doing simple addition), and she comes up with the same number of credits I do. She is happy. She smilingly tells me it's OK if I fail Angel.

There were things I didn't say to Angel's counselor since I'm a first-year teacher and don't want to make enemies—at least not yet. But here are another couple of facts about Angel's transcript. She is taking an advanced math course as an elective when she could have taken a number of other courses she would have had no trouble with. Compounding the error in judgment, she was taking an advanced math course as an elective even though she had a history of doing poorly in math. She had failed geometry just the year before and barely passed it in the summer. If she really did need a course to graduate she was badly mis-counseled into Algebra II. Like so many screwups, when I'm not angry, I attribute it to the unmanageable logistics of making placements in the urban school. When I am angry I can't help attributing it to incompetence. When I'm philosophically angry, I attribute it to an uncaring political society.

June 4: A Gratifying Moment with Angel

The following day, being very pleased with myself, I escort Angel over to the counselor's office so the counselor can tell her officially that she's graduating. The counselor gives me the credit for salvaging Angel's graduation. Angel smiles and tells the counselor, "He's smart. He went to college." I feel like telling Angel it had little to do with going to college. The counselor went to college too but there's too much to manage to get these things all right all the time.

June 4: Incompetence and Social Justice in General

I'm beginning to be weighed down by the possibility that all the experienced teachers who whine about incompetence all around them are at least in part right. Up to now I've given all the administrative staff the benefit of the doubt, but now I've turned my thoughts to how students are treated and I'm asking, how can kids overcome incompetence within the system when it's hard enough for many of them to just get by on their own?

Today I've decided to check up and see all those failure notices I've sent to the attendance office as requested, so students can be informed, have been received and filed properly. I choose a couple names as test cases. Their forms are nowhere to be found. And nobody in the office seems to react as if they had made an egregious error. Shit happens, no one's fault, too much to be on top of.

On the drive home I consider the social justice role I was educated to play and wonder how much I need to do to oversee that kids are treated justly and nobody falls through the cracks in the bureaucracy just because they have no one at home or at school to advocate for them.

June 5: Incompetence and Morale

As the term moves into its last couple of weeks, I've become somewhat pre-occupied by this question of incompetence in my school. I even wonder if some of the problems we all have are due to general incompetence rather than just logistical difficulty. I can't really see the source of this incompetence and am not typically a complainer, but I know that many teachers are talking about it all the time. My own view is that Principal Williams is competent, that he works hard and he cares, but I know many of the more experienced teachers feel that he's too narrow, too tunnel-visioned, too removed from them, and their input doesn't count for much. Maybe their input isn't worth much. One of the senior teachers I've talked to recently, a man who seems a bit more sanguine than most about the troubles we have here at Olympia High, told me something to the effect that the charge of incompetence is usually directed at those who are impeding something you are trying to accomplish. I'm not sure. I know that the kinds of problems we have here are pretty normal in most urban schools. At this point I'd have to conclude either that incompetence is endemic to all large comprehensive urban high schools or that the nature of the urban public school makes the job of even the most competent teachers and administrators more than difficult.

June 10: The Chess Club Doesn't Make the Cut

There are a number of after-school clubs that receive financial support, which means expenses for the activity plus salary for the teachers. All of the athletic teams fall in that category. So do the ethnic pride clubs. The chess club that I started with another teacher and gave my time to gratis this year is not approved for any kind of support for next year. I assume the turndown is occasioned by the fact chess doesn't particularly contribute to supporting ethnic identity like the Filipino club or the Ebony Nation or fall within the community service rubric that leads to outside financial support. The fact that the club itself brings together mixed ethnic groups to engage in nonviolent competition that is academic in nature doesn't seem to be a persuasive enough argument to encourage financial support. I intend to speak to the administration to secure a fuller explanation for their action. (They effectively manage to avoid the conversation.)

June 12: Another Lost Soul

I've been working with Thomas all year, sometimes obtaining positive results and sometimes failing because of his emotional instability. Thomas has conflicting commitments and has shown little interest in resolving them. On the one hand, he's smart enough to do well in school; on the other hand he seems to be driven to overcome the advantage of his intelligence. To complicate matters he seems committed to playing on the football team knowing he has to be in good academic standing to be allowed to do that. And as part of that commitment Thomas has given up coming to class high because he wants to get in shape for spring practice.

Unfortunately, when Thomas is not high, he is much more of a "pain in the ass." Yesterday, I kicked him out of class for gay bashing. He had become very violent toward an openly homosexual student in my class. Thomas is very aware of the standard I hold my students to regarding the acceptance of diversity in race, ethnicity, and sexual orientation.

Today Thomas and I have to endure another confrontation. He's sitting in class wearing his earphones. I tell him that he has a choice; he can give them to me and pick them up after class or he can take a referral slip and go to the guidance room. He knows if he is given one more referral to the guidance room he will be placed on the list for potential expulsion or a transfer to the continuation school. Students often are reluctant to give things up because they don't trust that they'll be given back. It's seemingly a matter of urban paranoia. It's true that some teachers take all confiscated items to the administration where they disappear into the mysterious processes of the upper bureaucracy.

Thomas tells me that I have a choice as well, I can forget about the Walkman, which he claims was turned off and not bothering anyone in the first place, or I can try to take it from him and he'll "kick my ass!" I don't think either option is particularly appealing.

I try to calm the situation by telling him that once he hands over the Walkman he'll have made himself ready for today's lesson, ready to learn. I hesitate to punish him for his threat for two reasons: (1) Thomas's threats are not to be taken seriously and (2) the administration is on the verge of booting him out. This I don't want. I have seen him perform well and know he can be a successful student, and I am trying to keep him from throwing away his academic possibilities in order to preserve his macho image.

I don't understand the dynamic of Thomas's refusal to hand over the Walkman when we both know he is teetering on the verge of being thrown out of school. Thomas demands to know why I care if he's ready to learn. I tell him I want him to pass the class and also retain his eligibility for football.

He then chooses to close the door on my support by telling me he doesn't want me to care about him. He's telling me to stay out of his life. It's really hard to "save" a student when it's clear he'd rather be booted out of school than "saved" by a teacher.

He then hands over his Walkman.

June 13: Rosario's Burden

It seems to me that many of my students, like Thomas, are victims of life conditions that are incompatible with school success. Rosario's unfortunate life condition is he feels he needs to fight all the time and he's too small and skinny to ever win. And since he's living in a male macho culture, he doesn't know he has the choice to strategically retreat. A couple weeks ago Rosario was badly mauled in a fight and was out of school for over a week. When he comes back he tells me he was fighting to uphold my honor, that some students were calling me a "lame" teacher and he came to my defense. Pure bull, of course, but it keeps me smiling all day. I continue telling Rosario that I'd like to see him learn that's it's ok to back away from a fight, but it's clear I'm dealing with a socialized condition that has taken too many years to develop to think I can undo it (or even know how to undo it) in the limited time I have to spend with him. I tell him he doesn't have to defend my honor any more; I can look after it myself.

It's not that Rosario fell behind by being injured and incapacitated. He was already hopelessly behind, but it seems to me there should be better accommodations made for students who can't make it to school than failing grades on all assignments. This, it seems to me, is too punitive a system.

June 13: Friday the 13th—Donald Freaks Out

Donald, a Puerto Rican boy, is normally respectful and well behaved on the surface but mischievous behind my back. Probably behind everybody's back. Donald is homophobic, and a few days ago he was cussing out an apparently gay student named Steven. At least if Steven isn't gay, he's quite adept at playing the role of someone who is flamboyantly, stereotypically gay. So I sent Donald to the guidance room and once again said something about respect for persons. A few days later, Donald is up at my desk tagging. When I call him on it he tells me someone had tagged on my desk and he was trying to erase it. I write him a referral and Donald snaps, trying to grab the referral from me. I send him outside and on his way out he asks Steven to come outside with him so they can fight it out. Steven stands up but I order him to sit down.

A few minutes later I hear my next-door neighbor Claire yelling at someone telling him, "You don't speak to a teacher like that!"

I quickly run out and discover Claire reprimanding Donald. Apparently Donald was outside alone swearing at the top of his lungs and Claire, who was giving a final exam, came out to check on what was going on and he continued swearing at her.

I ask Claire what's going on and Claire says something about his swearing. Donald interrupts her by saying, "I wasn't talking to you, bitch!"

Claire replied, "Well, now you are!"

I asked Donald forcefully to apologize to Claire but he refuses saying, "This is bullshit!"

Donald reached for the referral and we both tugged at it. He bumped into me hard. Then he gave up and started walking away. We asked a nearby security officer to take him to the guidance office. On the way he started walking away from the security officer who went to grab him, and he pushed the security officer away and swore at him. The officer then grabbed him hard and dragged him to the office where he started screaming at everybody; he was so out of control the sheriff's office was contacted and he was taken to juvenile hall. All this started from a little pencil tagging on my desk.

We all, including Steven and Claire, wrote reports about Donald's abusive behavior and I expect that's the last we'll see of him this year.

What I think is interesting is how so many similar events begin small and because of something in the chemistry or psychology of the student, the event spirals out of control. The student loses self-control, suddenly manifesting a hatred for all forms of authority. Just a few days before, another student found out he had failed the English proficiency exam preventing him from graduating, and he went crazy and started swearing and throwing chairs and four security guards had to hold him down. Eventually he settled down and the next day he came in and quietly took the exam again and passed it.

June 16: Some of Them Like Me

As the summer break approaches and I'm closing down my classes some students are telling me how much they like my class. This is baffling because I feel this has been a year where I haven't done a single thing right. I sense a kind of liberating feeling coming over me as I'm willing to believe I've positively affected some students in a small way.

I have to credit the end of the year with my being told that I'm liked because they've had me all year and never let me know it before. One student tells me I am the most caring teacher he has ever had. This remark is a welcome counterpoint to Thomas's comment that he doesn't want or need me to care about him. Apparently this student does and that's an important realization, that some can let themselves want to be cared about. Another of my more playful students tells me he likes me so much mine was the only class he didn't steal something from. Well, for this kid, that is quite a compliment.

June 16: The Felons in the Classroom

Today I notice that one of the students in my classroom is wearing an ankle bracelet, the kind that keeps track of juvenile offenders when they're on house arrest. He is a student who didn't do much work and didn't come to class very often so I hadn't noticed this before. Maybe this is the first time he's wearing it. This starts me reflecting about my school's policy of keeping the details of criminal behavior among the students private. Teachers are not privy to the type of crimes of students who are on probation, had been involved in, or even which students are on probation

The rationale for this is to protect student privacy. While I see and agree with the reasoning here, I'm wondering if this policy is justified in terms of the educational welfare of the student. Given my philosophy of openness and my desire that the gap between administrator knowledge and teacher knowledge should not be so wide, I'm not sure of my position here. Might we be better able to accommodate student needs if we were privy to this information?

There's something to the belief that the more we know about students, the better we can work with them. We might be able to get these students to talk about the trouble they've gotten into in a way that could point them in a better direction. Probation officers sometimes assume this role, but they too are overburdened by the same problems that confront the schools. And there is little structure in place for these officers to interact with teachers. Probation officers as a rule are not trained to navigate the educational system.

June 17: A Bad Taste in the Pedagogical Mouth

I was hoping to leave for the summer with more positive memories of the last days of the year than I was treated to. Unfortunately, four of my seniors in my best class (Algebra II) cheated on their final exam. What's more they cheated so damn poorly I couldn't pretend I didn't notice. Three of them had precisely the same answers as the fourth, who was the best student, and they also had all the wrong answers he did.

The seniors had to be tested a week before the rest of the class so they could participate in graduation activities. Because I was reviewing with the rest of the class for the final, the seniors had to be sent next door to another teacher's room with the exams and answer sheets. They returned the exams at the end of the period and that was the last I thought about the conditions under which they took the exam until I did the scoring.

The first student I interrogate (being careful not to accuse him of cheating since I'd been told by Anthony, my department chair, that could get messy) starts out lying about where he'd taken the test. I had already checked with the teacher I'd sent them to and the teacher he'd sent them to and knew they'd never arrived. Eventually, with a second student joining the questioning, they confess that they'd taken it under a tree in the yard without supervision.

I offer all of them a chance to retake the exam after school. Two of them say they'll take it but never show. They accept a failing grade. The other two retake it and both do considerably worse. They both fail. It is very disappointing. I can't say if the students are as disappointed as I am, but I'm guessing they aren't. The value for them in passing the course would be they would have qualified for higher education by completing Algebra II, which is a requirement for a University of California school or a state college. I know Dianne, who only needed four more percentage points to get into the state college she was accepted to, is horribly disappointed. I most likely would have given her the C− she needs had she not cheated. Because of the cheating she ends with an F in the class. I wish her the best and hope she can navigate the community college system well enough to move on to the state college or to one of the University of California campuses.

I'm left wondering why so many of our students cheat so poorly, so obviously, and why they don't try to stay below the radar. This is something that has been noted by every teacher with whom I have spoken. I have a hunch it has something to do with the fact that they don't think teachers care that much about them, that teachers give up on them, that they won't even take the time to check. When the clock hits 2:38, they're gone and they don't look back. I want to let them know I'm not in that company and that I do care. I will be giving a B to my very best student, Abraham, because he let students copy from him during the final. Of course, I have to consider the unlikely possibility that he did some copying too. At any rate I want to make a point of this by lowering his grade and if he comes to talk about why, I will tell him that cheating has consequences and let him take a retest of the final to earn back his A.

June 18: An Innocent Encounter

Benji, a tall African American student who is an average achiever and a better-than-average basketball player, is from the Deep South and has a southern accent as thick as honey. He's only been here a few weeks so I don't know him very well. He's a good-natured kid and I understand he will make a valuable member of the team. Today he wasn't in my Introduction to Algebra class. So, after school I'm standing in the parking lot talking to Leslie when to my surprise Benji appears and pleasantly asks me how I'm doing. I am of course surprised that a student who ditched my class wouldn't try to avoid running into me after school. I may be getting a reputation as someone who wouldn't be quick to blow the whistle.

I tell him I'm doing fine but would have been doing better if he'd shown up to class. I tell him I spent the whole period with my head on the desk crying, mourning his absence.

Benji puts on a huge smile and says with his rural southern accent, "Y'all is funnin' me. You didn't do no such thing. You was doin' graphin' the whole time."

I look at Leslie and she looks at me. We both have an astonished expression on our faces. We couldn't believe a student who wasn't an Algebra II student would ask somebody what went on in class when he wasn't there.

June 19: A Good Day for "Whitey"

Most classes have already taken their finals. After the exams I give a variety of fun gifts to kids who had done well in a variety of categories including the student with the best sense of humor. One girl in my Algebra II class, Holly, is half Vietnamese and half Mexican and looks as white as I do. She always gets teased for being white, like being called "white girl," but it seems like all the teasing is in fun. While giving out a present to Holly, who is the most improved student in the class, I said, "I want to give this gift to the only white student in the class," and went on to list her accomplishments. Everyone of course knows who I am talking about since she's the only one in the class who looks white. The remark is taken by everyone, including Holly, in the fun spirit in which it was intended. It is a happy ending to a very mixed year.

Analysis

In the miasma that is the overcrowded high school with low budgets and generally low expectations for student success, we have to wonder just how many others fall into Angel's leaky boat and how much time it would take one conscientious teacher to check the correctness of all his students' transcripts. What all is involved for a teacher then, as he goes about looking out for the welfare of students, besides doing the best teaching he can? Doesn't this kind of oversight expand the notion of teaching for the urban schoolteacher? It may not seem to matter in the logistics department in a school where half the students drop out or fail to graduate, but it could matter a great deal to the individual students who are deprived a graduation experience because no one's around to be sure that all receive the credits they've earned.

To be fair to the counselor in Angel's oversight, we can speculate that perhaps she was acting in Angel's general interest to have her take Algebra II, since the state colleges and the University of California require it. Paul doubts this, however, since Angel's career goal was to become a cosmetologist.

Experience with the system is beginning to show Paul how watchful human intervention in the urban school is crucial if all kids, particularly those most likely to fall through the cracks, are to receive the best possible treatment from the institution. The system that is in place to oversee student progress on an individual basis in urban high schools is taxed to the max. Something more is needed. Why, Paul wonders, hasn't this absence of oversight of individual students been dealt with as a high priority long before he arrived here? Priorities are, of course, tied to budget. Every teacher knows that. If something that needs to be done isn't being done, there is someone whom the school can't afford to pay not doing it.

The issue of teacher morale is a subject that has been looked at in a number of ways. We can raise the question here as to whether or not incompetence breeds low morale or the conditions that produce low morale also lead to incompetence. Probably some combination of both would be the explanation.

Two issues seem worthy of consideration here. As we look at the issue of teacher morale we can agree easily that incompetence of administrators and colleagues plays a part. Probably we can surmise from the data on where the quality teachers go and stay, that the urban school has the least qualified teachers (Darling-Hammond, Chung, Frelow 2002).

A second issue is that teacher morale degenerates over time if nothing is done to stop the bleeding. What adaptations do teachers who feel their morale sinking need to make to stop the downward spiral? We suspect that answers will be found in several areas: relations with administrators, personal rewards or gratifications, availability of parental support, and most of all, the degree to which teachers who work hard and really try will feel the students are responsive.

From both of our experiences we suspect that most urban schoolteachers lay out money for students from their own pockets. How much we can't know and we don't think a survey will reveal any dependable facts on the subject. Paul has spent about five hundred dollars on classroom materials and chess sets as well as volunteered his time. The sets are already available so he expects he'll be volunteering his time to run the chess club again next year since the school refused to support the activity financially.

Some clarity about the notion of choice has to be infused into the curriculum if a teacher wishes to integrate choice into the classroom. This seems to be much too humanistic an idea for the kind of school we are dealing with here, but nonetheless the idea of choice does not need to be totally abandoned by teachers with a humanistic bent. We are primarily talking about students having a choice about the kind of assignments they have to turn in and the basis for being evaluated. There also can be some choice in the area of classroom management. Paul does offer Thomas a choice in the matter of turning over the Walkman rather than be expelled from the class, but Thomas does not see this as a reasonable choice, nor does he see the act of being cared about as a choice he might want to consider.

There are many students at Olympia High who have to stay home to take care of younger brothers and sisters, and often parents or grandparents who are sick or injured. Unfortunately Paul doesn't have a clear sense of how to help students at home to catch up or keep up. What this really means is the society and the legislatures that support education are not willing to support what they consider to be not the business of the school. It may not be the business of the school but any teacher in Paul's kind of school knows that what happens in the home seriously affects what students can accomplish in the school.

By now it's quite clear to Paul that the reason for many fights is that very little things, things they forget about before the fight is over, set the fighters off. One fight between two girls that he broke up recently started because one of the girls thought the other had referred to her as a "bitch." After a battle between these two, where Paul got pushed around and security was called in, the fighting girls were dragged to the guidance office and the conflict was quickly resolved when, during mediation, it turned out she hadn't called her a bitch at all. They walked away friends.

So why do urban students tend to engage in so many fights that they can never justify on any grounds that they can remember once the fight is terminated with the consequence of suspension or expulsion? One obvious answer is that many of the kids in Paul's school, at least those in the Intro classes, feel like they don't have anything to lose or to gain.

The students in Paul's advanced class almost never get into fights or lose control of their emotions during their classes. By the time many of the students in the Intro classes get to be juniors they are so far behind they have no hope of graduating. They know it and they know the teachers know it. So what's to be done with this population? Apparently we need to provide them with something to gain.

There is something positive to be said about the need for privacy for students who have been convicted of crimes. Teachers who have this knowledge in advance could use it in ways that would be detrimental to the student. On the other hand, in a top-down authority system the people who do know are the least likely to be helpful. Students with records in the files of the principal are automatically on probation. They receive no counseling or indications that anyone cares about them. They are invisible as far as care goes, but they are watched carefully, suspiciously. This is an interesting paradox.

So, why was calling Holly "white" funny? We can't say exactly, but the fact the students didn't consider it a racially offensive comment made laughter possible. Paul was playing with the popular student conception that anything white or "whitewashed" did not belong in their "ghetto school." It seems that anything "whitewashed," displaying any aspect of whiteness, is in a general way objectionable. This is ostensibly rooted deep in the historical and contemporary relationships between lower-class black and Latino culture and middle- and upper-class white culture. It seems like it will be difficult for many of Paul's students to acquire much of the cultural capital required to be successful when they so readily shun the construct of "whiteness." Paul understands this relationship and chose to play with it. In a surreptitious pedagogical act, he tried to improve students' willingness to bring this dynamic to the surface while simultaneously having a good laugh.

The issue of the effect of skin color on a number of success variables has been widely researched (Frazier 1962; Drake and Cayton 1962; Bullough 1969; Edwards 1959) and it is no surprise to anyone who understands the invidious effects of white racism in literature and the entertainment media that everything favors the lighter-skinned minority. Significant differences in this direction have been found to be operating in such areas as judgments about intelligence (Lynn 2002), income and education (Allen, Telles, and Hunter 2000), and other experiences of discrimination.

This facet of varying degrees of skin darkness or lightness is, unfortunately, one dynamic that stays below the radar of the sociopolitical life of schools. Paul has reported on a number of brief encounters where some light-skinned African American students have taken ribbing from other darker-skinned African Americans. This is a tough issue for a white teacher to have to deal with, but it is something that does affect many actions and sometimes leads to fights. And even if fights had broken out based on this factor, what is any teacher to do besides deal with the symptoms and punish the fighting? There was one instance where Paul was asked to explain to the class the difference between an albino and someone with light skin. This didn't seem particularly touchy, though some students jokingly said they'd prefer being an albino because at least their whiteness would be a disease.

CHAPTER THIRTEEN

~

Conclusion

It seems appropriate at this juncture to reemphasize the fact we are not intending this work as a critique of Paul's teacher-education program, or teacher education in general. If that were the case we would have spent considerably more time on that kind of critique and suggested ways of improving the process. Paul was only one person experiencing his program and he experienced only the part of the program that was devoted to math teaching. At the same time it should be kept in mind that there are almost as many teacher-education programs in the country as there are universities and we are only dealing with one that orients its students to issues of social justice and the world of the inner-city school.

There are, we presume, many approaches to teacher education and a number of books and articles address the issue (Wideen and Grimett 1995; Gephart and Ayers 1988; McIntyre and Byrd 2000). The most provocative article we looked at (Weiner 2000) emphasizes the increasing complexity of issues that need to be addressed in the organizing of a teacher-education program for urban schools. The most confounding of these issues are the dynamics associated with school reform and the varying degrees to which schools and school districts are undergoing one kind of reform or another. Such issues as tracking students, or de-tracking them, increasing or decreasing segregation in schools and classrooms, increasing numbers of students with no or little knowledge of English, economic conditions that spur or retard financial support for schools, allocating resources to safety needs, advancing technology and access to it, and accommodating the curriculum to standardizations, all need to be addressed. What is to be the priority of a teacher-education program for urban schools? Weiner concludes that, despite extensive research in the last decade on urban schools, the results of this research were seldom applied to the way teachers for urban schools are prepared.

We are not focused on critique specifically but we do hope that highlighting encounters that first-year inner-city high school teachers with social justice goals deal with will suggest topics that teacher-education programs might consider treating. By indicating a legion of problem areas that first-year teachers, and we believe others, encounter on a regular basis and the way they feel about them, we hope to have contributed concrete, particular material for discussion and problem solving.

Now we want to turn to the summing-up portion of the book and we'll present it as a twofold commentary, the first from Paul in which he will describe what he thinks he learned from his experience, particularly the last part of the year when the repetition of events and student patterns led him to draw certain conclusions about what an urban teacher needs to understand.

The second, less extensive part of the conclusion will be from Carl who will try to filter Paul's experience through the lens of his own experience as a former inner-city secondary school teacher, a teacher educator, and an educational researcher.

Paul's Conclusion

I've become aware there are some students who, no matter how serious they are as classroom problems or how poor their achievement, I like working with. My favorite students are frequently the ones who don't give a damn about doing well in my class. Why would I feel that way? In general because if I can't work with the kids who need me the most, I don't think I can work in this business. I might as well find out sooner than later, while I still have time to change horses.

The fact is I am interested in kids with problems. Maybe it's because I think I can help them by talking with them, not necessarily about math and their difficulties with it. I think these students have interesting lives and I can help them succeed by gaining insight into them, if they will let me in.

This liking leads me to support these "problem" students and even overlook some of the negative things they do and push the positive things, academically as well as socially. A number of students deserved my extra effort, and I believe several benefited from it. I'm a little uneasy about playing favorites but at least I know I'm doing so for good rather than superficial reasons. I have an affinity for helping students who have ability and try to find ways of making it work for them despite their difficult personal situations.

Students who undeniably receive my extra effort are those who are getting by in school even if they have no resources in the home to help them along the way. The majority of the students in my classes have few resources outside the classroom. Richard, who did it all himself, is a prime example here, but I'm pretty sure he's an exception. Richard gave me the sense that he thrived from not needing support from persons or systems but I think he is a rare case. I hope he is not as rare as I think. It is exciting to watch Richard, and students like him, forge the path toward being the first members of their family to go to college.

In addition to enjoying working with bright students with difficult life circumstances, teaching here has brought me to an understanding of the nuances of gang life and its inevitable turn to violence. I hear conversations in class that inform me of the inner workings of gangs. I'm pretty sure my students tell me these things to try to shock me, or to reverse roles on me, where they become the pedagogues. What nine months of teaching here has taught me is that gangs operate like highly organized platoons of soldiers.

Rosario was beaten bloody because he was behind enemy lines. I've met his mother on several occasions and could feel her anguish over how badly he was hurt. When he came back to school his face was stitches and scars.

A similar beating was given to one of my several Jesuses. He was beaten around the head and neck with a baseball bat until he was unconscious, in a neighborhood where he "wasn't permitted." What overwhelms me more than anything is that my students are capable of such violence.

I've learned that the administration keeps a list of school violations on a large number of students who they think could cause trouble and when the student becomes central in a retaliation probability, his or her record can be used to justify a transfer to the continuation school. Let them beat him up over there. They're more used to dealing with it. This was true in the case of Jesus. After being beaten with a baseball bat over the weekend, Jesus was transferred out on Monday to avoid retaliation at our school.

One of my top Algebra II students, Gabriel, a tough-looking Latino boy, spends his nights tagging. He makes sure he's at school the next day alert and ready to learn. His attendance is good. The only day he missed my class he was in the criminal-courts building being arraigned for destruction of public property. I'm learning to expect apparent contradictions.

Another thing I learned in the latter part of the semester, because of my experience with Rosario and a number of other students who seem to be victims of the gang mentality, is that the administration has developed a much more sophisticated system of dealing with potential disruptions than I had imagined. Our administration seems to be totally on top of retaliation possibilities and, if at all possible, the student who can be expected to be involved in an act of retaliation (on either side) will be transferred out. Those students like Rosario, who are being suspended on a regular basis, are not in school able to learn.

On the issue of having "nothing left to lose," from my perspective it looks as if those enrolled in Introduction to Algebra are seen as students who need to be kept busy until they drop out or are arrested and sent to juvenile hall. This doesn't particularly threaten most of them; many of their homeys are already there and it can be a kind of a reunion. They brag about the various juvenile halls in which they have spent time. I knew during all of my adolescence—and even now—if I ever got arrested, it would ruin all my future plans. Many of my students don't have plans and they don't think anyone at the school has any plans for them either.

I've come to see how the continuation school is being used as a dumping ground for students who engage in violent behavior and are likely to participate in fights. The stated purpose of the continuation school is to help low-performing students improve their grades and earn their high school diplomas; since most of the violent kids are low performing, the transfers are justified on that basis.

Administration constantly alerts teachers to potential dangers. They also pass out flyers to students who, for the most part, already know about an impending battle. I don't think most of us teachers are privy to the system that operates to keep our school relatively free from serious conflicts. It's clear to me now that the principal and associate principals consider their roles as peacekeepers a serious responsibility with the full awareness that unless we feel we're working in a safe school, our academic goals will be undermined.

A striking factor to me of the end of the year practice of keeping failing students working is the expectation that we find ways to keep them motivated even if they are sure they are going to fail the class. Motivated to do what exactly? It's a mind-boggling conundrum. It's hard enough to keep them motivated if they think they have a chance to pass the class. It seems to me the issue of motivation, while generally important, takes on a different face when confronted with the need to make all motivation intrinsic. No one doubts that the carrot of grades and graduation are the principal motivating factors in school, but since so many students in the urban school don't care much about grades or going to college, the issue of the need for intrinsic motivation is paramount. If I am to remain an urban schoolteacher, I can see clearly that I will need to develop activities and tasks that provoke intrinsic interest. I think it's a real fallacy to assume that we can teach the same subject matter in the same way as is taught in middle-class schools. I don't think we even want to. There are emerging ideas, for example, in the field of math education that speaks to this notion of teaching math to urban youth using very different approaches than those used in traditional middle-class schools (Lehrer and Schauble 2000, 2005).

The idea of applying standards and comparisons based on standardized testing is intrinsically disadvantaging urban-school students and, since the tests wag the curriculum, I don't see how we can ever hope to compete with schools that take student motivation to succeed, and even excel, for granted.

My experience with the last meeting of our teacher-education group was extremely helpful in allowing me to see that my own difficulties are par for the course among our urban schoolteachers. I think, not only from sharing experiences but also from conversations with more experienced teachers in our schools, that the only answer I can come up with, to be able to at first survive and then prevail in the urban classroom, is to keep your spirits up and remain positive until you believe you've found your way. Certainly one year is not enough time for it to happen. I can't think of a more important thing to have learned.

At this stage of my thinking about things I have learned, I think it's important for me to consider the things I didn't learn but need to do much thinking about. For example, the case of Thomas and his disdain for my "caring" about him raises an important question for me to contemplate over the summer. I need to think through why some of my students, probably many, don't want to be "cared about" by a teacher, especially a white teacher. I've learned much about the futility of abstractions, so I'm pretty sure at this point telling students that I have a philosophical commitment to help students improve their life chances isn't going to fly. I need to come up with something more concrete, something I can accomplish in a class of forty students, fifty-three minutes a day, five days a week.

I have learned that in my school appropriate student placement is sometimes obstructed by bureaucratic maneuverings. Urban-school reform at a national level has been espousing the need for one teacher to have the same student for four years and the responsibility of being a parent surrogate for the student at the school site. He would be responsible for checking that students are enrolled in appropriate classes, checking grades, qualifications for college, as well as student behavior. I hope when I'm more experienced and confident I'll carve out some extra time to keep a closer watch on more students than I've had time for this year.

What have I learned this year that I think will help me in my work next year? That seems to be the central question. Well, one thing's for sure, I learned more from my mistakes than my successes, although many of the successes I have had came about from what I'm calling mistakes. I think my focus on developing a close relationship with my students cut two ways. Some students took advantage of it by taking the class and my rules of order less seriously than I wanted, but many responded well to knowing I had a caring relationship with them. I suppose I need to harden up and become more demanding with certain students, if I can figure out soon enough which ones will respond negatively to my overtures of friendship. Others will respond positively to my attempts to build a caring relationship. I don't want to have a carved-in-stone set of rules to follow. I need to take into account my own personality, which leads me to joke around with the students and get to know them as well as I can. The question appears to be, do I do the strict thing at first and then loosen up for certain individuals or do I stay soft and harden up for other individuals? Maybe it's both. There's enough conventional wisdom floating around from experienced teachers, but I think the individual personality of the teacher is a more important variable than any general wisdom takes into account. I don't know at this point how it's going to go but I'm still quite open on the subject.

I am, of course, angry and disappointed about my administration's decision to provide no funding for the chess club but that taught me a lesson in priorities. We have a higher membership and rate of attendance and less fighting than most other clubs that our campus sponsors and that should count for something—right? No, wrong! It doesn't count for much. You can expect good behavior from kids who volunteer to participate in a school activity. I heard through the grapevine that the decision was a matter of administrative politics. When representatives come to visit or audit our school they don't exclusively look at the teaching in classrooms or the scores on standardized tests. They look at extracurricular activities because these show identification with one's school. Student identification apparently correlates with student achievement. Apparently our administration does not see the chess club contributing to this identification. I think they're wrong.

Another thing I think I've learned, which may sound obvious, is that you don't lose students as much as you don't discover a way to find them. This understanding helped me face up to my naïve anger toward many students for what I considered to be their refusal to allow my teaching to improve their life conditions.

One of my classes never really responded to my attempts to engage them, and only a dozen or so of the students passed the class. I think this pattern is important to look at and one I need to reflect upon over the summer. The only answer I can think of at the moment that will bring students into the learning circle with me is to reconceptualize my curriculum. That's what I intend to work on this summer, although my first thought when I say that is, based upon my past year's experience, as soon as I develop a sound curriculum for a particular class I'll be given every math class to teach but that one. I know this is cynical but I've been told by others to expect it. Irrespective of the administrative manipulations, it is counter to mandates that a teacher should be developing his own curriculum. We are expected to stick to the mandated text and pacing guides. What can we say about a school where teachers have no say in what or how they teach?

There's a culture of mathematics I would like to be able to teach my students through some reform-based curricula. This culture deals with discourse: argument, inquiry, and proof. It's the way I learned it and it's why I love the subject. It seems investigating mathematical ideas to effectively frame persuasive arguments is important. This is the essence of mathematics. The district-mandated book has pushed me so far from anything that resembles mathematics. I've spent the whole year chasing "the standards."

Another thing I learned is that I need to manage my stress better on a daily basis; it is important to take days off when I'm overwhelmed with work. I need to keep myself from taking as many things as personally as I have, particularly when students get angry with me. Students who lose it are usually hitting out against a whole lot of things other than me. If I lose my control in these encounters, the student has taken the power away from me. The only thing that gets accomplished is a yelling match. Even if I win, I lose.

I think the more years I teach the more separation I will put between the student and myself. I will become older and more in control and my students will always be the same age. I need to stop taking failures personally, not that I think student failures are exclusively my fault, but the disappointment that comes from working hard with a student all semester or year and then watching them just quit on themselves (and me I suppose) in the end is hard to take.

My father, not necessarily playing devil's advocate, has challenged me to think about how much irritation I'm willing to put up with before I consider alternatives to teaching in schools like Olympia. I told him I'd teach here or schools like here as long as I felt I was making a positive difference. I'm not one to give up at the first sign of impossibility. Like I said somewhere earlier, I'm not the type to become cynical like my father, but then again he taught in my kind of school for six years fifty years ago. I'm not sure, to tell the truth, that much has changed but I haven't had time to tune in to the historical aspects of urban schooling.

Finally, and of important consequence, I learned that I do like teaching and I know I wouldn't trade where I teach for any middle-class or private school. I went into teaching to teach urban youth. The idea of social justice is more than just a concept I approve of. It's a feeling that leads to commitment. I want to give urban students the resources they are being denied by going to a school in an economically depressed community. If I change my mind about teaching in an urban school, it would be the same as changing my mind about teaching. There is no place to teach, from the perspective of social justice, but the urban school.

Carl's Impression of Paul's End of the Year Feelings

The first thing I need to say about Paul's experience in an inner-city school in comparison to my own is how little has changed in a half century. To a visitor the most obvious change is probably that teachers today no longer are required to wear suits and ties and dresses with hose—although some still do. One thing that has changed is there are many more experiments than earlier, attempts at restructuring within the mainstream of schooling: magnet schools, schools within schools, small schools, charter schools, decentralized school districts, etc.

But those are the observable differences and these experiments are small in number compared to ongoing traditional structures and processes of urban schooling. What hasn't changed in urban secondary schools is the never-ending number of confrontations between students and teachers, the recycling of problem students between teachers and schools, the emphasis on the test as the major basis for grading, the use of "guidance rooms" for students to cool out, the amount of fighting between students of different ethnic groups, the poor salaries that are paid to hard-working teachers, the authoritarian all-powerful principal, mindless reliance on standardized testing, and the many problems that could be relieved with adequate funding.

As we said in the introduction, the why of little change is already well known. In short, it is because despite political claims to the contrary, neither education nor children of the poor and probably children in general are high priorities in our high-powered economic culture. True, a lot of money is thrown at education, but, as in the case of No Child Left Behind financing, it is often not enough and focused on the wrong measures.

One other thing that hasn't changed and never will is that high school students will always be adolescents, which is not a problem in itself. What is the problem is that there are few programs in place to deal with emerging indicators of student aggression and depression in younger children, where perhaps something can be done about it before these untreated children arrive to terrorize the classrooms of U.S. urban schools. I don't think there is much emphasis in teacher-education programs or in-service programs that deal with the adolescent consciousness and especially evolving destructive tendencies. The consequence of this is that when troubled children become troubled adolescents and enter high school, it is probably too late to rehabilitate most of them within the limits of the school's resources. Therefore the choice of the day for acting-out behavior is punishment, always some form of punishment. It's just about the only weapon in the school's arsenal of discipline.

It's my opinion the one important thing Paul has learned by teaching in an urban school is that, for many students who don't succeed educationally, probably better than 50 percent according to Paul's calculations and the national statistics, the trouble is not in the fact that they can't learn the content but in the fact that the social conditions of their existence are obstacles to achievement. And it has become clear to him that a teacher's role, in his kind of school, is to deal with those conditions, or at least take them into account. This is not done by manipulating the home or street environment, which teachers can't do, but by knowing the students individually and convincing them there is someone here who cares about their development.

For some students punishment can extinguish deviant behavior, but I believe this is the exception. In general the urban adolescent consciousness does not yield to change easily. Paul knows it is the mind-set of many of his students that is the barrier to his idealistic goals. Many students have internalized the values of educational success and these students are likely to be helped and pushed by caring teachers. But it is Paul's opinion, and I would concur, that the majority of his students are far from convinced that school success is important to them. Again and again he hears from his students that relatives and friends in the community are doing very well thank you, without a high school diploma, much less a college one.

Paul has had to deal with the urban adolescent consciousness in a number of areas that are not specifically covered by the official handbook of school rules and regulations. Because of Paul's age and because he seems able to communicate an attitude of acceptance and even friendship, students rap with him about their thoughts and even their misadventures. Paul is sometimes surprised that students who know he is failing them will confide in him anyhow as if school failure is nothing they take personally. At least they are far from traumatized by it.

One such student, Chauncy, who has been on the road to total failure in school for years, has proudly confided to Paul that he probably makes more money in a month than Paul makes in a year. Paul has seen Chauncy flash hundred dollar bills. Chauncy, according to Paul, is a sweet kid who doesn't cause trouble, perhaps to protect his business interests.

Paul tries to communicate to Chauncy that there is more to life than making money; a career such as his as a teacher has intrinsic rewards far more important to him than making money. And furthermore, with an education, Paul has flexibility to pursue a number of different careers. In addition, he doesn't have to look behind him to see if somebody wants to move in on his territory or cancel him out altogether.

Paul is not so naïve as to believe that this will penetrate beyond Chauncy's smile. But as a first-year idealist he feels the need to lay his beliefs out front and see where they go. The fact is that Chauncy is talking fancy cars and king size TVs and cool clothes leading to lovely lasses, and Paul is talking intrinsic rewards like satisfaction with helping those who have a hard time helping themselves and giving students flexibility in their life choices. Chauncy's psychology is not atypical of the students he has and will continue to have in most of his classes. What Paul will have to contemplate over the summer is where he can go with his goals for his students and where it's foolish to even try to go.

Like any teacher who has just struggled through a first year, Paul has not shaken himself completely awake and sorted out in any systematic way exactly where he stands in relation to teaching in an urban school. He probably won't have done this by the time he begins again next fall. All he knows, as I read him, is that something's rotten in the state of urban education as he has experienced it, and the patterns that deny poor minority kids upward mobility are in place and they are more entrenched than he suspected. He is also of the belief that the same forces that account for why 30 percent of Los Angeles citizens live in poverty also account for why things don't get better for poor minority students. He still feels it shouldn't be all that difficult to get kids through high school in a condition where they can qualify for higher education. As far as he's concerned he hasn't lost sight of this goal even though he knows the statistics of high school graduation and college attendance tell him he's being monumentally unrealistic.

Throughout the year other more experienced teachers have told him to forget the "losers," to concentrate his limited energy on students who are there to learn, students who can still benefit from a high school education. This advice is not yet totally intelligible to him. What it means, given the classes he has taught this year, is they are telling him to write off more than half his students. The message he hears is let the students who show no interest in their education carve their own way to the economics of survival, to remain socioeconomically mired in the same condition they came in with. His education classes at the university, which were more than anything else about the politics of reproduction, seem to have hit the nail on the head. He now understands the sociological reasons that explain why his school has no college office but does have a career office, has no college counselors but does have seven security officers, has almost no AP classes but plenty of intro classes where more than 50 percent of the students fail every class.

One systemic problem that he keeps coming back to, which most troubles him, is the institutionalized process of student placement, the main criterion being where there is room to stick or squeeze them. He knows the logistical difficulties of overcrowded schools, but he also knows that in schools where parents play a key role students do not stay long in classes they shouldn't be in. Paul feels strongly that the school should play a role where parents can't or won't. Too many apologists for school failure point to the family as the chief culprit. For some reason, school personnel are let off the hook by this assignment of fault.

But, and this is a significant "but," with all that said, Paul has put aside his grievances and is hard at work planning his next year's classes. Sociological explanations for why students fail don't advance the cause of discovering new pedagogical tools to help students succeed. He has put himself in a position to spearhead a program of computerized math instruction for algebra and has hopes that the software will provide useful representations of mathematics concepts that the sterile, mandated textbook cannot.

As a personal note I am left with only positive feelings about Paul's choice to follow in the family tradition of working against the sociopolitical tide that keeps poor minorities from succeeding educationally on a larger scale than they do. It is my belief that there is nothing that succeeds in helping a young person mature as a professional more than being on the losing side of an important struggle. Paul knows that in the comprehensive urban high school victories can be personal whereas defeats are usually systemic.

Whereas he came into the education business as an idealist he is continuing as an idealistic realist with hopes he can make a difference. He still believes it is a struggle worthy of his efforts.

To be more precise I asked him toward the end of the summer how much longer he intends to teach in this school or any school of its type for that matter. He replied, "Until I get it right!" His meaning was unambiguous. He still hasn't decided how much his failure to touch more students is his own inexperience or the fault of the larger system. I suspect his long-range goal is to get a PhD and work in the area of math education and teacher training, but he doesn't want to do any of that until he's pretty sure he has something to offer, that he himself has solved, at least to a large extent, the problems he now faces on a daily basis.

References

Aber, J. L., C. Mitchell, R. Garfinkel, L. Allen, and E. Seidman. 1992. Indices of neighborhood impoverishment: Their associations with adolescent mental health and school achievement. Paper presented at the Conference on the Urban Underclass: Perspectives from the Social Sciences, Ann Arbor, MI.

Allen, W., E. Telles, and M. Hunter. 2000. Skin color, income and education: A comparison of African Americans and Mexican Americans. *National Journal of Sociology* 12 (1): 129–80.

Apple, M. 1979. *Ideology and Curriculum*. London: Routledge and Kegan Paul.

Augenblick, J., and A. Anderson. 1997. Equity and adequacy in school funding. *Future of Children* 7:63–78.

Balfanz, R., and N. Legters. 2006. The graduation rate crisis we know and what we can do about it. *Education Week Commentary*. July 12.

Brenner, N. D., T. R. Simon, E. G. Krug, and R. Lowry. 1999. Recent trends in violence-related behaviors among high school students in the United States. *JAMA* 282:440–46.

Bullough, B. 1969. *Social-Psychological Barriers to Housing Desegregation*. Los Angeles: University of California, Housing, Real Estate, and Urban Land Studies Program.

Bulman, R. C. 2002. Teachers in the 'hood: Hollywood's middle class fantasy. *Urban Review* 34 (3): 251–76.

Burnam, M. A., R. L. Hough, M. Karno, C. A. Escobar, and C. A. Telles. 1987. Acculturation and lifetime prevalence of psychiatric disorders among Mexican Americans in Los Angeles. *Journal of Health & Social Behavior* 28:89–102.

Byrnes, M. 2004. *Taking Sides: Clashing Views in Special Education*. New York: McGraw Hill.

Campbell, J. A. 1999. Health insurance coverage, 1998. *Current Population Reports.* Washington, DC: U.S. Department of Commerce.

Campbell, L. 2004. As strong as the weakest link: Urban high school dropout. *High School Journal* 87 (2): 16–24.

Carlie, M. K. 2002. Into the abyss: A personal journey into the world of street gangs. http://www.faculty.missouristate.edu/m/MichaelCarlie/site_map.htm (accessed December 16, 2005).

Cervantes, R. C., V. N. Salgado de Snyder, and A. M. Padilla. 1989. Post traumatic stress disorders among immigrants from Central America and Mexico. *Hospital and Community Psychiatry* 40:615–19.

Chaves, A. P., M. A. Diemer, D. L. Blustein, L. A. Gallagher, J. E. DeVoy, M. T. Casares, et al. 2004. Conceptions of work: The view from urban youth. *Journal of Counseling Psychology* 51 (3): 275–86.

Clark, B. 1960. The "cooling out" function in higher education. *American Journal of Sociology* 65 (6): 569–76.

Clark, C. 1998. The violence that creates school dropouts. *Multicultural Education* 6 (1): 19–22.

Coleman, J. S. 1961. *The Adolescent Society.* New York: Free Press of Glencoe.

———. 1969. *Equal Educational Opportunity.* Cambridge, MA: Harvard University Press.

Coleman, J. S., T. Hoffer, and S. Kilgore. 1982. *High School Achievement: Public, Catholic, and Private Schools Compared.* New York: Basic Books.

Committee on Increasing High School Students' Engagement and Motivation to Learn. 2004. *Engaging Schools: Fostering High School Students' Motivation to Learn.* Washington, DC: National Academies Press.

Darling-Hammond, L., R. Chung, and F. Frelow. 2002. Variations in teacher preparation. *Journal of Teacher Preparation* 53 (4): 286–302.

diSessa, A. A., et al. 1991. Inventing graphing: Meta-representational expertise in children. *Journal of Mathematical Behavior* 10 (2): 117–60.

Drake, S. C., and H. R. Cayton. 1962. *Black Metropolis.* New York: Harper and Row.

Dryfoos, J. G., and S. Maguire. 2002. *Inside Full Service Community School.* Thousand Oaks, CA: Corwin Press.

Duhaney, L. M. G. 2000. Culturally sensitive strategies for violence prevention. *Multicultural Education* 7 (4): 10–17.

Edwards, G. F. 1959. *The Negro Professional Class.* Glencoe, IL: Free Press.

Edwards, H. 1973. *Sociology of Sport.* Homewood, IL: Dorsey Press.

Eisner, C., ed. 2000. A report on ending social promotion: Early lessons learned in the efforts to end social promotion in the nation's public schools. Eric Document Reproduction Service No. ED448234.

Fallis, R. K., and S. Opotow. 2003. Are students failing school or are schools failing students? Class cutting in high school. *Journal of Social Issues* 59 (1): 103–19.

Fletcher, M. A. 1998. In L.A. a sense of future conflicts. *Washington Post*, April 7, A1–A2.

Fontaine, J. H. 1997. The sound of silence: Public school response to the needs of gay and lesbian youth. In *School Experiences of Gay and Lesbian Youth: The Invisible Minority*, ed. M. B. Harris, 101–9. Binghamton, NY: Harrington Press.

Frazier, F. E. 1962. *Black Bourgeoisie: The Rise of a New Middle Class in the United States*. New York: Collier Books.

Freire, P. 1973. *Pedagogy of the Oppressed*. New York: Seabury Press.

Friend, M. 2008. *Special Education: Contemporary Perspectives for School Professionals*. Boston: Allyn and Bacon.

Gardner, H. E. 1993. *Multiple Intelligences: Theory into Practice*. New York: Basic Books.

Garot, R., and J. Katz. 2003. Provocative looks: Gang appearance and dress codes in an inner city alternative school. *Ethnography* 4 (3): 421–54.

Gephart, W. G., and J. B. Ayers. 1988. *Teacher Education Evaluation*. Hamburg, Germany: Springer Press.

Gilmer, G., and M. Porter. 1998. Hairstyles talk a hit at NCTM! *International Study Group on Ethnomathematics (ISGEm) Newsletter* 13 (2): 5–6.

Ginsberg, R., H. Schwartz, G. Olson, and A. Bennett. 1987. Working conditions in urban schools. *Urban Review* 19 (1): 3–23.

Gomez, C. 2000. The continual significance of skin color: An exploratory study of Latinos in the northeast. *Hispanic Journal of Behavioral Sciences* 22 (1): 94–103.

Gordon, C. W. 1957. *The Social System of the High School: A Study in the Sociology of Adolescence*. New York: John Wiley.

Hanushek, E. A., J. F. Kain, and S. G. Rivkin. 2003. Why Public Schools Lose Teachers. Working Paper 8599, National Bureau of Economic Research, Cambridge, MA.

Hauck, W. E., and J. W. Thomas. 1972. The relationship of humor to intelligence, creativity, and intentional and incidental learning. *Journal of Experimental Education* 40:52–55.

Hauser, R. M., S. J. Simmons, and D. I. Pager. 2000. High school dropout, race-ethnicity, and social background from the 1970s to the 1990s. ERIC Document Reproduction Service No. ED 449277.

Hemmings, A. 2003. Fighting for respect in urban high schools. *Teachers College Record* 105 (3): 416–37.

Hernandez, T. K. 2007. Roots of anger: Long time prejudices, not economic rivalry fuel Latino-black tensions. *Los Angeles Times*, January 7, M1.

Heubert, J. P., and R. M. Hauser. 1999. *High Stakes: Testing for Tracking, Promotion, and Graduation*. Washington, DC: National Academy Press.

Holmes, C. T. 1989. *Grade Level Retention Effects: A Meta-Analysis of and Policies on Retention*. London: Falmer Press, 16–33.

Hunter, J. 2002. Juvenile Justice/Delinquency Prevention. Office of Justice Programs, U.S. Department of Justice, Washington, DC.

Jencks, C., and S. E. Mayer. 1990. The social consequences of growing up in a poor neighborhood. In *Inner-City Poverty in the United States*, eds. L. E. Lynn Jr. and M. G. H. McGeary, 111–86. Washington, DC: National Academy Press.

Johnson, L. 2002. "My eyes have been opened": White teachers and racial awareness. *Journal of Teacher Education* 53 (2): 153–67.

Juvenile Justice Bulletin. 2000. From the courthouse to the schoolhouse: Making successful transitions—school-based probation. http://www.ncjrs.gov/html/ojjdp/jjbul2000_02_1/prob.html (accessed January 13, 2003).

Kouyoumdjian, H., B. L. Zamboanga, and D. J. Hansen. 2003. *Clinical Psychology: Science & Practice* 10 (4): 394–422.

Kozol, J. 1991. *Savage Inequalities*. New York: Crown Publishers.

———. 2005. *The Shame of the Nation: The Restoration of Apartheid in America*. New York: Crown Publishers.

Lahey, B. B., R. Loeber, J. D. Burke, and B. Applegate. 2005. Predicting future antisocial personality disorder in males from a clinical assessment in childhood. *Journal of Consulting and Clinical Psychology* 73 (3): 389–99.

Lehrer, R., and L. Schauble. 2000. Modeling in mathematics and science. In *Advances in Instructional Psychology*. Vol. 5, ed. R. Glaser, 101–59. Mahwah, NJ: Lawrence Erlbaum Associates.

———. 2005. Developing modeling and argument in the elementary grades. In *Understanding Mathematics and Science Matters*, eds. T. A. Romberg, T. P. Carpenter, and F. Dremock, 29–53. Mahwah, NJ: Lawrence Erlbaum Associates.

Lehrer, R., M. Kobiela, and P. Weinberg. 2007.. Inquiring about space: Developing mathematical habits of mind. In *The Development of Spatial Literacy and Schooling*, organizer S. L. Golbeck. Symposium conducted at the June meeting of the Jean Piaget Society, The Netherlands.

Lesh, R., and R. Lehrer. 2003. Mathematical learning. In *Handbook of Psychology: Vol. 7, Educational Psychology*, eds. W. Reynolds and G. Miller, 357–91. Manhwah, NJ: Lawrence Earlbaum Associates.

Lewis, E. 2003. Playing the dozens. *Louisiana Weekly*, June 2.

Lortie, D. C. 1975. *Schoolteacher: A Sociological Study*. Chicago: University of Chicago Press.

Lott, B. 2002. Cognitive and behavioral distancing from the poor. *American Psychologist* 57 (2): 100–110.

Lynn, R. 2002. Skin color and intelligence in African Americans. *Population and Environment* 23 (4): 365–75.

McIntyre, D. J., and D. M. Byrd. 2000. *Teacher Education Yearbook VIII: Research on Effective Models for Teacher Education*. Thousand Oaks, CA: Corwin Press.

Medcalf, J. 2004. Co-operative learning: The social and intellectual outcomes of learning in groups. *Educational Psychology* 24 (3): 409–10.

Miller, T. W., R. Clayton, J. M. Miller, J. Bilyeu, J. Hunter, and R. F. Kraus. 2000. Violence in the schools: Clinical issues and case analysis for high-risk children. *Child Psychiatry and Human Development* 30 (4): 255–72.

Monroe, C. 2005. Why are "bad boys" always black?: Causes of disproportionality in school discipline and recommendations for change. *Clearing House* 79 (1): 45–50.

National Research Council. 2000. *How People Learn: Brain, Mind, Experience, and School*. Washington, DC: National Academy Press.

———. 2004. *Engaging Schools: Fostering High School Students' Motivation to Learn*. Washington, DC: National Academies Press.

Noguera, P. 2003. *City Schools and the American Dream: Reclaiming the Promise of Public Education*. New York: Teachers College Press.

Pastore, D. R., M. Fisher, and S. B. Friedman. 1996. Violence and mental health problems among urban high school students. *Journal of Adolescent Health* 18 (5): 320–24.

Paul, F. G. 2005. Grouping within Algebra I: A structural sieve with powerful effects for low-income, minority, and immigrant students. *Education Policy* 19 (2): 262–82.

Rareshide, S. W. 1993. Implications for teachers' use of humor in the classroom. ERIC Document Reproduction Service No. ED359165.

Ritsch, M. 2002. The old college try: Good grades? Not enough. An upscale school goes to bat to give its students an Ivy League edge. *Los Angeles Times*, April 21, E1–E3.

Rosenbloom, S. R., and N. Way. 2004. Experiences of discrimination among African-American, Asian American, and Latino adolescents in an urban high school. *Youth and Society* 35 (4): 420–51.

Saporito, S., W. L. Yancey, V. Louis. 2001. Quality, race, and the urban education marketplace reconsidered. *Urban Affairs Review* 37 (2): 267–76.

Sears, J. T. 1991. Educators, homosexuality and homosexual students. *Journal of Homosexuality* 22:29–79.

Seeman, M. 1959. On the meaning of alienation. *American Sociological Review* 24 (6): 783–91.

Sheets, R. H. 2002. "You're just a kid that's there"—Chicano Perception of Disciplinary Events. *Journal of Latinos & Education* 1 (2): 105–22.

Stevens, C. E. 2001. *Report to the Governor on Teacher Retention and Turnover*. Athens, GA: Standards Commission.

Viadero, D. 2002. Research on discipline not reaching schools, experts say. *Education Week* 18:10.

Walker-Barnes, C. J. 2001. Perceptions of risk factors for female gang involvement among African American and Hispanic women. *Youth & Society* 32 (3): 303–36.

Walters, A. S., and D. M. Hayes. 1998. Homophobia within schools: Challenging the culturally sanctioned dismissal of gay students and colleagues. *Journal of Homosexuality* 35 (2): 1–23.

Wasley, P. A., M. Fine, M. Gladden, N. E. Holland, S. P. King, E. Mosak, et al. 2000. Small schools, great strides: A study of new small schools in Chicago. Report of the Bank Street College of Education.

Weinberg, C. 1973. *Education is a Shuck*. Chicago: William Morrow.

———. 1989. Stress-reducing attitudes for teachers. *Teacher Education Quarterly* 16:73–84.

Weiner, L. 2000. Research in the 90s: Implications for urban teacher preparation. *Review of Educational Research* 70 (3): 369–406.

Weiss, L., and M. Fine. 1992. *Silenced Voices and Extraordinary Conversations*. New York: Teachers College Press.

Wideen, M. F., and P. P. Grimmett. 1995. *Changing Times in Teacher Education: Restructuring or Reconceptualization?* Bristol, PA: Falmer Press.

Wilson, T. C. 1995. Vietnam-era military service: A test of the class-bias thesis. *Armed Forces & Society* 21 (3): 461–71.

Index

~

About the Authors

Paul J. Weinberg graduated from the University of California, Los Angeles, with a bachelor of science in pure mathematics and a master's degree in mathematics education. He spent two years teaching mathematics at Leuzinger High School, a traditional urban school in Lawndale, California. He left Leuzinger to help with the start-up process of a public charter school in San Jose, California, working for the Leadership Public Schools organization as the mathematics department chair and head of assessment. He is currently doing doctoral work at Vanderbilt University's Peabody School of Education and Human Development. Within the Department of Teaching, Learning, and Diversity, his academic focus is mathematics and science education.

Carl Weinberg is a professor emeritus in the Graduate School of Education at UCLA where he taught sociology of education and curriculum studies. He began his teaching career in 1955 and taught in inner-city secondary schools in Philadelphia and Los Angeles for six years. For the past ten years of his tenure at UCLA he worked in teacher education where he introduced perspectives from humanistic and confluent education to prospective teachers.

DATE DUE

American Women of Letters
and the Nineteenth-Century Sciences